taste of home
busy family
FAVORITES

taste of home
BOOKS

REIMAN MEDIA GROUP, LLC · GREENDALE, WISCONSIN

taste of home

Reader's Digest

A TASTE OF HOME/READER'S DIGEST BOOK
© 2011 Reiman Media Group, LLC
5400 S. 60th St., Greendale WI 53129
All rights reserved.

Taste of Home and Reader's Digest are registered trademarks of The Reader's Digest Association, Inc.

Editor in Chief: Catherine Cassidy
Vice President, Executive Editor/Books: Heidi Reuter Lloyd
Creative Director: Howard Greenberg
North American Chief Marketing Officer: Lisa Karpinski
Food Director: Diane Werner RD
Senior Editor/Books: Mark Hagen
Editor: Janet Briggs

Associate Creative Director: Edwin Robles, Jr.
Content Production Manager: Julie Wagner
Design Layout Artist: Catherine Fletcher
Proofreader: Victoria Soukup Jensen
Recipe Asset System Manager: Coleen Martin
Premedia Supervisor: Scott Berger
Recipe Testing & Editing: Taste of Home Test Kitchen
Food Photography: Taste of Home Photo Studio
Administrative Assistant: Barb Czysz

The Reader's Digest Association, Inc.
President and Chief Executive Officer: Mary G. Berner
President, North American Affinities: Suzanne M. Grimes
President/Publisher Trade Publishing: Harold Clarke
Associate Publisher: Rosanne McManus
Vice President, Sales and Marketing: Stacey Ashton

For other Taste of Home books and products, visit us at **tasteofhome.com**

For more Reader's Digest products and information, visit **rd.com** (in the United States) or see **rd.ca** (in Canada).

Stock Photo Credits:
46368046, 46451110
wavebreakmedia, Ltd/Shutterstock Images LLC
19655542, 15490465, 19918573
Monkey Business Images/Shutterstock Images LLC
37858567
BlueOrange Studio/Shutterstock Images LLC

International Standard Book Number (10): 0-89821-839-X
International Standard Book Number (13): 978-0-89821-839-8
Library of Congress Control Number: 2010932790

Cover Photography
Photographers: Dan Roberts, Lori Foy
Food Stylists: Diane Armstrong, Kaitlyn Besasie
Set Stylists: Jennifer Bradley Vent, Stacey Genaw

Pictured on front cover: Apricot Chicken Drumsticks, p. 122 and Greek Pasta Salad, p.197.
Front cover insets (left to right): Swirled Dill Rolls, p. 215; Layered Lemon Pie, p. 227; and Crescent Turkey Casserole, p.139.
Pictured on back cover: Navy Bean Vegetable Soup, p. 37 and Peanut Butter Chocolate Pie, p. 231.

Printed in China
3 5 7 9 10 8 6 4

table of contents

Take Time for Dinner with 363 Half-Hour Recipes!

Dinnertime is an important way for families to connect and discuss the day's events. All too often, however, there can be a mad rush to cook a meal. With the **363** recipes in **Taste of Home Busy Family Favorites,** you can prepare a home-cooked supper in just **30 minutes** from prep to table, then have more time to spend with your family.

The recipes in this fabulous collection were selected because they are easy to make and are delicious, too. You'll find that they are kid-friendly, but they still appeal to adult palates. All of the ingredients are readily available in your supermarket, and most of the recipes use just a handful of ingredients.

Best of all, the recipes were shared by busy home cooks—just like you—who know the importance of making tasty, but quick meals. And, each dish was tested by a cooking professional at *Taste of Home*…the world's #1 cooking magazine. So, when you make one of these dishes, you can cook with confidence knowing that it will turn out well and that other families have been delighted with it.

When you page through this collection, you'll be impressed by the variety of foods and flavors. Here's just a sample:

Sandwiches and Salads are simple and filling dinners…and great for when it's too hot to cook.

Soups are ideal with a side salad or crusty bread for a hearty dinner on a blustery night. For lighter fare, serve just a cup of soup to whet appetites for the main course.

Entrees range from beef, pork and poultry to seafood, pasta and even meatless dishes, which means there is something to satisfy everyone's palate.

Sides will round out your meal…choose from side salads, veggies, potatoes, quick breads and grains.

Desserts will satisfy the desire for a sweet finale. The ones featured here do just that and take mere minutes to make.

The 30 minutes you take to prepare one of these mouthwatering dishes is time well spent, especially when your family sits down together at the dinner table. After all, with **Busy Family Favorites,** a memorable meal is only a few moments away.

busy family favorites

Sandwiches & Salads

Chicken Salad Sandwiches, p.10

Grilled Sourdough Clubs

Kristina Franklin • Clarkston, Washington

These toasty subs are filled with deli ham and turkey, bacon and cheese. They are hearty, nourishing and appeal to all ages. Best of all, they grill them up in just minutes, and they can be served as a meal in themselves!

12 slices sourdough bread

6 slices cheddar cheese

1/2 pound thinly sliced deli turkey

1/4 teaspoon garlic powder

1/2 pound thinly sliced deli ham

12 bacon strips, cooked and drained

2 tablespoons butter, softened

1. On six slices of bread, layer cheese and turkey; sprinkle with garlic powder. Top with ham, bacon and remaining bread. Spread butter over the top and bottom of each sandwich. Cook on an indoor grill or panini maker for 3-4 minutes or until bread is toasted and cheese is melted.

Yield: 6 servings.

Curried Chicken Salad Cups

Judy Ross • Freeport, Illinois

I love preparing this crisp salad for lunch meetings! Featuring crunchy fruit, slivered almonds and chicken, it brings lots of compliments.

3 cups cubed cooked chicken breast

1 cup dried cranberries

2 celery ribs, sliced

1/2 cup chopped red onion

1/2 cup chopped tart apple

1/3 cup slivered almonds, toasted

1/4 cup flaked coconut

DRESSING:

2/3 cup fat-free mayonnaise

3 tablespoons lemon juice

1 teaspoon fennel seed, crushed

1 teaspoon curry powder

1 teaspoon honey

1/8 teaspoon ground cinnamon

14 lettuce leaves

1. In a large bowl, combine first seven ingredients. In a small bowl, whisk the mayonnaise, lemon juice, fennel seed, curry, honey and cinnamon; add to the chicken mixture and mix well. Serve on lettuce leaves.

Yield: 7 servings.

Pear Chicken Salad

Rebecca Baird • Salt Lake City, Utah

This beautiful change-of-pace salad is sprinkled with feta cheese, sweetened cranberries and walnuts for extra pop and crunch.

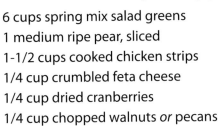

6 cups spring mix salad greens

1 medium ripe pear, sliced

1-1/2 cups cooked chicken strips

1/4 cup crumbled feta cheese

1/4 cup dried cranberries

1/4 cup chopped walnuts *or* pecans

DRESSING:

1/4 cup olive oil

2 tablespoons orange juice

2 tablespoons white wine vinegar

1-1/2 teaspoons sugar

1/2 teaspoon grated orange peel

1/8 teaspoon salt

Dash pepper

1. On each of four salad plates, arrange the greens, pear, chicken, feta cheese, cranberries and nuts. In a small bowl, whisk the dressing ingredients; drizzle over salads.

Yield: 4 servings.

Refreshing Shrimp Salad

Taste of Home Test Kitchen

Avocado, strawberries and shrimp are wonderful together in this very refreshing and light salad. Balsamic or raspberry vinaigrette dressings go well with the salad, as do Asian inspired dressings.

1 package (5 ounces) spring mix salad greens

1 pound cooked medium shrimp, peeled and deveined

1 large navel orange, peeled and sectioned

1 medium ripe avocado, peeled and sliced

1 cup sliced fresh strawberries

1/2 cup thinly sliced onions

Salad dressing of your choice

1. On each of four serving plates, arrange salad greens, shrimp, orange, avocado, strawberries and onions. Drizzle with dressing.

Yield: 4 servings.

Colorful Beef Wraps

Robyn Cavallaro • Easton, Pennsylvania

I stir-fry a combination of sirloin steak, onions and peppers for these hearty wraps. Spreading a little fat-free ranch salad dressing inside the tortillas really jazzes up the taste.

1 boneless beef sirloin steak (1 pound), cut into thin strips

3 garlic cloves, minced

1/4 teaspoon pepper

3 tablespoons reduced-sodium soy sauce, *divided*

3 teaspoons olive oil, *divided*

1 medium red onion, cut into wedges

1 jar (7 ounces) roasted sweet red peppers, drained and cut into strips

1/4 cup dry red wine *or* reduced-sodium beef broth

6 tablespoons fat-free ranch salad dressing

6 flour tortillas (8 inches)

1-1/2 cups torn iceberg lettuce

1 medium tomato, chopped

1/4 cup chopped green onions

1. In a large nonstick skillet coated with cooking spray, saute the beef, garlic, pepper and 2 tablespoons soy sauce in 2 teaspoons oil until meat is no longer pink. Remove and keep warm.

2. Saute onion in remaining oil for 2 minutes. Stir in the red peppers, wine and remaining soy sauce; bring to a boil. Return beef to pan; simmer for 5 minutes or until heated through.

3. Spread the ranch dressing over one side of each tortilla; sprinkle with the lettuce, tomato and green onions. Spoon about 3/4 cup beef mixture down the center of each tortilla; roll up.

Yield: 6 servings.

busy family favorites

Ginger Salmon Salad

Nancee Melin • Tucson, Arizona

After trying something similar at a restaurant, I duplicated this salad from taste and memory at home. It's a cinch to prepare and comes together in no time. If you prefer, you can easily change the fruit depending on what is in season. Whenever I serve it to company, people always tell me they love it.

2/3 cup lime juice

1/2 cup honey

1/2 teaspoon minced fresh gingerroot

4 salmon fillets (6 ounces *each*), skin removed

1/4 teaspoon salt

1 package (5 ounces) spring mix salad greens

1 cup sliced peeled mango

1. In a small bowl, combine lime juice, honey and ginger; set aside 1/2 cup for serving.

2. Place fillets on a broiler pan coated with nonstick cooking spray. Spoon 1/2 cup lime juice mixture over salmon. Broil 4-6 in. from the heat for 4-5 minutes on each side or until fish flakes easily with a fork, basting occasionally with remaining lime juice mixture. Sprinkle with salt.

3. Divide salad greens among four plates; top with salmon and mango. Drizzle with reserved lime juice mixture.

Yield: 4 servings.

Havarti Turkey Hero

Agnes Ward • Stratford, Ontario

Everyone enjoys the combination of chutney and chopped peanuts in this sandwich. I like to make it when I have company in the afternoon or at night after a game of cards.

1/3 cup mango chutney

2 tablespoons reduced-fat mayonnaise

2 tablespoons chopped unsalted peanuts

Dash cayenne pepper

1 loaf (1 pound) French bread, halved lengthwise

3/4 pound thinly sliced deli turkey

6 lettuce leaves

2 ounces thinly sliced Havarti cheese

1 medium Red Delicious apple, cored and cut into thin rings

1. In a small bowl, combine the chutney, mayonnaise, peanuts and cayenne; spread evenly over the cut side of bread bottom.

2. Layer with the turkey, lettuce, cheese and apple. Replace the bread top. Cut into eight slices.

Yield: 8 servings.

sandwiches & salads

10-Minute Taco Salad

Cindy Stephan • Owosso, Michigan

Mom often made this hearty main-dish salad for my three brothers and me when we were growing up. Now it's one of my husband's favorite meals.

2 cans (16 ounces *each*) chili beans, undrained

1 package (10-1/2 ounces) corn chips

2 cups (8 ounces) shredded cheddar cheese

4 cups chopped lettuce

2 small tomatoes, chopped

1 small onion, chopped

1 can (2-1/4 ounces) sliced ripe olives, drained

1-1/4 cups salsa

1/2 cup sour cream

1. In a small saucepan, cook beans over medium-low heat until heated through.

2. Place corn chips on a large platter. Top with beans, cheese, lettuce, tomatoes, onion, olives, salsa and sour cream. Serve immediately.

Yield: 8 servings.

Chicken Salad Sandwiches

Shannon Tucker • Land O' Lakes, Florida

I made these simple, yet special, sandwiches for a birthday party. Tangy cranberries and crunchy celery pep up the chicken. Leftover turkey works well, too!

1/2 cup mayonnaise

2 tablespoons honey Dijon mustard

1/4 teaspoon pepper

2 cups cubed rotisserie chicken

1 cup (4 ounces) shredded Swiss cheese

1/2 cup chopped celery

1/2 cup dried cranberries

1/4 cup chopped walnuts

1/2 teaspoon dried parsley flakes

8 lettuce leaves

16 slices pumpernickel bread

1. In a large bowl, combine the mayonnaise, mustard and pepper. Stir in the chicken, cheese, celery, cranberries, walnuts and parsley.

2. Place lettuce on eight slices of bread; top each with 1/2 cup chicken salad and remaining bread.

Yield: 8 servings.

Bacon Avocado Wraps

Taste of Home Test Kitchen

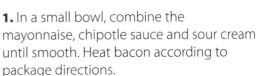

A variety of flavored flour tortillas are now available and would add a nice variation to this tasty and simple recipe.

1/3 cup mayonnaise

2 tablespoons chipotle sauce

1 tablespoon sour cream

1 package (2.1 ounces) ready-to-serve fully cooked bacon

4 flour tortillas (8 inches)

4 large lettuce leaves

1 large tomato, sliced

2 medium ripe avocados, peeled and sliced

1. In a small bowl, combine the mayonnaise, chipotle sauce and sour cream until smooth. Heat bacon according to package directions.

2. Spread chipotle mayonnaise over tortillas; layer with lettuce, tomato, bacon and avocado slices. Roll up tightly.

Yield: 4 servings.

sandwiches & salads

11

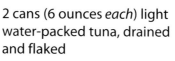

Herbed Tuna Sandwiches

Marie Connor • Virginia Beach, Virginia

A delightful combination of herbs and reduced-fat cheese make this simple tuna sandwich stand out.

2 cans (6 ounces *each*) light water-packed tuna, drained and flaked

2 hard-cooked eggs, chopped

1/3 cup fat-free mayonnaise

1/4 cup minced chives

2 teaspoons minced fresh parsley

1/2 teaspoon dried basil

1/4 teaspoon onion powder

8 slices whole wheat bread, toasted

1/2 cup shredded reduced-fat cheddar cheese

1. In a small bowl, combine the first seven ingredients. Place four slices of toast on an ungreased baking sheet; top with tuna mixture and sprinkle with cheese.

2. Broil 3-4 in. from the heat for 1-2 minutes or until cheese is melted. Top with remaining toast.

Yield: 4 servings.

Tarragon Crab Sandwiches

Taste of Home Test Kitchen

Imitation crabmeat gets a boost of flavor from tarragon and hot pepper sauce. Serve this crab spread with bacon on sourdough bread for a truly delicious sandwich.

1 package (16 ounces) imitation crabmeat, chopped

1/3 cup chopped celery

1/3 cup mayonnaise

1 tablespoon chopped green onion

2 teaspoons minced fresh tarragon

2 to 3 drops hot pepper sauce

1/8 teaspoon salt

1/8 teaspoon pepper

12 ready-to-serve fully cooked bacon strips

12 slices sourdough bread, toasted

6 lettuce leaves

6 slices tomato

1. In a large bowl, combine crabmeat and celery. In a small bowl, combine the mayonnaise, onion, tarragon, pepper sauce, salt and pepper. Pour over crabmeat mixture and toss to coat.

2. Cook bacon according to package directions. On six bread slices, layer with lettuce, tomato, bacon and crab mixture. Top with remaining bread.

Yield: 6 servings.

Warm Beef and Spinach Salad

Linda Eggers • Albany, California

Sliced beef and tasty onions top this simple spinach salad. The dressing is thick, hearty and tangy, and is just the thing to bring it all together. Plus, you can put it on the table in no time!

1/2 cup reduced-fat sour cream

2 tablespoons fat-free milk

1 tablespoon horseradish

1 tablespoon prepared mustard

SALAD:

1 small red onion, sliced and separated into rings

1 pound deli roast beef, cut into thin strips

1 package (6 ounces) fresh baby spinach

2 plum tomatoes, cut into 1/4-inch slices

1. In a small bowl, combine the sour cream, milk, horseradish and mustard; set aside.

2. In a large nonstick skillet coated with cooking spray, cook and stir onion over medium-high heat until tender. Add beef; cook and stir until heated through.

3. In a salad bowl, combine spinach and tomatoes. Add beef mixture and dressing; toss to coat.

Yield: 4 servings.

Home Run Slugger Sub

Cathy Runyon • Allendale, Michigan

I trimmed long French bread to make these hearty hoagies look like baseball bats.

1 French bread baguette (1 pound and 20 inches long)

1/4 pound thinly sliced fully cooked ham

1/4 pound thinly sliced bologna

1/4 pound thinly sliced hard salami

4 romaine leaves

6 slices Swiss cheese

6 slices Colby cheese

1 medium tomato, sliced

1. With a sharp knife, cut one end of the baguette in the shape of a baseball bat handle. Slice loaf in half lengthwise.

2. On the bottom half, layer with ham, bologna, salami, romaine, cheeses and tomato. Replace top. Secure with toothpicks if necessary. Cut into slices.

Yield: 8 servings.

Salami Pork Sub

Shirley Nordblum • Youngsville, Pennsylvania

Our family used to drive 22 miles to enjoy these subs at a restaurant. After the place was torn down to make room for a highway, I was able to get the recipe. Now I fix them at home all the time.

1 loaf (1 pound) unsliced French bread

12 slices salami

16 slices cooked pork (1/8 inch thick)

8 slices provolone cheese

24 thin dill pickle slices

Lettuce leaves

1/4 cup mayonnaise

2 tablespoons prepared mustard

1. Cut the bread in half lengthwise. On the bottom half, layer with salami, pork, cheese, pickles and lettuce.

2. Combine mayonnaise and mustard; spread over cut side of top half of loaf. Replace bread top. Cut into fourths.

Yield: 4 servings.

Crunchy Crab Salad

Stephanie Hamilton • Rupert, Idaho

I frequently serve this cool salad at home and at social functions. It's super simple to make and has a deliciously unique flavor.

1 can (6 ounces) crabmeat, drained, flaked and cartilage removed

1 package (10 ounces) frozen peas, thawed

1 cup chopped celery

1 small onion, chopped

3/4 cup mayonnaise

1 tablespoon lemon juice

1 teaspoon soy sauce

1/4 teaspoon garlic salt

1/4 teaspoon curry powder

1 can (3 ounces) chow mein noodles

1/2 cup slivered almonds

1. In a large bowl, combine the crab, peas, celery and onion; set aside. Combine the mayonnaise, lemon juice, soy sauce, garlic salt and curry powder; add to the crab mixture and toss to coat. Stir in the chow mein noodles and almonds.

Yield: 6 servings.

busy family favorites

Bistro Turkey Sandwiches

Veronica Callaghan • Glastonbury, Connecticut

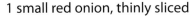

Sweet and savory flavors combine in this quick, healthy sandwich. The apples give an unexpected crunch, but you can substitute them with pears for a tasty change.

1 small red onion, thinly sliced

4 teaspoons brown sugar, *divided*

1 tablespoon olive oil

1/4 teaspoon salt

1/8 teaspoon cayenne pepper

1/4 cup Dijon mustard

1 tablespoon apple cider *or* unsweetened apple juice

6 wheat sandwich buns, split

6 Bibb *or* Boston lettuce leaves

1 medium pear, peeled and thinly sliced

1 pound cooked turkey breast, thinly sliced

1/4 cup loosely packed basil leaves

6 tablespoons crumbled Gorgonzola cheese

1. In a small skillet over medium heat, cook onion and 1 teaspoon brown sugar in oil for 8-10 minutes or until golden brown, stirring frequently. Stir in salt and cayenne.

2. Combine the mustard, apple cider and remaining brown sugar; spread over bun bottoms. Layer with lettuce, pear, turkey, basil and cheese. Top with caramelized onion. Replace tops.

Yield: 6 servings.

Beef Sandwiches Au Jus

Marge Miller • Atlantic Mine, Michigan

My hearty sandwiches are served with individual ramekins of well-seasoned bouillon for dipping. This recipe is a favorite of ours when time is of the essence. Guests always rave when I prepare it, too. Nobody leaves the table hungry.

2 cups water

1 tablespoon beef bouillon granules

1/2 teaspoon pepper, *divided*

1/4 teaspoon crushed red pepper flakes

1/8 teaspoon garlic salt

1 medium onion, thinly sliced

1 small green pepper, thinly sliced

4 tablespoons butter, *divided*

1/4 teaspoon salt

1 pound beef top sirloin steak, cut into 1/2-inch strips

4 French rolls, split

4 slices provolone cheese

1. In a large saucepan, combine the water, bouillon, 1/4 teaspoon pepper, pepper flakes and garlic salt. Bring to a boil. Reduce heat; simmer, uncovered, for 15-20 minutes.

2. Meanwhile, in a large skillet, saute onion and green pepper in 2 tablespoons butter until tender; remove and keep warm. Sprinkle salt and remaining pepper over the beef.

3. In the same skillet, cook beef in remaining butter over medium-high heat until no longer pink. Spoon onto roll bottoms; top with cheese and onion mixture. Replace roll tops. Serve with au jus.

Yield: 4 servings.

TIP

A frittata is a great choice for breakfast. But you can turn it into a hearty lunch or dinner by using the open-faced omelet as a sandwich filling. Simply cook the frittata as the recipe directs, then place a piece between two slices of substantial bakery bread, such as sourdough or focaccia. Include sliced tomato and fresh spinach leaves, if you would like, for a quick sandwich that's sure to satisfy.

busy family favorites

Chow Mein Tuna Salad

Marilyn Coomer • Louisville, Kentucky

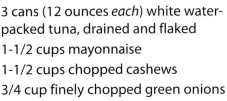

You'll enjoy the crunchiness of the chow mein noodles in this delicious spin on traditional tuna salad.

3 cans (12 ounces *each*) white water-packed tuna, drained and flaked

1-1/2 cups mayonnaise

1-1/2 cups chopped cashews

3/4 cup finely chopped green onions

3 jars (2 ounces *each*) diced pimientos, drained and finely chopped

3 tablespoons finely chopped green pepper

3 tablespoons sour cream

1 tablespoon cider vinegar

3/4 teaspoon salt

3 cups chow mein noodles

1. Place tuna in a large bowl; set aside. In another large bowl, combine the mayonnaise, cashews, onions, pimientos, green pepper, sour cream, vinegar and salt.

2. Pour over tuna and toss to coat. Serve with chow mein noodles.

Yield: 6 servings.

Chicken Pesto Wraps

Gary Phile • Ravenna, Ohio

This makes a really quick meal for us. My wife likes to add a dollop of sour cream in her sandwich, and I sometimes use tomato basil sauce.

1/2 pound ground chicken

1 tablespoon canola oil

1/4 cup sun-dried tomato pesto

4 flour tortillas (8 inches), warmed

1/2 cup shredded part-skim mozzarella cheese

8 grape tomatoes, cut in half

4 slices red onion, separated into rings

1 cup shredded lettuce

1. In a large skillet, cook chicken in oil over medium heat for 5-6 minutes or until juices run clear; drain.

2. Spread pesto over each tortilla; spoon chicken down the center. Layer with the cheese, tomatoes, onion and lettuce; roll up.

Yield: 4 servings.

Roast Beef Barbecue

Agnes Ward • Stratford, Ontario

When I'm in a hurry and want something good, this sandwich fills the bill. It tastes great with a salad and pork and beans on the side. Instead of using ketchup, I occasionally use barbecue sauce with a little Tabasco for extra zip.

2/3 pound thinly sliced deli roast beef

1/2 cup water

1/4 cup ketchup

1 tablespoon brown sugar

1/2 teaspoon prepared mustard

1/4 teaspoon hot pepper sauce

1/8 teaspoon salt

1/8 teaspoon pepper

1/8 teaspoon chili powder

4 hamburger buns, split

1. In a small saucepan, combine the first nine ingredients. Cook over medium-high heat for 4-6 minutes or until heated through. Serve on buns, using a slotted spoon.

Yield: 4 servings.

Waldorf Tuna Salad

Shirley Glaab • Hattiesburg, Mississippi

I dress up tuna salad deliciously with apple, raisins, dates and walnuts...then drizzle it all with a tangy yogurt dressing.

2 cans (6 ounces *each*) light water-packed tuna, drained and flaked

1 large red apple, chopped

1/3 cup chopped celery

1/3 cup raisins

1/3 cup chopped dates

1/4 cup chopped walnuts

1/2 cup fat-free plain yogurt

1/4 cup reduced-fat mayonnaise

4 lettuce leaves

1/4 cup shredded reduced-fat Monterey Jack cheese

1. In a large bowl, combine the tuna, apple, celery, raisins, dates and walnuts. Combine yogurt and mayonnaise; add to tuna mixture and toss to coat. Serve on lettuce-lined plates; sprinkle with the cheese.

Yield: 4 servings.

busy family favorites

Balsamic Chicken Salad

Rebecca Lindamood • Belfast, New York

This is a fast, elegant and tasty alternative to frozen dinners. My husband fell in love with this main course the first time I served it and he regularly requests that I make it.

6 boneless skinless chicken breast halves (4 ounces *each*), cut into 3-inch strips

4 tablespoons olive oil, *divided*

1/2 teaspoon minced garlic

1/4 cup balsamic vinegar

1-1/2 cups halved cherry tomatoes

1 tablespoon minced fresh basil *or* 1 teaspoon dried basil

1/4 teaspoon salt

1/8 teaspoon pepper

6 cups torn mixed salad greens

1. In a large skillet, saute chicken in 1 tablespoon oil until no longer pink. Add garlic; cook 1 minute longer. Remove from the pan.

2. In the same skillet, bring vinegar to a boil. Add the chicken, tomatoes, basil, salt, pepper and remaining oil; cook and stir until heated through. Divide salad greens among six plates; top with chicken mixture.

Yield: 6 servings.

Bacon-Topped Grilled Cheese

Nita Crosby • St. George, Utah

Sourdough bread adds a delicious twist to an all-American lunch classic. My robust version gets its heartiness from bacon and extra flavor from the onion, sour cream and oregano.

4 slices part-skim mozzarella cheese

8 slices sourdough bread

2 large tomatoes, thinly sliced

8 bacon strips, cooked

4 tablespoons sour cream

4 tablespoons finely chopped onion

1/4 teaspoon dried oregano

4 slices cheddar cheese

2 tablespoons butter, softened

1. Place mozzarella cheese on four bread slices; layer each with a fourth of the tomato slices, two bacon strips, 1 tablespoon sour cream, 1 tablespoon onion, a pinch of oregano and one slice of cheddar cheese. Top with remaining bread.

2. Butter outsides of sandwiches. In a small skillet over medium heat, toast sandwiches for 3-4 minutes on each side or until cheese is melted.

Yield: 4 servings.

Chicken Caesar Salad

Kim Blanda • Neptune, New Jersey

After tasting this salad at a friend's going-away party, I made sure to request the recipe. Now I fix it for my husband just about every week. It's great with a potato or pasta side dish and chunks of crusty bread.

6 cups torn romaine

1 pound boneless skinless chicken breasts, cooked and cut into strips

2 cups seasoned salad croutons

3/4 cup shredded Parmesan cheese

1/2 teaspoon salt

6 tablespoons olive oil

1/3 cup lemon juice

3 to 4 garlic cloves, minced

1/4 teaspoon coarsely ground pepper

1. In a large salad bowl, combine the romaine, chicken, croutons, Parmesan cheese and salt.

2. In a small bowl, whisk the oil, lemon juice, garlic and pepper. Pour over the salad; toss to coat.

Yield: 4-6 servings.

busy family favorites

Southwestern Panini

Janet Miller • Midland, Texas

I'm a busy wife, mother, grandmother and great-grandmother who loves to cook. This warm, hearty sandwich is a convenient way for me to serve a complete meal.

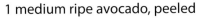

1 medium ripe avocado, peeled

1/2 teaspoon sugar

1/2 teaspoon garlic salt

1/2 teaspoon lemon juice

8 slices oat bread

1/2 pound thinly sliced deli ham

4 slices Swiss cheese

2 tablespoons butter

1. In a small bowl, mash the avocado with sugar, garlic salt and lemon juice. Spread over four slices of bread; layer with ham and cheese. Top with remaining bread.

2. Spread butter over both sides of sandwiches. Cook on an indoor grill for 2-3 minutes or until bread is browned and cheese is melted.

Yield: 4 servings.

Supreme Pizza Tortillas

Jill Flory • Covington, Ohio

Hungry for scratch pizza, but too busy to fix one, I put together these delicious tortillas. Canadian bacon is a good substitute for ham, and cheddar or Swiss cheese work as well as mozzarella. Extra sauce makes a great sandwich dip.

1/2 pound ground beef

1/2 pound bulk pork sausage

1/2 cup chopped onion

1/2 cup chopped green pepper

1 can (4 ounces) mushroom stems and pieces, drained and chopped

1 can (2-1/4 ounces) sliced ripe olives, drained

1/2 pound fully cooked ham, thinly sliced

8 flour tortillas (10 inches), room temperature

2 cups pizza sauce, *divided*

40 slices pepperoni

40 banana pepper rings

2 cups (8 ounces) shredded part-skim mozzarella cheese

1. In a large skillet, cook beef, sausage, onion and green pepper over medium heat until meat is no longer pink; drain. Stir in mushrooms and olives; set aside.

2. Place one slice of ham on each tortilla; top with about 1/2 cup beef mixture. Drizzle each with 3 tablespoons pizza sauce. Layer with pepperoni, banana pepper rings and cheese. Fold sides of tortillas over filling; secure with toothpicks.

3. Place in two 13-in. x 9-in. baking dishes. Bake, uncovered, at 400° for 10-15 minutes or until cheese is melted. Warm the remaining pizza sauce; serve with wraps.

Yield: 8 servings.

busy family favorites

TIP

Don't settle for ho-hum mayonnaise when building a sandwich. Jazz up the mayo by adding some chopped sun-dried tomatoes, chopped olives and garlic, prepared horseradish, pesto sauce or ground mustard.

Tuna Salad Wraps

Ivy Abbadessa • Loxahatchee, Florida

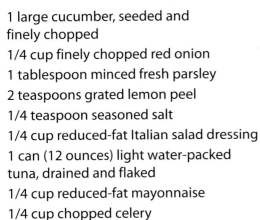

Usually, I make my tuna salad the night before, so the flavors have more time to blend. Plus, the sandwiches go together quickly for a neat and compact meal.

1 large cucumber, seeded and finely chopped

1/4 cup finely chopped red onion

1 tablespoon minced fresh parsley

2 teaspoons grated lemon peel

1/4 teaspoon seasoned salt

1/4 cup reduced-fat Italian salad dressing

1 can (12 ounces) light water-packed tuna, drained and flaked

1/4 cup reduced-fat mayonnaise

1/4 cup chopped celery

1/4 cup chopped green onions

6 flour tortillas (8 inches), room temperature

1. In a small bowl, combine the first six ingredients. In another bowl, combine the tuna, mayonnaise, celery and green onions.

2. Spread 1/4 cup tuna mixture over each tortilla; top with 1/3 cup cucumber mixture. Fold in sides of tortillas and roll up.

Yield: 6 servings.

sandwiches & salads

Hot Italian Ham Subs

Leann Hillmer • Sylvan Grove, Kansas

I got the idea for this recipe when I tried to duplicate a delicious deli sandwich I enjoyed while traveling. Serve it with a nice green salad for a hearty lunch or supper.

1/2 cup olive oil
1/4 cup red wine vinegar
1 tablespoon Dijon mustard
1 teaspoon sugar
1/2 teaspoon pepper
1/2 teaspoon minced fresh basil
1/4 teaspoon salt
4 submarine buns, split
12 slices deli ham
12 slices tomato
12 slices part-skim mozzarella cheese
12 fresh basil leaves
4 slices sweet onion, halved
8 slices provolone cheese

1. In a small bowl, whisk the first seven ingredients. Generously drizzle dressing over cut sides of buns.

2. On bun bottoms, layer the ham, tomato and mozzarella cheese. On bun tops, layer the basil leaves, onion and provolone cheese. Place on a baking sheet.

3. Broil 6-8 in. from the heat for 2-3 minutes or until cheese is melted. Place bun tops over bottoms; serve immediately.

Yield: 4 servings.

Roast Beef Tortilla Wraps

Taste of Home Test Kitchen

Cumin, chili powder and cayenne pepper give the cream cheese spread in these extraordinary sandwiches a wonderfully mild Southwestern flavor.

2 tablespoons cream cheese, softened
2 tablespoons mayonnaise
1/2 teaspoon ground cumin
1/4 teaspoon salt
1/4 teaspoon chili powder
1/8 teaspoon cayenne pepper
4 flour tortillas (10 inches), warmed
4 leaf lettuce leaves
1/2 pound thinly sliced deli roast beef
8 thin slices tomato
4 slices red onion, separated into rings

1. In a small bowl, beat the cream cheese, mayonnaise, cumin, salt, chili powder and cayenne until smooth.

2. Spread 1 tablespoon on one side of each tortilla; top with lettuce, roast beef, tomato and onion; roll up tightly. Cut on a diagonal.

Yield: 4 servings.

busy family favorites

Brickyard Bistro Sandwich

Taste of Home Test Kitchen

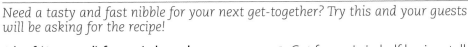

Need a tasty and fast nibble for your next get-together? Try this and your guests will be asking for the recipe!

1 loaf (1 pound) focaccia bread

2 tablespoons olive oil

1 tablespoon balsamic vinegar

2 teaspoons minced fresh oregano

1 teaspoon minced fresh rosemary

2 slices red onion, separated into rings

2 ounces sliced deli smoked turkey

2 ounces thinly sliced hard salami

2 ounces sliced deli roast beef

2 ounces sliced provolone cheese

1 plum tomato, sliced

2 lettuce leaves

1. Cut focaccia in half horizontally. In a small bowl, combine the oil, vinegar, oregano and rosemary; brush over cut sides of bread.

2. On bread bottom, layer with onion, turkey, salami, roast beef, cheese, tomato and lettuce; replace bread top. Cut the sandwich into four wedges.

Yield: 4 servings.

Guacamole Turkey Subs

Marci McDonald • Armarillo, Texas

This may sound like a strange combination, but it is the best sub you'll ever eat!

1 package (3 ounces) cream cheese, softened

1/3 cup prepared guacamole

1/4 cup picante sauce

3 submarine sandwich buns (about 8 inches), split

1-1/2 cups shredded lettuce

1 medium tomato, thinly sliced

9 slices smoked deli turkey

9 bacon strips, cooked and drained

1. In a large bowl, combine the cream cheese, guacamole and picante sauce; spread over cut side of buns.

2. On bun bottoms, layer half of the lettuce, all of the tomato, turkey and bacon, then remaining lettuce. Replace tops. Cut sandwiches in half; wrap in plastic wrap. Refrigerate until serving.

Yield: 6 servings.

Reuben Slaw Sandwiches

Taste of Home Test Kitchen

Prepared coleslaw helps make these tasty sandwiches quick and easy to put together.

1-1/2 cups deli coleslaw

2 tablespoons stone-ground mustard

6 submarine buns, split

3/4 pound thinly sliced deli corned beef

12 dill pickle slices

12 slices Swiss cheese, halved

1. In a small bowl, combine coleslaw and mustard. Spread about 2 tablespoons over each bun half. Top with the corned beef, pickles and cheese.

2. Place sandwiches on a baking sheet. Broil 4-6 in. from the heat for 3 minutes or until cheese is melted.

Yield: 6 servings.

Sirloin Steak Sandwiches

Marlene Wiczek • Little Falls, Minnesota

This is a fun sandwich to pack into a brown bag lunch. If a microwave is available, warm it just enough to melt the cheese.

1 beef top sirloin steak (1 pound)

4 onion rolls, split

1/4 cup mayonnaise

2 to 4 tablespoons prepared mustard

4 teaspoons prepared horseradish

4 slices Swiss cheese

1. Grill steak, uncovered, over medium heat for 5-8 minutes on each side or until meat reaches desired doneness (for medium-rare, a meat thermometer should read 145°; medium, 160°; well-done, 170°).

2. Spread cut side of roll tops with mayonnaise, mustard and horseradish. Slice steak diagonally; place on roll bottoms. Top with cheese and roll tops.

Yield: 4 servings.

busy family favorites

Soups

Taco Soup, p. 44

Beef Soup in a Hurry

Loellen Holley • Topock, Arizona

I need just a few canned goods to stir up this comforting microwave mixture. I call this "throw-together soup." Serve it with a green salad and hot bread or rolls. You can also simmer this soup in a slow cooker.

1 can (24 ounces) beef stew

1 can (14-1/2 ounces) stewed tomatoes, cut up

1 can (10-3/4 ounces) condensed vegetable beef soup, undiluted

1 can (8-3/4 ounces) whole kernel corn, drained

1/8 teaspoon hot pepper sauce

1. Combine all ingredients in a microwave-safe bowl. Cover and microwave on high for 2-3 minutes or until heated through, stirring once.

Yield: 6 servings.

EDITOR'S NOTE: This recipe was tested in a 1,100-watt microwave.

Potato-Clam Soup in Bread Bowls

Cheryl Cor • Auburn, Washington

This heartwarming main course helps my husband get a swift yet satisfying meal on the table when I'm at work. He loves clam chowder and this simple recipe lets him prepare it in just minutes.

2 cans (18.8 ounces *each*) ready-to-serve chunky baked potato with cheddar and bacon bits soup

2 cans (6-1/2 ounces *each*) chopped clams, drained

1 bacon strip, cooked and crumbled

1 teaspoon minced chives

1 teaspoon dried parsley flakes

1 teaspoon dried rosemary, crushed

1/4 teaspoon pepper

5 round loaves (8 ounces *each*) sourdough bread

1. In a large saucepan, combine the soup, clams, bacon, chives, parsley flakes, rosemary and pepper; heat through.

2. Meanwhile, cut a thin slice off the top of each loaf; set aside. Hollow out loaves, leaving 3/4-in. shells (discard removed bread or save for another use). Ladle soup into bread bowls; replace tops.

Yield: 5 servings.

busy family favorites

Hot Italian Sausage Soup

Dan Bute • Ottawa, Illinois

Loaded with zesty sausage and an array of veggies, this soup will hit the spot! A hint of brown sugar balances the heat with a little sweetness, making it a real crowd-pleaser. I'm part owner of a small tavern, and on Saturdays, we provide soups and deli sandwiches free of charge. Our patrons love this one.

1 pound bulk hot Italian sausage

1 can (14-1/2 ounces) Italian stewed tomatoes

1 can (8 ounces) tomato sauce

1 cup frozen Italian vegetables

3/4 cup julienned green, sweet red *and/or* yellow pepper

1/4 cup chopped onion

1/4 cup white wine *or* chicken broth

1 teaspoon brown sugar

1 teaspoon minced fresh parsley

1/2 teaspoon Italian seasoning

1/8 teaspoon salt

1/8 teaspoon pepper

1. In a large skillet, cook sausage over medium heat until no longer pink.

2. Meanwhile, in a large saucepan, combine the remaining ingredients. Bring to a boil. Reduce heat; cover and simmer for 10 minutes or until vegetables are tender.

3. Drain sausage; add to soup and heat through.

Yield: 4 servings.

Rocky Ford Chili

Karen Sikora • Phoenix, Arizona

When my brother and sister were in grade school in little Rocky Ford, Colorado, this comforting chili dish was served in the school cafeteria. My siblings described it to my mother so she could duplicate it at home. We all enjoy preparing it for our own families now.

2 cans (14.3 ounces *each*) chili with beans

1 package (10 ounces) frozen corn

4 cups corn chips

1 cup shredded lettuce

1 cup (4 ounces) shredded Mexican cheese blend

1 can (2-1/4 ounces) sliced ripe olives, drained

1/4 cup sour cream

1/4 cup salsa

1. In a large microwave-safe bowl, cook chili and corn on high for 2-4 minutes or until heated through. Place corn chips in four large soup bowls; top with chili mixture, lettuce, cheese, olives, sour cream and salsa.

Yield: 4 servings.

EDITOR'S NOTE: This recipe was tested in a 1,100-watt microwave.

Shrimp 'n' Chicken Noodle Soup

Todd Schaal • Lake City, Minnesota

Give dinner a Thai twist with this recipe. It's a wonderful way to dress up ramen noodles.

1/4 cup chopped sweet onion

3 green onions, sliced

1 can (4 ounces) mushroom stems and pieces, drained

2 teaspoons olive oil

2 teaspoons minced garlic

3/4 cup frozen cooked salad shrimp, thawed

1 teaspoon dried rosemary, crushed

1/4 teaspoon lemon-pepper seasoning

2 cans (14-1/2 ounces *each*) chicken broth

1 cup cubed cooked chicken

1 package (3 ounces) chicken ramen noodles

2 tablespoons crumbled cooked bacon, optional

1. In a large saucepan, saute onions and mushrooms in oil. Add the garlic; cook 1 minute longer. Stir in the shrimp, rosemary and lemon-pepper. Cook for 3-4 minutes or until vegetables are tender.

2. Stir in the broth, chicken, ramen noodles and contents of seasoning packet if desired. Bring to a boil. Reduce heat; cover and simmer for 6-8 minutes or until noodles are tender. Garnish with bacon if desired.

Yield: 4 servings.

busy family favorites

Spinach Tortellini Soup

Cindy Politowicz • Northville, Michigan

Tortellini, spinach and tomatoes are a pleasing combination in this tasty soup. Don't forget the sprinkle of Parmesan cheese.

3/4 cup chopped onion

1 teaspoon minced garlic

1 tablespoon olive oil

2 cans (14-1/2 ounces *each*) reduced-sodium chicken broth

2 cups water

1 teaspoon sugar

1/4 teaspoon salt

1/4 teaspoon pepper

1 package (9 ounces) refrigerated cheese tortellini

1 can (14-1/2 ounces) diced tomatoes, undrained

1 package (10 ounces) frozen chopped spinach, thawed

3 tablespoons shredded Parmesan cheese

1. In a large saucepan, saute onion and garlic in oil until tender. Add the broth, water, sugar, salt and pepper. Bring to a boil. Add tortellini; cook for 7-9 minutes or until tender, stirring occasionally.

2. Reduce heat. Stir in tomatoes and spinach; heat through. Just before serving, sprinkle with Parmesan cheese.

Yield: 6 servings (about 2 quarts).

Tuscan Turkey Soup

Marie McConnell • Shelbyville, Illinois

Use your leftover Thanksgiving turkey to make this quick, creamy soup chock-full of pumpkin and beans to feed hungry family and friends. It's simply fabulous!

1 cup chopped onion

1 cup chopped celery

2 tablespoons olive oil

1 teaspoon minced garlic

2 cans (14-1/2 ounces *each*) chicken broth

2 cups cubed cooked turkey

1 can (15 ounces) solid-pack pumpkin

1 can (15 ounces) white kidney *or* cannellini beans, rinsed and drained

1/2 teaspoon salt

1/2 teaspoon dried basil

1/4 teaspoon pepper

Grated Parmesan cheese, optional

1. In a large saucepan, saute onion and celery in oil until tender. Add the garlic; cook 1 minute longer. Stir in the broth, turkey, pumpkin, beans, salt, basil and pepper. Bring to a boil.

2. Reduce heat; simmer, uncovered, for 10-15 minutes or until heated through, stirring occasionally. Serve with cheese if desired.

Yield: 8 servings (2 quarts).

Gumbo in a Jiffy

Amy Flack • Homer City, Pennsylvania

This gumbo recipe could not be any easier to make. Try it on a busy weeknight with a side of crusty bread for dipping!

3 Italian turkey sausage links, sliced

1 can (14-1/2 ounces) diced tomatoes with green peppers and onions, undrained

1 can (14-1/2 ounces) reduced-sodium chicken broth

1/2 cup water

1 cup uncooked instant rice

1 can (7 ounces) whole kernel corn, drained

1. In a large saucepan, cook sausage until no longer pink; drain. Stir in the tomatoes, broth and water; bring to a boil. Stir in rice and corn; cover and remove from the heat. Let stand for 5 minutes.

Yield: 6 servings.

Egg Drop Soup

Amy Corlew-Sherlock • Lapeer, Michigan

We start many stir-fry meals with this easy Egg Drop Soup, which cooks in just minutes flat. There are many recipe variations, but we like the addition of cornstarch to thicken the soup and give it a rich, golden color. I got the recipe from my grandma's old cookbook.

3 cups chicken broth

1 tablespoon cornstarch

2 tablespoons cold water

1 egg, lightly beaten

1 green onion, sliced

1. In a large saucepan, bring broth to a boil over medium heat. Combine cornstarch and water until smooth; gradually stir into broth. Bring to a boil; cook and stir for 2 minutes or until thickened.

2. Reduce heat. Drizzle beaten egg into hot broth, stirring constantly. Remove from the heat; stir in onion.

Yield: 4 servings.

busy family favorites

Minestrone with Turkey

Angela Goodman • Kaneohe, Hawaii

I remember my mom making this soup; now I make it as often as I can. It's a good way to use up leftover vegetables. Sometimes I add a can of rinsed and drained kidney or garbanzo beans.

1 medium onion, chopped

1 medium carrot, sliced

1 celery rib, sliced

1 tablespoon olive oil

1 garlic clove, minced

4 cups chicken broth *or* homemade turkey stock

1 can (14-1/2 ounces) diced tomatoes, undrained

2/3 cup *each* frozen peas, corn and cut green beans, thawed

1/2 cup uncooked elbow macaroni

1 teaspoon salt

1/4 teaspoon dried basil

1/4 teaspoon dried oregano

1/4 teaspoon pepper

1 bay leaf

1 cup cubed cooked turkey

1 small zucchini, halved lengthwise and cut into 1/4-inch slices

1/4 cup grated Parmesan cheese, optional

1. In a Dutch oven, saute the onion, carrot and celery in oil until tender. Add garlic; cook 1 minute longer. Add the broth, vegetables, macaroni and seasonings.

2. Bring to a boil. Reduce heat; simmer, uncovered, for 5 minutes. Add turkey and zucchini; cook until zucchini is crisp-tender. Discard bay leaf. Serve with Parmesan cheese if desired.

Yield: 6 servings (2 quarts).

Chinese Chicken Soup

Taste of Home Test Kitchen

This attractive, simple soup begins with frozen stir-fry vegetables. Convenient refrigerated minced gingerroot adds to the Oriental flavor.

3 cans (14-1/2 ounces *each*) chicken broth

1 package (16 ounces) frozen stir-fry vegetable blend

2 cups cubed cooked chicken

1 teaspoon minced fresh gingerroot

1 teaspoon soy sauce

1/4 teaspoon sesame oil

1. In a large saucepan, combine all ingredients. Bring to a boil. Reduce heat; cover and simmer for 15 minutes or until heated through.

Yield: 6 servings.

Vegetable Bean Soup

Lillian Palko • Napa, California

Full of kidney beans, celery, spinach, carrot, zucchini and tomatoes, my comforting broth is ideal to serve on crisp autumn days with a loaf of crusty bread or warm biscuits.

1 can (16 ounces) kidney beans, rinsed and drained

1 medium zucchini, cubed

1 medium carrot, diced

2 celery ribs, chopped

3 green onions, sliced

1/4 cup chopped fresh spinach

3 tablespoons quick-cooking barley

3 cans (14-1/2 ounces *each*) reduced-sodium chicken broth

1/4 cup minced fresh parsley

1 garlic clove, minced

1/2 teaspoon garlic salt

1 can (14-1/2 ounces) Italian diced tomatoes, undrained

1. In a large saucepan, combine the beans, zucchini, carrot, celery, onions, spinach, barley, broth, parsley, garlic and garlic salt. Bring to a boil. Reduce heat; cover and simmer for 10-12 minutes or until the barley and vegetables are tender.

2. Add the tomatoes; heat through.

Yield: 8 servings (2 quarts).

busy family favorites

Pesto Minestrone

Natalie Cataldo • Des Moines, Iowa

I rely on store-bought pesto to provide mild flavor to this chunky tortellini and vegetable soup. If you don't like zucchini, use another vegetable.

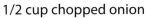

1/2 cup chopped onion

2 teaspoons olive oil

1 teaspoon minced garlic

2-1/4 cups water

2 cups frozen mixed vegetables

1 can (14-1/2 ounces) vegetable broth

3/4 teaspoon dried oregano

1/2 teaspoon salt

1/2 teaspoon pepper

1 package (9 ounces) refrigerated cheese tortellini

2 cups diced zucchini

2 tablespoons prepared pesto

1. In a large saucepan, saute onion in oil until tender. Add garlic; cook 1 minute longer. Stir in the water, mixed vegetables, broth, oregano, salt and pepper. Bring to a boil. Reduce heat; cover and simmer for 3 minutes.

2. Add the tortellini, zucchini and pesto. Simmer, uncovered, 7-9 minutes longer or until pasta and vegetables are tender.

Yield: 4 servings.

Country Sausage Soup

Grace Meyer • Galva, Kansas

Savory pork sausage makes this a hearty fix when I don't know what to prepare for supper.

3/4 pound bulk pork sausage

1 can (14-1/2 ounces) diced tomatoes, undrained

1 can (14-1/2 ounces) chicken broth

1 teaspoon dried thyme

3/4 to 1 teaspoon dried rosemary, crushed

1/4 teaspoon pepper

1 can (15-1/2 ounces) great northern beans, rinsed and drained

1 can (15 ounces) garbanzo beans *or* chickpeas, rinsed and drained

1. In a large saucepan, cook sausage over medium heat until no longer pink; drain. Stir in the tomatoes, broth, thyme, rosemary and pepper. Bring to a boil. Stir in the beans; heat through.

Yield: 4 servings.

Tortellini Soup

Donna Morgan • Hend, Tennessee

I like to top bowls of this tasty soup with a little grated Parmesan cheese...and serve it with crusty bread to round out the meal.

2 garlic cloves, minced
1 tablespoon butter
3 cans (14-1/2 ounces *each*) reduced-sodium chicken broth *or* vegetable broth
1 package (9 ounces) refrigerated cheese tortellini
1 can (14-1/2 ounces) diced tomatoes with green chilies, undrained
1 package (10 ounces) frozen chopped spinach, thawed

1. In a large saucepan, saute garlic in butter for 1 minute. Stir in the broth. Bring to a boil. Add tortellini; cook for 7-9 minutes or until tender. Stir in the tomatoes and spinach; heat through.

Yield: 5 servings.

Bow Tie Beef Soup

Lee Anne McBride • Austin, Texas

Usually I turn the page when I see a long list of ingredients, but this one didn't seem so bad. After fixing it, I think it's one of the best and easiest one-dish meals I've made.

2 cups sliced zucchini
1 can (14-1/2 ounces) beef broth
1 cup uncooked bow tie pasta
3/4 cup water
1/2 teaspoon dried oregano
1/4 to 1/2 teaspoon dried thyme
1/4 to 1/2 teaspoon crushed red pepper flakes
1-1/2 pounds ground beef
1 cup chopped onion
2 teaspoons minced garlic
4 plum tomatoes, cut into chunks
1/4 cup minced fresh basil
1/2 cup shredded Parmesan cheese

1. In a Dutch oven, combine the first seven ingredients. Bring to a boil. With a spoon, press pasta into broth mixture. Reduce heat; cover and simmer for 15 minutes or until pasta is tender, stirring once.

2. Meanwhile, in a large skillet, cook the beef, onion and garlic over medium heat until meat is no longer pink; drain.

3. Add the beef mixture, tomatoes and basil to the broth mixture; heat through. Garnish with Parmesan cheese.

Yield: 8 servings (about 2 quarts).

busy family favorites

Navy Bean Vegetable Soup

Bean Education and Awareness Network • Scottsbluff, Nebraska

Beans add extra texture and flavor to this vegetable soup. It's hearty and filling!

3 medium carrots, sliced

1-1/2 cups chopped onions

1 cup sliced celery

1 tablespoon canola oil

2 to 3 garlic cloves, minced

2 cans (14-1/2 ounces *each*) chicken broth

2 cans (15 ounces *each*) navy *or* great northern beans, rinsed and drained, *divided*

2 cups fresh broccoli florets

1/2 teaspoon salt

1/2 teaspoon dried rosemary, crushed

1/4 teaspoon dried thyme

1/4 teaspoon pepper

1 cup fresh baby spinach, optional

1. In a Dutch oven, saute the carrots, onions and celery in oil until tender. Add garlic; cook 1 minute longer. Stir in broth, one can of beans, broccoli and seasonings; bring to a boil. Reduce heat; simmer, uncovered, for 5-7 minutes.

2. Place remaining beans in a blender; cover and process until smooth. Add to the soup with spinach if desired; simmer for 2 minutes or until heated through.

Yield: 8 servings (2 quarts).

Basil Turkey Soup

Taste of Home Test Kitchen

After a busy day of shopping, it's easy to put together this soup with leftover turkey and frozen vegetables. It tastes like it simmered all day!

2 cups beef broth

2-1/2 cups frozen mixed vegetables

1 can (14-1/2 ounces) diced tomatoes, undrained

3/4 cup uncooked small shell pasta

3/4 teaspoon dried basil

3/4 teaspoon pepper

2-1/2 cups cubed cooked turkey

2-1/2 teaspoons dried parsley flakes

1. In a large saucepan, combine the first six ingredients. Bring to a boil. Reduce heat; cover and simmer for 7-10 minutes or until the pasta and vegetables are tender. Stir in the turkey and parsley; heat through.

Yield: 6 servings.

White Chili with Chicken

Christy Campos • Richmond, Virginia

Folks who enjoy a change from traditional tomato-based chilies will enjoy this version. The flavorful blend has tender chunks of chicken, white beans and just enough zip.

1 medium onion, chopped

1 jalapeno pepper, seeded and chopped, optional

1 tablespoon canola oil

2 garlic cloves, minced

4 cups chicken broth

2 cans (15-1/2 ounces *each*) great northern beans, rinsed and drained

2 tablespoons minced fresh parsley

1 tablespoon lime juice

1 to 1-1/4 teaspoons ground cumin

2 tablespoons cornstarch

1/4 cup cold water

2 cups cubed cooked chicken

1. In a large saucepan, cook onion and jalapeno if desired in oil until tender. Add garlic; cook 1 minute longer. Stir in the broth, beans, parsley, lime juice and cumin; bring to a boil. Reduce heat; cover and simmer for 10 minutes, stirring occasionally.

2. Combine cornstarch and water until smooth; gradually stir into chili. Add chicken. Bring to a boil; cook and stir for 2 minutes or until thickened.

Yield: 6 servings.

EDITOR'S NOTE: When cutting hot peppers, disposable gloves are recommended. Avoid touching your face.

busy family favorites

Pasta Beef Soup

Brenda Jackson • Garden City, Kansas

This tasty soup can be prepared in no time. Handy canned goods, tomato juice and a frozen pasta-vegetable medley make this recipe flavorful and fast.

1 pound lean ground beef (90% lean)

2 cans (14-1/2 ounces *each*) beef broth

1 package (16 ounces) frozen pasta with broccoli, corn and carrots in garlic-seasoned sauce

1-1/2 cups tomato juice

1 can (14-1/2 ounces) diced tomatoes, undrained

2 teaspoons Italian seasoning

1/4 cup shredded Parmesan cheese, optional

1. In a large saucepan, cook beef over medium heat until no longer pink; drain. Add the broth, pasta with vegetables, tomato juice, tomatoes and Italian seasoning; bring to a boil. Reduce heat; cover and simmer for 10 minutes or until vegetables are tender. Serve with cheese if desired.

Yield: 6 servings.

Veggie Chowder

Vicki Kerr • Portland, Maine

This thick soup features fresh potatoes, carrots and corn. It would also be nice alongside sandwiches for a complete meal.

2 cups reduced-sodium chicken broth
2 cups cubed peeled potatoes
1 cup chopped carrots
1/2 cup chopped onion
1 can (14-3/4 ounces) cream-style corn
1 can (12 ounces) fat-free evaporated milk
3/4 cup shredded reduced-fat cheddar cheese
1/2 cup sliced fresh mushrooms
1/4 teaspoon pepper
2 tablespoons real bacon bits

1. In a large saucepan, combine the broth, potatoes, carrots and onion. Bring to a boil. Reduce heat; simmer, uncovered, for 10-15 minutes or until the vegetables are tender.

2. Add the corn, milk, cheese, mushrooms and pepper. Cook and stir 4-6 minutes longer or until heated through. Sprinkle with bacon.

Yield: 7 servings.

Turkey Bean Chili

LaRita Lang • Lincoln, Nebraska

This is a fast, easy recipe that tastes great. It won a ribbon at the Nebraska State Fair.

2 cups cubed cooked turkey breast
2 cans (14-1/2 ounces *each*) diced tomatoes, undrained
1 can (15 ounces) black beans, rinsed and drained
1 can (15 ounces) great northern beans, rinsed and drained
1 cup barbecue sauce
1 medium onion, chopped
1 teaspoon chili powder
1 teaspoon ground cumin

1. In a large saucepan, combine all ingredients. Bring to a boil. Reduce heat; simmer, uncovered, for 10 minutes or until heated through.

Yield: 6 servings.

Zippy Chicken Soup

Linda Lashley • Redgranite, Wisconsin

This spicy, satisfying soup is quick to make but tastes like it simmered all day. If you're lucky enough to have leftovers, it's delicious reheated!

1/2 pound boneless skinless chicken breasts, cut into 1-inch cubes

2 cans (14-1/2 ounces *each*) reduced-sodium chicken broth, *divided*

2 cups frozen corn

1 can (15 ounces) black beans, rinsed and drained

1 can (10 ounces) diced tomatoes and green chilies, undrained

1 jalapeno pepper, seeded and chopped

2 tablespoons minced fresh cilantro

3 teaspoons chili powder

1/2 teaspoon ground cumin

1 tablespoon cornstarch

18 tortilla chips

Shredded reduced-fat Mexican cheese blend, optional

1. In a large nonstick saucepan or Dutch oven coated with cooking spray, cook chicken over medium heat for 4-6 minutes or until no longer pink. Set aside 2 tablespoons of broth; add remaining broth to pan. Stir in the corn, beans, tomatoes, jalapeno, cilantro, chili powder and cumin. Bring to a boil. Reduce heat; simmer, uncovered, for 15 minutes.

2. Combine the cornstarch and reserved broth until smooth; gradually stir into soup. Bring to a boil; cook and stir for 2 minutes or until thickened. Top each serving with tortilla chips. Garnish with cheese if desired.

Yield: 6 servings.

EDITOR'S NOTE: When cutting hot peppers, disposable gloves are recommended. Avoid touching your face.

ABC Vegetable Soup

Taste of Home Test Kitchen

All you need for this down-home soup is a handful of ingredients, including fun alphabet pasta and convenient frozen veggies. It's ideal for nights when there is a frost in the air.

1/2 cup uncooked alphabet pasta

3 cans (14-1/2 ounces *each*) beef broth

1 package (16 ounces) frozen mixed vegetables

1/2 teaspoon dried thyme

1/2 teaspoon dried basil

1/4 teaspoon pepper

1. Cook pasta according to package directions. In a large saucepan, combine the remaining ingredients. Bring to a boil. Reduce heat; cover and simmer for 5 minutes or until vegetables are tender. Drain pasta; stir into soup.

Yield: 6-8 servings.

Low-Fat Clam Chowder

Linda Tindel • Avondale, Arizona

You'd never guess that a rich and creamy clam chowder could be low-fat, but this one is! With lots of potatoes, turkey bacon and seasonings, this slimmed-down version is loaded with fabulous flavor.

2 turkey bacon strips, diced

1 cup chopped onion

2 cups cubed red potatoes

2 cans (6-1/2 ounces *each*) minced clams, undrained

1 cup reduced-sodium chicken broth

1 cup chopped celery

1/2 teaspoon dried basil

1/2 teaspoon dried thyme

1/2 teaspoon reduced-sodium seafood seasoning

1/2 teaspoon salt-free lemon-pepper seasoning

1/8 teaspoon white pepper

1 tablespoon all-purpose flour

1-1/2 cups fat-free half-and-half

1. In a large nonstick saucepan, cook bacon and onion over medium heat until onion is tender. Add the potatoes, clams, broth, celery and seasonings. Bring to a boil. Reduce heat; cover and simmer for 12-15 minutes or until vegetables are tender.

2. In a small bowl, combine flour and half-and-half until smooth; stir into potato mixture. Bring to a boil; cook and stir for 2 minutes or until thickened.

Yield: 4 servings.

busy family favorites

Pasta Fagioli Soup

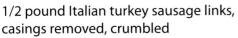

Brenda Thomas • Springfield, Missouri

My husband enjoys my version of this dish so much, he doesn't order it at restaurants anymore. With fresh spinach, pasta and seasoned sausage, this fast-to-fix soup eats like a meal.

1/2 pound Italian turkey sausage links, casings removed, crumbled

1 small onion, chopped

1-1/2 teaspoons canola oil

1 garlic clove, minced

2 cups water

1 can (15-1/2 ounces) great northern beans, rinsed and drained

1 can (14-1/2 ounces) diced tomatoes, undrained

1 can (14-1/2 ounces) reduced-sodium chicken broth

3/4 cup uncooked elbow macaroni

1/4 teaspoon pepper

1 cup fresh spinach leaves, cut into strips

5 teaspoons shredded Parmesan cheese

1. In a large saucepan, cook sausage over medium heat until no longer pink; drain and set aside. In the same pan, saute onion in oil until tender. Add garlic; saute 1 minute longer.

2. Add the water, beans, tomatoes, broth, macaroni and pepper; bring to a boil. Cook, uncovered, for 8-10 minutes or until macaroni is tender.

3. Reduce heat to low; stir in sausage and spinach. Cook for 2-3 minutes or until spinach is wilted. Garnish with cheese.

Yield: 5 servings.

Vegetarian White Bean Soup

Taste of Home Test Kitchen

We simmered up this fresh-tasting meatless soup with two kinds of beans, making for a satisfying entree. Round out the meal with warm dinner rolls.

2 small zucchini, quartered lengthwise and sliced

1 cup *each* chopped onion, celery and carrots

2 tablespoons canola oil

3 cans (14-1/2 ounces *each*) vegetable broth

1 can (15-1/2 ounces) great northern beans, rinsed and drained

1 can (15 ounces) white kidney or cannellini beans, rinsed and drained

1 can (14-1/2 ounces) diced tomatoes, undrained

1/2 teaspoon dried thyme

1/2 teaspoon dried oregano

1/4 teaspoon pepper

1. In a large saucepan, saute the zucchini, onion, celery and carrots in oil for 5-7 minutes or until crisp-tender. Add the remaining ingredients. Bring to a boil. Reduce heat; cover and simmer for 15 minutes or until vegetables are tender.

Yield: 7 servings.

Taco Soup

Jennifer Villarreal • Texas City, Texas

This hefty, popular taco soup offers a bright assortment of colors and flavors. Garnish with shredded cheese, sour cream or sliced jalapenos if you like.

1-1/2 pounds ground beef

1 envelope taco seasoning

2 cans (15-1/4 ounces *each*) whole kernel corn, undrained

2 cans (15 ounces *each*) Ranch Style beans (pinto beans in seasoned tomato sauce)

2 cans (14-1/2 ounces *each*) diced tomatoes, undrained

Crushed tortilla chips and shredded cheddar cheese

Flour tortillas, warmed

1. In a Dutch oven, cook beef over medium heat until no longer pink; drain. Stir in the taco seasoning, corn, beans and tomatoes. Cover and simmer for 15 minutes or until heated through, stirring occasionally. Place tortilla chips in soup bowls; ladle soup over top. Sprinkle with cheese. Serve with tortillas.

Yield: 8 servings (about 2 quarts).

Clam Chowder

Melba Horne • Macon, Georgia

Here's a quick chowder that's been in my family for quite a few years. I make a big pot to take to an annual party at work and it's always a hit. Served with crusty bread and a salad, it's the perfect meal when there is a chill in the air.

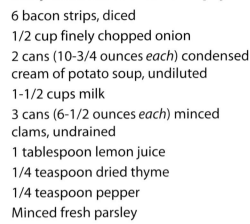

6 bacon strips, diced

1/2 cup finely chopped onion

2 cans (10-3/4 ounces *each*) condensed cream of potato soup, undiluted

1-1/2 cups milk

3 cans (6-1/2 ounces *each*) minced clams, undrained

1 tablespoon lemon juice

1/4 teaspoon dried thyme

1/4 teaspoon pepper

Minced fresh parsley

1. In a large skillet, cook bacon over medium heat until crisp. Using a slotted spoon, remove to paper towels; drain, reserving 1 tablespoon drippings.

2. In the same skillet, saute onion in reserved drippings until tender. Stir in soup and milk. Add the clams, lemon juice, thyme, pepper and bacon; cook until heated through. Garnish with parsley.

Yield: 5 servings.

Chicken Tortilla Soup

Marianne Morgan • Traverse City, Michigan

The fresh lime and cilantro in this zesty soup reminds me of warmer climates.

3 corn tortillas (6 inches), cut into 1/4-inch strips

4 teaspoons olive oil, *divided*

1/4 teaspoon salt

3/4 pound boneless skinless chicken breasts, cut into 1/2-inch chunks

1 large onion, chopped

5 cups reduced-sodium chicken broth

1 pound red potatoes, cut into 1/2-inch cubes

1 cup frozen corn

1 can (4 ounces) chopped green chilies

1/4 cup minced fresh cilantro

1/4 teaspoon pepper

3 tablespoons lime juice

1. In a large resealable plastic bag, combine tortilla strips, 1 teaspoon oil and salt. Seal bag and shake to coat. Arrange tortilla strips on an ungreased baking sheet. Bake at 400° for 8-10 minutes or until crisp, stirring once. Remove to paper towels to cool.

2. In a large saucepan, saute chicken in remaining oil until no longer pink and lightly browned. Add onion; cook and stir until onion is tender. Add broth and potatoes.

3. Bring to a boil. Reduce heat; cover and simmer for 10 minutes. Add the corn, chilies, cilantro and pepper. Cook until heated through. Stir in lime juice. Garnish with tortilla strips.

Yield: 6 servings.

Meatball Vegetable Soup

Marcia Piaskowski • Plantsville, Connecticut

This satisfying soup uses frozen meatballs. It cooks on the stovetop in half an hour, but I often double the recipe and simmer it in the slow cooker for easy preparation.

2/3 cup uncooked medium pasta shells

4 cups chicken broth

1 can (14-1/2 ounces) diced tomatoes, undrained

1 can (10-1/2 ounces) condensed French onion soup, undiluted

12 frozen fully cooked Italian meatballs (1/2 ounce *each*), thawed and quartered

1-1/2 cups chopped fresh spinach

1 cup frozen sliced carrots, thawed

3/4 cup canned kidney beans, rinsed and drained

3/4 cup garbonzo beans *or* chickpeas, rinsed and drained

1. Cook pasta according to package directions.

2. Meanwhile, combine the remaining ingredients in a Dutch oven. Bring to a boil. Reduce heat; cover and simmer for 15 minutes or until vegetables are tender. Drain pasta and stir into the soup.

Yield: 6-8 servings (about 2-1/2 quarts).

White Bean 'n' Ham Soup

Bissy Crosby • Columbia, Missouri

This soup is economical, quick and yummy! While canned beans make this hearty main dish a fast fix, you can save money by soaking and cooking dry beans instead.

2 cans (15-1/2 ounces *each*) great northern beans, rinsed and drained

2 medium carrots, diced

1 small onion, chopped

2 tablespoons butter

2-1/4 cups water

1-1/2 cups cubed fully cooked ham

1/2 teaspoon salt

1/8 to 1/4 teaspoon white pepper

1 bay leaf

1. Mash one can of beans; set aside. In a large saucepan, saute the carrots and onion in butter. Stir in the water, ham, seasonings and whole and mashed beans; cook over medium heat until heated through. Discard bay leaf.

Yield: 6 servings.

busy family favorites

Makeover Creamy Seafood Soup

Mildred Fasig • Stephens City, Virginia

This slimmed-down version of seafood soup has only half the cholesterol, a fourth of the fat and half the calories of the original recipe.

1/2 pound uncooked medium shrimp, peeled and deveined

1/2 pound bay scallops

2 tablespoons butter, *divided*

2 celery ribs, thinly sliced

1 medium sweet red pepper, finely chopped

1 medium onion, finely chopped

1/4 cup all-purpose flour

2 cups fat-free milk

2 cups half-and-half cream

1/4 cup sherry *or* reduced-sodium chicken broth

1 tablespoon minced fresh thyme *or* 1 teaspoon dried thyme

1/2 teaspoon salt

1/4 teaspoon cayenne pepper

1/8 teaspoon ground nutmeg

1. In a Dutch oven, saute shrimp and scallops in 1 tablespoon butter until shrimp turn pink. Remove and set aside.

2. In the same pan, saute the celery, red pepper and onion in remaining butter until tender. Sprinkle with flour; stir until blended. Gradually stir in the remaining ingredients. Bring to a boil; cook and stir for 2 minutes or until thickened. Return seafood to the pan; heat through.

Yield: 6 servings.

"Apres-Ski" Soup

Nancy Hamlin • Littleton, Colorado

Apres ski, French for "after skiing," refers to the social time directly after getting off the slopes, and this microwave soup is perfect for the occasion. Chock-full of healthy veggies, this one will warm you from head to toe.

1 tablespoon butter

1-1/4 cups cubed acorn squash

1 carrot, thinly sliced

1 medium leek (white portion only), thinly sliced

3 cans (14-1/2 ounces *each*) reduced-sodium chicken broth

1 small zucchini, halved and sliced

1/2 cup uncooked elbow macaroni

1 bay leaf

1/2 teaspoon dried basil

1/4 teaspoon dried thyme

1/8 teaspoon salt

1/8 teaspoon pepper

1. Place butter in a 3-qt. microwave-safe bowl; microwave on high for 20-30 seconds or until melted. Add the squash, carrot and leek; stir to coat. Cover and cook on high for 6 minutes.

2. Stir in the remaining ingredients; cover and cook on high for 12-14 minutes or until vegetables and macaroni are tender, stirring twice. Discard bay leaf.

Yield: 6 servings.

EDITOR'S NOTE: This recipe was tested in a 1,100-watt microwave.

Garlic-Basil Tortellini Soup

Linda Kees • Boise, Idaho

This soup is so tasty and filling it can be served as a main dish meal.

2 garlic cloves, minced

1 teaspoon butter

2 cans (14-1/2 ounces *each*) reduced-sodium chicken broth *or* vegetable broth

1/2 cup water

1/3 cup minced fresh basil

1/4 teaspoon pepper

2-1/2 cups frozen cheese tortellini

1 can (19 ounces) white kidney beans *or* cannellini beans, rinsed and drained

2 tablespoons balsamic vinegar

1/4 cup shredded Parmesan cheese

1. In a large saucepan, saute garlic in butter until tender. Stir in the broth, water, basil and pepper. Bring to a boil. Stir in tortellini. Reduce heat; simmer, uncovered, for about 3 minutes or until tortellini begins to float.

2. Stir in beans and vinegar; heat through. Sprinkle with Parmesan cheese.

Yield: 4 servings.

busy family favorites

Broccoli Cheese Soup

Jean Pare • Vermilion, Alberta
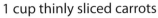

This is a colorful soup easily made in the microwave oven. The orange carrots contrast nicely with the green broccoli.

1 cup thinly sliced carrots

2 tablespoons plus 1 cup water, *divided*

1 package (16 ounces) frozen broccoli florets, thawed

2-1/2 cups milk

1/4 cup all-purpose flour

2 teaspoons chicken bouillon granules

1/2 teaspoon salt

1/4 teaspoon pepper

1 cup (4 ounces) shredded cheddar cheese

1. In a 2-qt. microwave-safe dish, combine carrots and 2 tablespoons water. Cover and microwave on high for 2 minutes; stir. Cover and cook 2 minutes longer or until tender. Add broccoli. Cover and microwave for 2 minutes; stir. Cover and cook 1 to 1-1/2 minutes longer or until vegetables are tender. Stir in milk.

2. In a small bowl, combine the flour, bouillon, salt and pepper; stir in remaining water until smooth. Stir into broccoli mixture. Cover and microwave on high for 6-7 minutes or until mixture is boiling and thickened, stirring every minute. Stir in cheese until melted.

Yield: 4-5 servings.

EDITOR'S NOTE: This recipe was tested in a 1,100-watt microwave.

Kielbasa Cabbage Soup

Marcia Wolff • Rolling Prairie, Indiana

A friend brought samples of this recipe to a soup-tasting class sponsored by our extension homemakers club. It was a great hit with my family. The mix of sausage, apples and vegetables makes a different and flavorful combination.

3 cups coleslaw mix

2 medium carrots, chopped

1/2 cup chopped onion

1/2 cup chopped celery

1/2 teaspoon caraway seeds

2 tablespoons butter

1 carton (32 ounces) chicken broth

3/4 to 1 pound smoked kielbasa *or* Polish sausage, cut into 1/2-inch pieces

2 medium unpeeled Golden Delicious apples, chopped

1/4 teaspoon pepper

1/8 teaspoon salt

1. In a large saucepan, saute the coleslaw mix, carrots, onion, celery and caraway seeds in butter for 5-8 minutes or until vegetables are crisp-tender. Stir in the remaining ingredients.

2. Bring to a boil. Reduce heat; simmer, uncovered, for 20 minutes, stirring occasionally.

Yield: 6 servings (2 quarts).

Spicy Chicken Rice Soup

Mary Shaver • Jonesboro, Arkansas

I'm a member of the Craighead County Farm Bureau Women's Committee, and one of our main promotions is rice. This easy soup contains rice and is loaded with flavor.

2 cans (14-1/2 ounces *each*) chicken broth

3 cups cooked rice

2 cups cubed cooked chicken

1 can (15-1/4 ounces) whole kernel corn, undrained

1 can (11-1/2 ounces) V8 juice

1 cup salsa

1 can (4 ounces) chopped green chilies, drained

1/2 cup chopped green onions

2 tablespoons minced fresh cilantro

1/2 cup shredded Monterey Jack cheese, optional

1. In a large saucepan, combine the first nine ingredients. Bring to a boil. Reduce heat; cover and simmer for 15 minutes or until heated through. Sprinkle with cheese if desired.

Yield: 8 servings.

busy family favorites

Beef

Asparagus Beef Stir-Fry, p. 58

Skillet Beef Tamales

Deb Williams • Peoria, Arizona

This Southwestern skillet dinner is cheesy and delicious, and it doesn't taste light at all! It is sure to be a family favorite.

1 pound lean ground beef (90% lean)

1/3 cup chopped green pepper

1/3 cup chopped sweet red pepper

2 cups salsa

3/4 cup frozen corn

2 tablespoons water

6 corn tortillas (6 inches), halved and cut into 1/2-inch strips

3/4 cup shredded reduced-fat cheddar cheese

5 tablespoons fat-free sour cream

1. In a large nonstick skillet coated with cooking spray, cook beef and peppers over medium heat until meat is no longer pink; drain. Stir in the salsa, corn and water; bring to a boil.

2. Stir in tortilla strips. Reduce heat; cover and simmer for 10-15 minutes or until tortillas are softened. Sprinkle with cheese; cover and cook 2-3 minutes longer or until cheese is melted. Serve with sour cream.

Yield: 5 servings.

Peanut Beef Stir-Fry

Rita Reifenstein • Evans City, Pennsylvania

Peanut butter lends a subtle flavor to this no-fuss beef dish. For a change of pace, try ground beef. We like the stir-fry served over noodles.

5 teaspoons cornstarch

1 can (14-1/2 ounces) beef broth

2 tablespoons soy sauce

2 tablespoons creamy peanut butter

1/2 teaspoon sugar

Dash pepper

1 beef top sirloin steak (1 pound), thinly sliced

1 cup sliced onion

1 cup sliced celery

2 tablespoons canola oil

1 teaspoon minced garlic

1. In a large bowl, combine the cornstarch, broth, soy sauce, peanut butter, sugar and pepper until smooth; set aside. In a large skillet or wok, stir-fry the beef, onion and celery in oil for 5-8 minutes or until meat is no longer pink. Add the garlic; cook 1 minute longer.

2. Stir cornstarch mixture and add to the pan. Bring to a boil; cook and stir for 1-2 minutes or until thickened.

Yield: 4 servings.

Beef 'n' Asparagus Pasta

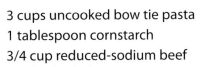

Elaine Norgaard • Penn Valley, California

I like to offer this stir-fry over penne pasta, but feel free to use whatever variety you have on hand. If you leave the beef out, it also makes a filling meatless dish.

3 cups uncooked bow tie pasta

1 tablespoon cornstarch

3/4 cup reduced-sodium beef broth, *divided*

1 beef top sirloin steak (1 pound), cut into 2-inch strips

1 tablespoon olive oil

1 pound fresh asparagus, trimmed and cut into 1-inch pieces

4 green onions, chopped

4 garlic cloves, minced

1 cup sliced fresh mushrooms

1 large tomato, diced

1 teaspoon dried basil

1/2 teaspoon dried oregano

1/2 cup dry red wine *or* additional reduced-sodium beef broth

2 tablespoons sliced ripe olives, drained

1/2 teaspoon salt

1/4 teaspoon pepper

1. Cook pasta according to package directions. In a small bowl, combine cornstarch and 1/4 cup broth until smooth; set aside.

2. Meanwhile, in a large nonstick skillet or wok, stir-fry beef in oil for 1 minute or until meat is no longer pink. Add the asparagus, onions and garlic; stir-fry for 2 minutes. Add the mushrooms, tomato, basil and oregano; stir-fry 2 minutes longer or until vegetables are crisp-tender.

3. Add the wine, olives, salt, pepper and remaining broth. Stir cornstarch mixture and gradually stir into skillet. Bring to a boil; cook and stir for 2 minutes or until thickened. Drain pasta; serve with the beef mixture.

Yield: 4 servings.

Beef 'n' Bacon Lo Mein

Stephanie Francis • Yale, Iowa

This special dish is not tricky to fix, and it's very hearty. Even kids and my meat-and-potatoes husband like it.

1/2 pound sliced bacon, diced

1/2 pound beef flank steak, cut into thin strips

2 tablespoons canola oil, *divided*

1 cup fresh broccoli florets

1 cup fresh cauliflowerets

1 medium carrot, cut into thin 2-inch strips

1 small onion, cut into wedges

1 teaspoon minced fresh gingerroot

1 cup sliced fresh mushrooms

1 can (8 ounces) sliced water chestnuts, drained

2 garlic cloves, minced

1 tablespoon beef bouillon granules

1 cup boiling water

1/4 cup soy sauce

3 tablespoons cornstarch

3/4 cup cold water

1/2 pound thin spaghetti, cooked and drained

1. In a large skillet, cook bacon until crisp; remove to paper towels to drain. Discard drippings. In the same skillet, stir-fry beef in 1 tablespoon oil until no longer pink, about 2 minutes. Remove beef and pan juices; keep warm.

2. In the same skillet, saute the broccoli, cauliflower, carrot, onion and ginger in remaining oil for 3 minutes. Add the mushrooms, water chestnuts and garlic; cook and stir 2 minutes longer. Dissolve bouillon in boiling water; stir into vegetables.

3. Stir in soy sauce and beef with pan juices. Combine cornstarch and cold water until smooth; add to the pan. Bring to a boil; cook and stir for 1-2 minutes or until thickened. Stir in bacon and spaghetti.

Yield: 4 servings.

TIP

An easy way to dice bacon is to cut it with kitchen scissors. Cut the slices in half lengthwise and stack them on top of each other. Then, cut widthwise into small pieces.

busy family favorites

Orange Beef Teriyaki

Nella Parker • Hersey, Michigan

This entree is my favorite anytime stir-fry. When my family comes to visit, it satisfies them fast.

1 can (11 ounces) mandarin oranges

1 tablespoon cornstarch

1-1/2 pounds beef top sirloin steak, thinly sliced

2 tablespoons canola oil

1/2 cup soy sauce

2 tablespoons honey

1-1/2 teaspoons ground ginger

1 garlic clove, minced

Hot cooked rice

Green onion and orange peel curls, optional

1. Drain oranges, reserving juice; set oranges aside. In a small bowl, combine cornstarch and 2 tablespoons reserved juice until smooth; set aside.

2. In a large skillet or wok, stir-fry beef in oil. Add the soy sauce, honey, ginger and remaining juice. Cover and cook over medium heat for 5-10 minutes or until meat is tender. Add garlic; cook 1 minute longer.

3. Stir cornstarch mixture and add to the pan. Bring to a boil; cook and stir for 2 minutes or until thickened. Stir in the oranges. Serve with rice. Garnish with green onions and curls if desired.

Yield: 4-6 servings.

Beefy Tomato Rice Skillet

Ellyn Graebert • Yuma, Arizona

I put this dinner together one day with what I had on hand.

1 pound ground beef
1 cup chopped celery
2/3 cup chopped onion
1/2 cup chopped green pepper
1 can (11 ounces) whole kernel corn, drained
1 can (10-3/4 ounces) condensed tomato soup, undiluted
1 cup water
1 teaspoon Italian seasoning
1 cup uncooked instant rice

1. In a large skillet over medium heat, cook the beef, celery, onion and pepper until meat is no longer pink and vegetables are tender; drain.

2. Add the corn, soup, water and Italian seasoning; bring to a boil. Stir in rice; cover and remove from the heat. Let stand for 10 minutes.

Yield: 6 servings.

Thai Beef Stir-Fry

Janet Lowe • Kennewick, Washington

The flavor of this stir-fry is very similar to restaurant-style Thai dishes.

2 tablespoons cornstarch
3/4 cup water
2 tablespoons plus 1-1/2 teaspoons chunky peanut butter
4 tablespoons soy sauce, *divided*
1-1/2 pounds beef top sirloin steak, thinly sliced
1/4 teaspoon pepper
2 tablespoons olive oil
1 *each* medium green, sweet red and yellow pepper, julienned
1 can (8 ounces) bamboo shoots, drained
1/2 cup julienned carrot
1/2 teaspoon crushed red pepper flakes
1-1/2 teaspoons minced garlic
Hot cooked rice

1. In a small bowl, combine cornstarch and water until smooth. Stir in peanut butter and 3 tablespoons soy sauce; set aside.

2. In a skillet, stir-fry the beef, pepper and remaining soy sauce in oil until meat is no longer pink; remove and keep warm. Add peppers, bamboo shoots, carrot and pepper flakes; stir-fry for 2-3 minutes or until tender. Add garlic; cook 1 minute longer.

3. Stir cornstarch mixture and add to the pan. Bring to a boil; cook and stir for 1 minute or until thickened. Return beef mixture to the pan. Serve with rice.

Yield: 6 servings.

busy family favorites

Grilled Sirloin Steaks

Taste of Home Test Kitchen

These tender steaks are treated to a buttery topping that's mixed with garlic, parsley and cumin. Delicious!

2 tablespoons prepared mustard

1/4 teaspoon pepper

4 boneless beef petite sirloin steaks (5 ounces *each*)

1/4 cup butter, softened

3 tablespoons minced fresh parsley

1 teaspoon minced garlic

1/2 teaspoon ground cumin

1. Combine mustard and pepper; rub over both sides of steaks. Grill, covered, over medium heat or broil 4 in. from the heat for 4-5 minutes on each side or until meat reaches desired doneness (for medium-rare, a meat thermometer should read 145°; medium, 160°; well-done, 170°).

2. In a small bowl, combine the butter, parsley, garlic and cumin. Serve with steaks.

Yield: 4 servings.

Southwestern Goulash

Vikki Rebholz • West Chester, Ohio

I had some extra cilantro in the fridge and didn't want to throw it away. Instead, I came up with this delightful and filling family recipe. Everyone just loved it!

1 cup uncooked elbow macaroni

1 pound lean ground beef (90% lean)

1 medium onion, chopped

1 can (28 ounces) diced tomatoes, undrained

2/3 cup frozen corn

1 can (8 ounces) tomato sauce

1 can (4 ounces) chopped green chilies

1/2 teaspoon ground cumin

1/2 teaspoon pepper

1/4 teaspoon salt

1/4 cup minced fresh cilantro

1. Cook macaroni according to package directions. Meanwhile, in a Dutch oven over medium heat, cook beef and onion until meat is no longer pink; drain. Stir in the tomatoes, corn, tomato sauce, chilies, cumin, pepper and salt. Bring to a boil. Reduce heat; simmer, uncovered, for 3-4 minutes or until heated through.

2. Drain macaroni; add to meat mixture. Stir in cilantro and heat through.

Yield: 6 servings.

Burritos Made Easy

Jennifer McKinney • Washington, Illinois

These quick burritos are packed with savory bean and beef filling that tastes of the Southwest.

1 pound ground beef

1/4 cup chopped onion

1 can (15 ounces) chili with beans

1-1/4 cups chunky salsa

1/4 cup chopped green chilies

8 flour tortillas (8 inches), warmed

8 slices process American cheese

Taco sauce and shredded lettuce, optional

1. In a large skillet, cook beef and onion over medium heat until meat is no longer pink; drain. Stir in the chili, salsa and chilies. Bring to a boil. Reduce heat; simmer, uncovered, for 5 minutes.

2. Spoon about 1/2 cupful beef mixture off center on each tortilla. Top each with a slice of cheese; roll up. Serve with taco sauce and lettuce if desired.

Yield: 8 burritos.

Asparagus Beef Stir-Fry

Linda Flynn • Ellicott City, Maryland

I love Filet Mignon, but not its price! While grocery shopping, I picked up a more affordable beef cut. I brought it home and came up with this recipe. Now I cook it once a week, plus my husband loves taking the leftovers to work.

1 pound beef tenderloin roast, cubed

1 green onion, sliced

1/2 teaspoon salt

1/4 teaspoon pepper

1 tablespoon canola oil

2 garlic cloves, minced

1 pound fresh asparagus, trimmed and cut into 2-inch pieces

1/2 pound sliced fresh mushrooms

1/4 cup butter, cubed

1 tablespoon soy sauce

1-1/2 teaspoons lemon juice

Hot cooked rice

1. In a wok or large skillet, stir-fry the beef, onion, salt and pepper in oil for 3-5 minutes. Add garlic; cook 1 minute longer. Remove and keep warm.

2. In the same pan, stir-fry asparagus and mushrooms in butter until asparagus is tender. Return beef mixture to the pan. Stir in soy sauce and lemon juice; heat through. Serve with rice.

Yield: 4 servings.

busy family favorites

Skillet Beef and Potatoes

Taste of Home Test Kitchen

To shorten the cooking time for this meal, I precook unpeeled potato slices in the microwave. Fresh rosemary adds a nice flavor to this skillet entree.

3 medium potatoes, halved and cut into 1/4-inch slices

1/3 cup water

1/2 teaspoon salt

1 pound beef top sirloin steak, cut into thin strips

2 teaspoons garlic pepper blend

1/2 cup chopped onion

3 tablespoons olive oil, *divided*

1-1/2 teaspoons minced fresh rosemary

1. Place potatoes, water and salt in a microwave-safe dish. Cover and microwave on high for 6-10 minutes or until potatoes are tender; drain.

2. Season beef with pepper blend. In a large skillet, stir-fry beef and onion in 2 tablespoons oil for 5 minutes or until beef is no longer pink. Meanwhile, in another skillet, stir-fry potatoes in remaining oil for 5 minutes or until browned. Stir in beef mixture. Sprinkle with rosemary.

Yield: 4 servings.

Stovetop Beef Stew

Mitzi Sentiff • Annapolis, Maryland

I use a packaged pot roast dinner jazzed up with a few additional ingredients to give this dish a slow-cooked flavor. Serve it with a salad and dinner rolls for a delicious meal.

1 package (24 ounces) frozen Yankee pot roast skillet dinner

1 can (14-1/2 ounces) diced tomatoes with roasted garlic, undrained

1 cup reduced-sodium beef broth

1/2 cup dry red wine *or* additional reduced-sodium beef broth

1/2 cup sliced celery

1/2 teaspoon pepper

1/8 to 1/4 teaspoon dried marjoram

1 package (9 ounces) frozen peas and pearl onions

2 tablespoons minced fresh parsley

1. In a large saucepan, combine the pot roast dinner, tomatoes, broth, wine, celery, pepper and marjoram. Bring to a boil. Reduce heat; cover and simmer for 8 minutes.

2. Stir in peas and onions; cook 7-9 minutes longer or until onions are tender. Sprinkle with parsley.

Yield: 4 servings.

Tangy Beef Stroganoff

Joan Roth • Jackson, New Jersey

If you're looking for a supper that's simple and yummy, this stroganoff fills the bill. I combine ketchup and Worcestershire in a creamy sauce for this satisfying beef dish.

1 pound beef top sirloin steak, thinly sliced

1 tablespoon butter

1 medium onion, sliced

1/2 teaspoon minced garlic

1 can (10-3/4 ounces) condensed cream of mushroom soup, undiluted

1 cup (8 ounces) sour cream

1 jar (6 ounces) sliced mushrooms, drained

2 tablespoons ketchup

2 teaspoons Worcestershire sauce

Hot cooked noodles

1. In a large skillet, saute beef in butter until no longer pink; drain. Add onion; cook for 3-4 minutes or until onion is tender. Add garlic; cook 1 minute longer.

2. Stir in the soup, sour cream, mushrooms, ketchup and Worcestershire sauce; heat through (do not boil). Serve with noodles.

Yield: 5 servings.

busy family favorites

Beef Fried Rice

Taste of Home Test Kitchen

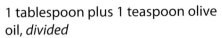

End the day with Asian flavors. Moist beef strips partner with crisp asparagus and coleslaw in this standout medley.

1 tablespoon plus 1 teaspoon olive oil, *divided*

3 eggs, lightly beaten

3 beef top sirloin steaks (5 ounces *each*), cut into thin strips

2-1/2 cups coleslaw mix

1/2 pound fresh asparagus, trimmed and cut into 1-1/2-inch pieces

1/2 cup chopped onion

4 cups cold cooked instant rice

3 tablespoons butter, cubed

3 tablespoons soy sauce

1/8 teaspoon pepper

1. In a large skillet or wok, heat 1 tablespoon oil until hot. Add eggs; cook and stir over medium heat until completely set. Remove and keep warm.

2. In the same pan, stir-fry the beef, coleslaw, asparagus and onion in remaining oil for 4-6 minutes or until beef is no longer pink and vegetables are crisp-tender.

3. Add rice and butter; cook and stir over medium heat for 1-2 minutes or until heated through. Add eggs; stir in soy sauce and pepper.

Yield: 6 servings.

Bow Tie Beef Skillet

Tammy Perrault • Lancaster, Ohio

When I have an active afternoon, this is the recipe I choose to make for supper. It comes together in 30 minutes and is always delicious.

1 pound ground beef

1/2 teaspoon salt

1/8 teaspoon pepper

2 cups uncooked bow tie pasta

1 can (14-1/2 ounces) diced tomatoes, drained

1-1/3 cups beef broth

1 can (8 ounces) tomato sauce

1 tablespoon Worcestershire sauce

3 medium yellow summer squash, thinly sliced

3/4 cup chopped green pepper

1 cup (4 ounces) shredded Parmesan cheese, *divided*

1. In a large skillet, cook beef over medium heat until no longer pink; drain. Sprinkle with salt and pepper. Stir in the pasta, tomatoes, broth, tomato sauce and Worcestershire sauce. Bring to a boil. Reduce heat; cover and simmer for 10-12 minutes.

2. Add squash and green pepper. Cook, uncovered, for 3-4 minutes or until pasta and vegetables are tender, stirring occasionally. Add 1/2 cup cheese; cook 1-2 minutes longer or until cheese is melted. Sprinkle with remaining cheese.

Yield: 5 servings.

Zesty Meatballs

Debbie Segate • Grande Prairie, Alberta

Molasses adds a touch of sweetness to the tangy sauce that covers these moist meatballs. Serve them over egg noodles for a flavorful meal.

1/3 cup finely chopped onion

2 egg whites, lightly beaten

1/4 cup fat-free milk

2 teaspoons prepared mustard

1/2 teaspoon salt

3/4 cup graham cracker crumbs

3/4 pound lean ground beef (90% lean)

3/4 pound lean ground turkey

BARBECUE SAUCE:

1/2 cup packed brown sugar

3 tablespoons cornstarch

1/2 cup cider vinegar

1/2 cup ketchup

1/2 cup molasses

1/4 cup orange juice concentrate

2 tablespoons Dijon mustard

2 tablespoons reduced-sodium soy sauce

1/4 teaspoon hot pepper sauce

6 cups hot cooked yolk-free noodles

1. Place onion in a small microwave-safe bowl; cover and microwave on high for 1-1/2 minutes or until tender. In a large bowl, combine the egg whites, milk, mustard, salt, cracker crumbs and onion. Crumble beef and turkey over mixture and mix well.

2. Shape into 1-1/4-in. balls. Place meatballs on a rack coated with cooking spray in a shallow baking pan. Bake at 375° for 15-18 minutes or until the meat is no longer pink; drain.

3. Meanwhile, in a large saucepan, combine brown sugar and cornstarch. Stir in vinegar until smooth. Add the ketchup, molasses, orange juice concentrate, mustard, soy sauce and hot pepper sauce. Bring to a boil; cook and stir for 2 minutes or until thickened. Add meatballs; heat through. Serve with noodles.

Yield: 6 servings.

EDITOR'S NOTE: This recipe was tested in a 1,100-watt microwave.

busy family favorites

Speedy Salisbury Steak

Cindy Stephenson • Bullard, Texas

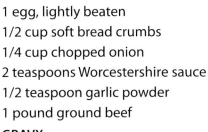

Ground beef patties get fast family appeal when covered in a tasty gravy with nice chunks of mushrooms. This is great served over rice or mashed potatoes. It also freezes well.

1 egg, lightly beaten

1/2 cup soft bread crumbs

1/4 cup chopped onion

2 teaspoons Worcestershire sauce

1/2 teaspoon garlic powder

1 pound ground beef

GRAVY:

2 tablespoons all-purpose flour

1 can (14-1/2 ounces) beef broth

1/4 cup ketchup

1 tablespoon Worcestershire sauce

1/4 teaspoon dried basil

1 jar (4-1/2 ounces) sliced mushrooms, drained

Mashed potatoes

1. In a large bowl, combine the first five ingredients. Crumble beef over mixture and mix well. Shape into four patties; place in a shallow 2-qt. microwave-safe dish.

2. Cover and microwave at 70% power for 5-6 minutes. Meanwhile, in a small bowl, combine flour and broth until smooth. Stir in the ketchup, Worcestershire sauce, basil and mushrooms.

3. Turn patties; drain. Pour gravy over patties. Cover and microwave at 70% power for 5-6 minutes or until a meat thermometer reads 160° and juices run clear. Gently stir gravy; cover and let stand for 5 minutes. Serve with mashed potatoes.

Yield: 4 servings.

EDITOR'S NOTE: This recipe was tested in a 1,100-watt microwave.

Ravioli Skillet

Taste of Home Test Kitchen

It's easy to dress up store-bought ravioli and make it special with prosciutto and mozzarella.

1 pound ground beef

3/4 cup chopped green pepper

1 ounce prosciutto *or* deli ham, chopped

3 cups spaghetti sauce

3/4 cup water

1 package (25 ounces) frozen cheese ravioli

1 cup (4 ounces) shredded part-skim mozzarella cheese

1. In a large skillet, cook the beef, green pepper and prosciutto over medium heat until meat is no longer pink; drain.

2. Stir in spaghetti sauce and water; bring to a boil. Add ravioli. Reduce heat; cover and simmer for 7-9 minutes or until ravioli is tender, stirring once. Sprinkle with cheese. Simmer, uncovered, 1-2 minutes longer or until cheese is melted.

Yield: 4 servings.

Philly Cheesesteak Pizza

Anne Zirkle • South Riding, Virginia

Mushrooms aren't just for pizza—but you must admit, the two go pretty well together. I added mushrooms to this combination of my husband's favorite foods—pizza and Philly Cheesesteak.

1 prebaked 12-inch pizza crust

1 medium onion, thinly sliced and separated into rings

1 small sweet red pepper, cut into 1/8-inch strips

1 tablespoon olive oil

2 garlic cloves, minced

1/2 pound thinly sliced deli roast beef, cut into 1/4-inch strips

1 jar (6 ounces) sliced mushrooms, drained

1 teaspoon dried oregano

1 teaspoon dried basil

1/4 teaspoon salt

1/4 teaspoon pepper

1 cup (4 ounces) shredded part-skim mozzarella cheese

1/2 cup shredded Parmesan cheese

1. Place crust on a 14-in. pizza pan; set aside. In a large skillet, saute onion and red pepper in oil for 3-5 minutes or until crisp-tender. Add garlic; cook 1 minute longer. Add beef and mushrooms; cook and stir for 3-5 minutes or until heated through. Drain. Stir in the seasonings.

2. Spread meat mixture over crust to within 1/2 in. of edge. Combine the cheeses; sprinkle over pizza. Bake at 350° for 15 minutes or until the crust is golden and the cheese is melted. Cut into wedges.

Yield: 4-6 servings.

busy family favorites

Italian Patty Melts

Taste of Home Test Kitchen

End the day on a fun note with an easy-to-make sandwich. Either serve these Italian-style burgers as a sandwich or open-faced with extra sauce.

1 egg
1/2 cup spaghetti sauce, *divided*
3 tablespoons seasoned bread crumbs
1/4 teaspoon pepper
1 pound ground beef
2 tablespoons butter, melted
1/4 teaspoon dried basil
1/4 teaspoon dried parsley flakes
1/8 teaspoon garlic powder
8 slices Italian bread
1/2 cup shredded part-skim mozzarella cheese

1. In a large bowl, combine the egg, 1/4 cup spaghetti sauce, bread crumbs and pepper. Crumble beef over mixture and mix well. Shape into four oval patties; set aside.

2. Combine butter and seasonings; brush over both sides of bread. In a large skillet, toast bread until lightly browned; set aside.

3. In the same skillet, cook patties over medium heat for 4-6 minutes on each side or until no longer pink.

4. Spoon remaining sauce over patties; sprinkle with cheese. Cover and cook for 1 minute or until cheese is melted. Place burgers on four slices of toast; top with remaining toast.

Yield: 4 servings.

Broiled Sirloin Steaks

Karol Chandler-Ezell • Nacogdoches, Texas

A flavorful rub gives these steaks a delicious flavor.

2 tablespoons lime juice

1 teaspoon onion powder

1 teaspoon garlic powder

1/4 teaspoon ground mustard

1/4 teaspoon dried oregano

1/4 teaspoon dried thyme

4 beef top sirloin steak (5 ounces *each*)

1 cup sliced fresh mushrooms

1. In a small bowl, combine the first six ingredients; rub over both sides of steaks.

2. Broil 4 in. from the heat for 7 minutes. Turn steaks; top with mushrooms. Broil 7-8 minutes longer or until meat reaches desired doneness (for medium-rare, a meat thermometer should read 145°; medium, 160°; well-done, 170°) and mushrooms are tender.

Yield: 4 servings.

Beef 'n' Bean Enchiladas

Linda Lundmark • Martinton, Illinois

The entire recipe is cooked in the microwave...so it's ready in mere minutes!

3 tablespoons all-purpose flour

1 teaspoon salt, *divided*

1/4 teaspoon paprika

1-1/2 cups 2% milk

1 can (10 ounces) enchilada sauce

1 cup (4 ounces) shredded cheddar cheese

1 can (2-1/4 ounces) sliced ripe olives, drained

3/4 pound ground beef

1 medium onion, chopped

1 can (9 ounces) bean dip

1 can (4 ounces) chopped green chilies

1/8 teaspoon pepper

1 large tomato, seeded and diced

9 white *or* yellow corn tortillas (6 inches), warmed

1. In a 1-qt. microwave-safe bowl, combine the flour, 1/2 teaspoon salt, paprika, milk and enchilada sauce until smooth. Microwave, uncovered, on high for 1-1/2 minutes; stir. Cook 3-4 minutes longer or until thickened, stirring every minute. Stir in cheese and olives; set aside.

2. Place beef and onion in a microwave-safe dish. Cover and microwave on high for 3-4 minutes or until meat is no longer pink; drain. Stir in the bean dip, chilies, pepper and remaining salt.

3. Spoon about 1/3 cup meat mixture and 1 tablespoon of diced tomato down the center of each tortilla; roll up tightly. Place enchiladas seam side down in an ungreased 11-in. x 7-in. microwave-safe dish. Top with sauce. Microwave, uncovered, on high for 7-8 minutes or until bubbly around the edges, rotating dish twice.

Yield: 4 servings.

EDITOR'S NOTE: This recipe was tested in a 1,100-watt microwave.

busy family favorites

Salsa Sloppy Joes

Krista Collins • Concord, North Carolina

This zippy, skillet sloppy joe recipe is not only effortless but also mouthwatering.

1 pound ground beef

1-1/3 cups salsa

1 can (10-3/4 ounces) condensed tomato soup, undiluted

1 tablespoon brown sugar

8 hamburger buns, split

1. In a large skillet, cook beef over medium heat until no longer pink; drain. Stir in the salsa, soup and brown sugar. Cover and simmer for 10 minutes or until heated through. Spoon 1/2 cup onto each bun.

Yield: 8 servings.

Fajita Skillet

Taste of Home Test Kitchen

This recipe gives you authentic fajita flavor in 30 minutes without using a mix! Pineapple and tomato combine for a real treat that will have everybody coming back for seconds.

2 flour tortillas (10 inches), cut into 1/2-inch strips

3 tablespoons olive oil, *divided*

1/2 pound boneless skinless chicken breasts, cut into strips

1/2 pound beef top sirloin steak, cut into thin strips

1 medium green pepper, sliced

1 small onion, sliced

2 tablespoons soy sauce

2 teaspoons brown sugar

1/2 teaspoon chili powder

1/2 teaspoon ground cumin

1/4 teaspoon pepper

1 teaspoon cornstarch

2 tablespoons lime juice

1 cup cubed fresh pineapple

1 medium tomato, coarsely chopped

1. In a large skillet, fry tortilla strips in 2 tablespoons oil on both sides for 1 minute or until golden brown. Drain on paper towels.

2. In the same skillet, cook the chicken, beef, green pepper, onion, soy sauce, brown sugar, chili powder, cumin and pepper in remaining oil for 3-4 minutes or until chicken is no longer pink.

3. In a small bowl, combine cornstarch and lime juice until smooth; add to the pan. Bring to a boil; cook and stir for 1 minute or until thickened. Stir in pineapple and tomato; heat through. Serve with tortilla strips.

Yield: 4 servings.

Two-Meat Spaghetti Sauce

Shirley Klinner • Medford, Wisconsin

I can put this hearty dish together, make a salad and have supper on the table in 30 minutes flat. It's one of my favorite hurry-up meals.

10 ounces uncooked spaghetti
1/2 pound ground beef
2 packages (3 ounces *each*) sliced pepperoni
1 cup water
1 can (8 ounces) tomato sauce
1 can (6 ounces) tomato paste
1 can (4 ounces) mushroom stems and pieces, drained
2 tablespoons dried minced onion
2 tablespoons dried parsley flakes
1 teaspoon dried oregano
1 teaspoon chili powder
3/4 to 1 teaspoon sugar
1/2 teaspoon garlic powder

1. Cook spaghetti according to package directions; drain. Meanwhile, in a large skillet, cook beef and pepperoni over medium heat until the beef is no longer pink; drain.

2. Stir in the water, tomato sauce, tomato paste, mushrooms, onion, parsley, oregano, chili powder, sugar and garlic powder.

3. Bring to a boil. Reduce heat; simmer, uncovered, for 15-20 minutes or until heated through. Serve with the spaghetti.

Yield: 5 servings.

Wiener Schnitzel

Emma West • Leoma, Tennessee

If you have the time, chill the veal for 30 minutes after coating, making the recipe more convenient while preparing other foods.

4 veal cutlets (4 ounces *each*)
3/4 teaspoon salt
3/4 teaspoon pepper
1/2 cup all-purpose flour
2 eggs, lightly beaten
3/4 cup dry bread crumbs
1/4 cup butter, cubed
4 lemon slices

1. Sprinkle veal with salt and pepper. Place the flour, eggs and bread crumbs in separate shallow bowls. Coat veal with flour, then dip in eggs and coat with crumbs.

2. In a large skillet over medium heat, cook veal in butter for 2-3 minutes on each side or until no longer pink. Serve with lemon.

Yield: 4 servings.

Steak Sandwich Kabobs

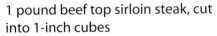

Taste of Home Test Kitchen

Seasoned steak skewers are grilled with bread and veggies and topped with provolone cheese for a fantastic dinner. Coleslaw, spruced up with chopped walnuts, is a great side for the kabobs.

1 pound beef top sirloin steak, cut into 1-inch cubes

1 teaspoon steak seasoning

1 medium sweet red pepper, cut into 1-inch chunks

6 ounces focaccia bread, cut into 1-inch cubes

1 medium onion, cut into 1-inch chunks

1 tablespoon olive oil

3 slices provolone cheese, cut into strips

2 cups deli coleslaw

1/2 cup chopped walnuts

1. Sprinkle beef with steak seasoning. Alternately thread the beef, red pepper, bread cubes and onion onto four metal or soaked wooden skewers; brush with oil.

2. Grill, covered, over medium heat for 8-10 minutes or until meat reaches desired doneness, turning occasionally. Top with cheese; grill 1-2 minutes longer or until cheese is melted.

3. In a small bowl, combine coleslaw and walnuts. Serve with kabobs.

Yield: 4 servings.

EDITOR'S NOTE: This recipe was tested with McCormick's Montreal Steak Seasoning. Look for it in the spice aisle.

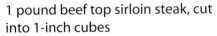

Vegetable Beef Ragout

Taste of Home Test Kitchen

Prepared beef tips and gravy can be found in the meat section of your grocery store. Add your favorite vegetables to this tasty convenience item for a quick and delicious meal.

1 cup sliced fresh mushrooms

1/2 cup chopped onion

1 tablespoon canola oil

1 package (17 ounces) refrigerated beef tips with gravy

1 package (14 ounces) frozen sugar snap peas, thawed

1 cup cherry tomatoes, halved

Hot cooked pasta, optional

1. In a large skillet, saute mushrooms and onion in oil until tender. Add the beef tips with gravy, peas and tomatoes; heat through. Serve over pasta if desired.

Yield: 4 servings.

Chicken-Fried Steaks

Denice Louk • Garnett, Kansas

These crispy steaks will earn raves when you serve them for dinner. My husband asks me to prepare this recipe regularly. I like it because it's so easy to make.

2-1/4 cups all-purpose flour, *divided*

2 teaspoons baking powder

3/4 teaspoon *each* salt, onion powder, garlic powder, chili powder and pepper

2 eggs, lightly beaten

1-2/3 cups buttermilk, *divided*

4 beef cubed steaks (4 ounces each)

Oil for deep-fat frying

1-1/2 cups 2% milk

1. In a shallow bowl, combine 2 cups flour, baking powder and seasonings. In another shallow bowl, combine eggs and 1 cup buttermilk. Dip each cubed steak in buttermilk mixture, then roll in flour mixture. Let stand for 5 minutes.

2. In a large skillet, heat 1/2 in. of oil on medium-high. Fry steaks for 5-7 minutes. Turn carefully; cook 5 minutes longer or until coating is crisp and meat is no longer pink. Remove steaks and keep warm.

3. Drain, reserving 1/3 cup drippings; stir remaining flour into drippings until smooth. Cook and stir over medium heat for 2 minutes. Gradually whisk in milk and remaining buttermilk. Bring to a boil; cook and stir for 2 minutes or until thickened. Serve with steaks.

Yield: 4 servings (2 cups gravy).

busy family favorites

Flank Steak with Couscous

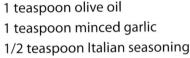

Taste of Home Test Kitchen

It takes just minutes to broil this nicely seasoned flank steak that's served with made-in-minutes couscous. If you prefer, a pound of sirloin steak can be used instead of the flank steak in this recipe.

1 teaspoon olive oil
1 teaspoon minced garlic
1/2 teaspoon Italian seasoning
1/4 teaspoon pepper
1/8 teaspoon salt
1 beef flank steak (1 pound)
2 packages (5.8 ounces *each*) roasted garlic and olive oil couscous
3/4 cup diced roasted sweet red peppers, drained
1/2 cup Italian salad dressing

1. In a small bowl, combine the first five ingredients; rub over flank steak. Broil 4 in. from the heat for 7-8 minutes on each side or until meat reaches desired doneness (for medium-rare, a meat thermometer should read 145°; medium, 160°; well-done, 170°).

2. Meanwhile, cook couscous according to package directions. Stir in roasted peppers. Thinly slice steak across the grain; drizzle with Italian dressing. Serve with couscous.

Yield: 4 servings.

Grilled Bacon Burgers

Wanda Holoubek • Omaha, Nebraska

I really like cooking and having family or friends over. These juicy burgers always go over big at get-togethers.

1 egg
1/2 cup shredded cheddar cheese
2 tablespoons chopped onion
2 tablespoons soy sauce
2 tablespoons ketchup
1/4 teaspoon pepper
1 pound ground beef
5 bacon strips
5 hamburger buns, split
Leaf lettuce, tomato slices and onion slices, optional

1. In a small bowl, combine the egg, cheese, onion, soy sauce, ketchup and pepper. Crumble beef over mixture and mix well. Shape into five patties. Wrap a bacon strip around each; secure with a toothpick.

2. Grill patties, uncovered, over medium-hot heat for 5-6 minutes on each side or until a meat thermometer reads 160° and juices run clear. Discard toothpicks. Serve on buns with lettuce, tomato and onion if desired.

Yield: 5 servings.

Spanish Noodles 'n' Ground Beef

Kelli Jones • Peris, California

Bacon adds flavor to this comforting stovetop supper my mom frequently made when I was growing up. Now I prepare it for my family.

1 pound ground beef

1 small green pepper, chopped

1/3 cup chopped onion

3-1/4 cups uncooked medium egg noodles

1 can (14-1/2 ounces) diced tomatoes, undrained

1 cup water

1/4 cup chili sauce

1 teaspoon salt

1/8 teaspoon pepper

4 bacon strips, cooked and crumbled

1. In a large skillet, cook the beef, green pepper and onion over medium heat until meat is no longer pink; drain. Stir in the noodles, tomatoes, water, chili sauce, salt and pepper.

2. Cover and cook over low heat for 15-20 minutes or until the noodles are tender, stirring frequently. Top with bacon.

Yield: 5 servings.

Sloppy Joe Under a Bun

Trish Bloom • Ray, Michigan

I usually keep a can of sloppy joe sauce in the pantry, because our kids love sloppy joes. But sometimes I don't have buns on hand. With this fun casserole, we can still enjoy the flavor in a flash. The bun-like crust is made with biscuit mix.

1-1/2 pounds ground beef

1 can (15-1/2 ounces) sloppy joe sauce

2 cups (8 ounces) shredded cheddar cheese

2 cups biscuit/baking mix

2 eggs, lightly beaten

1 cup 2% milk

1 tablespoon sesame seeds

1. In a large skillet, cook beef over medium heat until no longer pink; drain.

2. Stir in sloppy joe sauce. Transfer to a lightly greased 13-in. x 9-in. baking dish; sprinkle with cheese.

3. In a large bowl, combine the biscuit mix, eggs and milk just until blended. Pour over cheese; sprinkle with sesame seeds. Bake, uncovered, at 400° for 25 minutes or until golden brown.

Yield: 8 servings.

busy family favorites

Beef Pitas with Yogurt Sauce

Taste of Home Test Kitchen

Serve a Greek menu with our tasty version of a traditional gyro. With tender seasoned beef and sauteed onions, this dish is sure to be a hit. Top it with a very easy-to-make yogurt sauce that doubles as a dip for warmed pita chips.

1 cup (8 ounces) fat-free plain yogurt

1/4 cup minced fresh parsley

1/2 teaspoon minced garlic

1/8 teaspoon salt

PITAS:

1 teaspoon dried oregano

1 teaspoon minced fresh rosemary

1/2 teaspoon salt

1/4 teaspoon pepper

1 pound beef top sirloin steak, cut into thin strips

1 large sweet onion, sliced

4 teaspoons olive oil, *divided*

4 whole pita breads, warmed

1. For sauce, in a small bowl, combine the yogurt, parsley, garlic and salt. Refrigerate until serving.

2. In a large resealable plastic bag, combine the oregano, rosemary, salt and pepper; add beef. Seal bag and toss to coat.

3. In a large nonstick skillet, saute onion in 2 teaspoons oil until golden brown. Remove and keep warm. Saute beef in remaining oil until no longer pink.

4. Serve beef and onion on pitas with yogurt sauce.

Yield: 4 servings.

Asian Beef and Noodles

Laura Stenberg • Wyoming, Minnesota

Stir-fry recipes translate to one-dish family fare that is long on flavor but short on prep time and cleanup. This light and colorful dish takes only five ingredients.

1 pound lean ground beef (90% lean)

2 packages (3 ounces *each*) Oriental ramen noodles, crumbled

2-1/2 cups water

2 cups frozen broccoli stir-fry vegetable blend

1/4 teaspoon ground ginger

2 tablespoons thinly sliced green onion

1. In a large skillet, cook beef over medium heat for 4-5 minutes or until no longer pink; drain. Add the contents of one ramen noodle flavoring packet; stir until dissolved. Remove beef and keep warm.

2. In the same skillet, combine the water, vegetables, ginger, noodles and contents of remaining flavoring packet. Bring to a boil. Reduce heat; cover and simmer for 3-4 minutes or until noodles are tender, stirring occasionally. Return beef to the pan; cook for 2-3 minutes or until heated through. Stir in onion.

Yield: 4 servings.

Cuban Ground Beef Hash

Adrianna Still Cruz • Weston, Florida

Called "picadillo" in Spanish, this distinctive hash is terrific served over white rice...or inside plain omelets for a hearty breakfast.

1-1/2 pounds ground beef

1 medium green pepper, chopped

1 medium onion, chopped

1 can (14-1/2 ounces) diced tomatoes, undrained

3 tablespoons tomato paste

1/3 cup raisins

1/3 cup sliced pimiento-stuffed olives

1 tablespoon cider vinegar

3 garlic cloves, minced

2 teaspoons ground cumin

1/2 teaspoon salt

1/2 teaspoon pepper

1/2 cup frozen peas

Hot cooked rice

1. In a large skillet, cook the beef, green pepper and onion over medium heat until meat is no longer pink; drain. Stir in the tomatoes, tomato paste, raisins, olives, vinegar, garlic, cumin, salt and pepper.

2. Bring to a boil. Reduce heat; cover and simmer for 5 minutes. Add peas; cover and cook 5 minutes longer or until heated through. Serve with rice.

Yield: 6 servings.

Supreme Pizza Burgers

Anna Rhyne • Kershaw, South Carolina

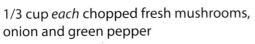

One night I couldn't decide what I wanted more, pizza or hamburgers, so I combined the two. Now my daughter, Amelia, is quite pleased every time we have pizza burgers!

1/3 cup *each* chopped fresh mushrooms, onion and green pepper

1/3 cup chopped ripe olives

10 slices turkey pepperoni

2 tablespoons tomato paste

2 teaspoons Italian seasoning

1/4 teaspoon garlic powder

1/4 teaspoon salt

1/4 teaspoon pepper

1/3 cup seasoned
bread crumbs

1 pound lean ground beef (90% lean)

4 whole wheat hamburger buns, split

4 slices provolone cheese

4 tablespoons pizza sauce

OPTIONAL TOPPINGS:
Sliced ripe olives, fresh mushrooms *and/or* green pepper rings

1. In a food processor, combine the vegetables, olives, pepperoni, tomato paste and seasonings; cover and pulse just until blended. Transfer to a large bowl; stir in bread crumbs. Crumble beef over mixture and mix well. Shape into four patties.

2. Using long-handled tongs, moisten a paper towel with cooking oil and lightly coat the grill rack. Grill burgers, covered, over medium heat or broil 4 in. from the heat for 5-7 minutes on each side or until a meat thermometer reads 160° and juices run clear.

3. Serve on buns with cheese and pizza sauce. Add toppings if desired.

Yield: 4 servings.

Southwestern Beef Strips

Taste of Home Test Kitchen

Mexican seasoning gives this filling main dish some zip.

1-1/2 pounds beef top sirloin steak, cut into thin strips
1 medium onion, sliced
1 medium sweet red pepper, cut into thin strips
2 tablespoons taco seasoning
1/4 teaspoon salt
1/4 teaspoon pepper
2 tablespoons canola oil
1 can (15 ounces) black beans, rinsed and drained
1-1/2 cups frozen corn, thawed
1/2 cup picante sauce
2 teaspoons dried cilantro flakes
Hot cooked fettuccine, optional

1. In a large skillet, stir-fry the beef, onion, red pepper strips, taco seasoning, salt and pepper in oil until the meat is no longer pink.

2. Stir in the beans, corn, picante sauce and cilantro; heat through. Serve with fettuccine if desired.

Yield: 6 servings.

Swedish Meatballs

Sheryl Ludeman • Kenosha, Wisconsin

This recipe relies on ingredients we always have on hand and doesn't dirty many dishes.

1 small onion, chopped
1 egg
1/4 cup seasoned bread crumbs
2 tablespoons 2% milk
1/2 teaspoon salt
1/8 teaspoon pepper
1 pound ground beef
SAUCE:
1 can (10-3/4 ounces) condensed cream of mushroom soup, undiluted
1/2 cup sour cream
1/4 cup 2% milk
1 tablespoon dried parsley flakes
1/4 teaspoon ground nutmeg, optional
Hot cooked noodles

1. In a large bowl, combine the onion, egg, bread crumbs, milk, salt and pepper. Crumble beef over mixture and mix well. Shape into 1-in. meatballs, about 24.

2. Place in a shallow 1-1/2-qt. microwave-safe dish. Cover and microwave on high for 7-1/2 minutes or until meat is no longer pink; drain.

3. Combine the soup, sour cream, milk, parsley and nutmeg if desired; pour over meatballs. Cover and cook on high for 5-6 minutes or until heated through. Serve with noodles.

Yield: 4 servings.

EDITOR'S NOTE: This recipe was tested in a 1,100-watt microwave.

busy family favorites

Hearty Penne Beef

Taste of Home Test Kitchen

This is comfort food at its finest! The best of everything is found here.

1-3/4 cups uncooked penne pasta
1 pound ground beef
1 teaspoon minced garlic
1 can (15 ounces) tomato puree
1 can (14-1/2 ounces) beef broth
1-1/2 teaspoons Italian seasoning
1 teaspoon Worcestershire sauce
1/4 teaspoon salt
1/4 teaspoon pepper
2 cups chopped fresh spinach
2 cups (8 ounces) shredded part-skim mozzarella cheese

1. Cook pasta according to package directions. Meanwhile, in a Dutch oven, cook beef over medium heat until meat is no longer pink. Add garlic; cook 1 minute longer. Drain. Stir in the tomato puree, broth, Italian seasoning, Worcestershire sauce, salt and pepper.

2. Bring to a boil. Reduce heat; simmer, uncovered, for 10-15 minutes or until slightly thickened. Add spinach; cook for 1-2 minutes or until spinach is wilted.

3. Drain pasta; stir into beef mixture. Sprinkle with cheese; cover and cook for 3-4 minutes or until cheese is melted.

Yield: 4 servings.

Steaks with Peppery Onions

Dee Faulding • Santa Barbara, California

This recipe name couldn't be more fitting as skillet-cooked rib eye steaks get a burst of flavor from caramelized onions.

3 medium onions, sliced
1 teaspoon salt
1 teaspoon pepper
2 tablespoons olive oil
1 tablespoon butter
1 teaspoon minced garlic
4 beef ribeye steaks
(6 ounces *each*)

1. In a skillet over medium heat, cook onions, salt and pepper in oil and butter for 15-20 minutes or until onions are golden brown, stirring frequently. Add garlic; cook 1 minute longer.

2. Broil steaks 3-4 in. from the heat for 6-8 minutes on each side or until meat reaches desired doneness (for medium-rare, a meat thermometer should read 145°; medium, 160°; well-done, 170°). Serve with onion mixture.

Yield: 4 servings.

Ground Beef a la King

Taste of Home Test Kitchen

Instead of using puff pastry shells, this tasty dish can be served over mashed potatoes, too.

1 package (10 ounces) frozen puff pastry shells
1 pound fresh baby carrots, cut in half
1-1/4 cups water, *divided*
1-1/2 pounds lean ground beef (90% lean)
1 package (8 ounces) sliced baby portobello mushrooms
2 tablespoons chopped shallots
3 tablespoons all-purpose flour
1 can (10-1/2 ounces) condensed beef broth, undiluted
1/4 cup tomato paste
1/4 cup dry red wine
1 tablespoon minced fresh tarragon
1/2 teaspoon salt
1/4 teaspoon pepper

1. Bake pastry shells according to package directions. In a microwave-safe bowl, combine the carrots and 1 cup of water. Cover and microwave on high for 8-10 minutes or until crisp-tender.

2. In a skillet, cook beef, mushrooms and shallots over medium heat until meat is no longer pink; drain. Combine flour and broth until smooth. Add broth mixture, tomato paste, wine, seasonings and remaining water to skillet. Bring to a boil; cook and stir for 2 minutes or until thickened.

3. Drain carrots; add to skillet. Bring to a boil. Reduce heat; cover and simmer for 15 minutes. Remove top of pastry shells; fill with beef mixture.

Yield: 6 servings.

EDITOR'S NOTE: This recipe was tested in a 1,100-watt microwave.

busy family favorites

Grilled Beef Fajitas

Taste of Home Test Kitchen

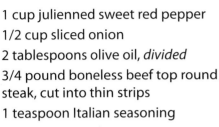

Grilling the tortillas gives them just the right amount of crunch. And the red pepper and cream cheese in the filling makes them taste extra special.

1 cup julienned sweet red pepper

1/2 cup sliced onion

2 tablespoons olive oil, *divided*

3/4 pound boneless beef top round steak, cut into thin strips

1 teaspoon Italian seasoning

1/4 teaspoon salt

1/4 teaspoon pepper

1/4 cup spreadable chive and onion cream cheese

4 flour tortillas (8 inches), warmed

1. In a large skillet, saute red pepper and onion in 1 tablespoon oil until crisp-tender; remove and set aside.

2. In the same skillet, saute the steak, Italian seasoning, salt and pepper in remaining oil for 2-4 minutes or until meat reaches desired doneness. Return vegetables to the pan; heat through.

3. Spread 1 tablespoon of cream cheese off-center on each tortilla; top with beef mixture. Fold in sides and roll up. Cook on a panini maker or indoor grill for 3-4 minutes or until tortilla is browned.

Yield: 4 servings.

Family Flank Steak

Bernadette Bennett • Waco, Texas

I wanted to try something new with beef, so I created this recipe. Now, I prepare the entree a few times a month. The sauce adds wonderful flavor, and it is versatile enough to go with just about any meat.

1 beef flank steak (1 pound)
1 tablespoon canola oil
1/4 cup dry red wine *or* beef broth
1 tablespoon Worcestershire sauce
1 teaspoon minced fresh basil *or* 1/2 teaspoon dried basil

MUSHROOM WINE SAUCE:
1 cup sliced fresh mushrooms
3/4 cup beef broth
1/4 cup dry red wine *or* additional beef broth
1/4 cup chopped green onions
1 teaspoon butter
1 teaspoon pepper
2 teaspoons cornstarch
1 tablespoon cold water

1. In a large skillet, brown steak in oil. Stir in the wine, Worcestershire sauce and basil. Bring to a boil. Reduce heat; simmer, uncovered, for 2-4 minutes on each side or until meat reaches desired doneness (for medium-rare, a meat thermometer should read 145°; medium, 160°; well-done, 170°). Remove steak and keep warm.

2. To the skillet, add the mushrooms, broth, wine, onions, butter and pepper. Bring to a boil. Reduce heat; simmer, uncovered, for 5 minutes or until mushrooms are tender.

3. Combine cornstarch and water until smooth; gradually stir into sauce. Bring to a boil; cook and stir for 1 minute or until thickened. Thinly slice steak across the grain; serve with sauce.

Yield: 4 servings.

TIP The way a cooked flank steak is sliced will affect its tenderness. Flank steak should be cut across the grain. If you hold the knife at a 45° angle when cutting, the slices will be a little larger.

busy family favorites

Ginger Sirloin Strips

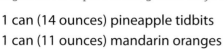

Jill Cox • Lincoln, Nebraska

A wonderful blend of fruity flavors with just the right touch of ginger makes this fabulous stir-fry dish a winner with our family. I came up with the recipe one night while experimenting with ways to do something new with beef strips.

1 can (14 ounces) pineapple tidbits

1 can (11 ounces) mandarin oranges

2 tablespoons cornstarch

1-1/2 pounds beef top sirloin steak, cut into strips

4-1/2 teaspoons minced fresh gingerroot

1 tablespoon olive oil

1 can (14 ounces) whole-berry cranberry sauce

1 cup thinly sliced green onions

Hot cooked rice

1. Drain pineapple and oranges, reserving juice; set fruit aside. In a small bowl, combine cornstarch and juices until smooth; set aside.

2. In a large skillet or wok, stir-fry beef and ginger in oil until meat is no longer pink. Add the cranberry sauce, onions and pineapple. Stir cornstarch mixture and gradually add to skillet; cook and stir until slightly thickened. Gently stir in oranges. Serve with rice.

Yield: 7 servings.

Sweet-and-Sour Beef

Brittany McCloud • Kenyon, Minnesota

This healthful stir-fry recipe is a family favorite. I've used a variety of meats and apples and sometimes replace the green onion with yellow onion. It always tastes great!

1 pound beef top sirloin steak, cut into 1/2-inch cubes

1 teaspoon salt

1/2 teaspoon pepper

3 teaspoons canola oil, *divided*

1 large green pepper, cut into 1/2-inch pieces

1 large sweet red pepper, cut into 1/2-inch pieces

2 medium tart apples, chopped

1/2 cup plus 2 tablespoons thinly sliced green onions, *divided*

2/3 cup packed brown sugar

1/2 cup cider vinegar

1 tablespoon cornstarch

2 tablespoons cold water

Hot cooked rice, optional

1. Sprinkle beef with salt and pepper. In a large nonstick skillet or wok coated with cooking spray, stir-fry beef in 2 teaspoons oil until no longer pink. Remove and keep warm.

2. In the same pan, stir-fry peppers and apples in remaining oil for about 3 minutes. Add 1/2 cup green onions. Stir-fry 2-3 minutes longer or until peppers are crisp-tender. Remove and keep warm.

3. Add brown sugar and vinegar to pan; bring to a boil. Combine cornstarch and water until smooth; stir into brown sugar mixture. Return to a boil; cook and stir for 2 minutes or until thickened and bubbly.

4. Return beef and vegetable mixture to pan; heat through. Garnish with remaining onions. Serve with rice if desired.

Yield: 4 servings.

TIP Sweet red peppers are usually more expensive than green peppers. Be sure to purchase them when they are on sale. Wash and dry them before cutting into strips, chunks or cubes and freezing. Add them to soups, stews or stir-fries. As long as they are cooked, the texture will be fine.

busy family favorites

Pork

Busy-Day Pork Chops, p. 91

Pork Medallions With Asian Flair

Dianne Luehring • Edmond, Oklahoma

When I became serious about losing weight and getting healthy, my kids missed the Chinese delivery that I used to order so frequently. I combined a few recipes to come up with this quick and tasty winner.

1 pork tenderloin (1 pound), halved and thinly sliced
1 tablespoon sesame oil
1/4 cup sherry *or* reduced-sodium chicken broth
3 tablespoons reduced-sodium soy sauce
1 tablespoon brown sugar
1 tablespoon hoisin sauce
1 garlic clove, minced
1/8 teaspoon cayenne pepper
Hot cooked brown rice, optional

1. In a large nonstick skillet, saute pork in oil in batches until no longer pink. Remove and keep warm. Add the remaining ingredients to the pan; cook and stir over medium heat for 3-4 minutes or until thickened.

2. Return pork to the pan; heat through. Serve with rice if desired.

Yield: 4 servings.

Tortellini Alfredo

Chris Snyder • Boulder, Colorado

I jazz up refrigerated tortellini with ham, mushrooms, peas and my homemade Alfredo sauce for a fast supper. When we're having company, I prepare the dinner shortly before guests arrive, put it in a casserole dish and keep it warm in the oven.

2 packages (9 ounces *each*) refrigerated cheese tortellini
1/2 cup chopped onion
1/3 cup butter, cubed
1-1/2 cups frozen peas, thawed
1 cup thinly sliced fresh mushrooms
1 cup cubed fully cooked ham
1-3/4 cups heavy whipping cream
1/4 teaspoon coarsely ground pepper
3/4 cup grated Parmesan cheese
Shredded Parmesan cheese, optional

1. Cook tortellini according to package directions. Meanwhile, in a large skillet, saute onion in butter until tender. Add the peas, mushrooms and ham; cook until mushrooms are tender. Stir in cream and pepper; heat through. Stir in the grated Parmesan cheese until melted.

2. Drain the tortellini and place in a serving dish; add the sauce and toss to coat. Sprinkle with shredded Parmesan cheese if desired.

Yield: 4-6 servings.

busy family favorites

Mediterranean Pork and Orzo

Mary Relyea • Canastota, New York

Is there a food group not represented in this flavorful and fabulous meal-in-a-bowl? It's one of my family's wholesome favorites.

2 pork tenderloins (3/4 pound *each*)

1 teaspoon coarsely ground pepper

2 tablespoons olive oil

3 quarts water

1-1/4 cups uncooked orzo pasta

1/4 teaspoon salt

1 package (6 ounces) fresh baby spinach

1 cup grape tomatoes, halved

3/4 cup crumbled feta cheese

1. Rub pork with pepper; cut into 1-in. cubes. In a large nonstick skillet, cook pork in oil over medium heat for 8-10 minutes or until no longer pink.

2. Meanwhile, in a large saucepan, bring water to a boil. Stir in orzo and salt; cook, uncovered, for 8 minutes. Stir in spinach; cook 45-60 seconds longer or until orzo is tender and spinach is wilted.

3. Add tomatoes to the pork; cook and stir for 1 minute or until heated through. Drain orzo mixture; toss with pork mixture and feta cheese.

Yield: 6 servings.

Apple-Spiced Pork

Linda Murray • Allenstown, New Hampshire

The sweet and savory combination serves up fall flavors. I've passed this recipe on many times! It also works well with ground pork or cubed leftover pork roast.

2 cups uncooked yolk-free noodles

1 pork tenderloin (1 pound), halved lengthwise and cut into 1/2-inch slices

1/4 cup chopped celery

2 tablespoons chopped onion

1 tablespoon canola oil

2 medium tart apples, chopped

1/3 cup raisins

1 tablespoon brown sugar

1/2 teaspoon seasoned salt

1/4 to 1/2 teaspoon ground cinnamon

4-1/2 teaspoons cornstarch

1 can (14-1/2 ounces) reduced-sodium beef broth

2 tablespoons chopped walnuts

1. Cook noodles according to package directions; drain. Meanwhile, in a large skillet, brown pork with celery and onion in oil; drain. Add the apples, raisins, brown sugar, seasoned salt and cinnamon. Cook and stir over medium heat for 8-10 minutes or until pork is no longer pink and vegetables are tender.

2. In a small bowl, combine cornstarch and broth until smooth; gradually add to the pork mixture. Bring to a boil; cook and stir for 2 minutes or until thickened. Serve with noodles. Sprinkle with walnuts.

Yield: 4 servings.

Maple Ham Steak

Jean Tayntor • Eaton, New York

This main course is very simple to make, but has a great flavor that everyone will enjoy.

1 bone-in fully cooked ham steak (about 2 pounds and 3/4 inch thick)

1/2 cup maple syrup, *divided*

1. Grill ham, uncovered, over medium-hot heat for 5-7 minutes on each side or until a meat thermometer reads 140°, basting frequently with 1/4 cup syrup. Warm remaining syrup to serve with ham.

Yield: 6 servings.

TIP Processing maple syrup is labor intensive, which is why it is so expensive. Maple syrup is graded from AA to C with AA being light in color with a mild flavor and C being dark in color with a strong flavor. Store open containers of maple syrup in the refrigerator.

busy family favorites

Sweet 'n' Tangy Pork Chops

Dennis Wolcott • Blossburg, Pennsylvania

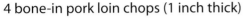

These pork chops bring flavor to the table like none other. They are so easy to make...try serving them tonight!

4 bone-in pork loin chops (1 inch thick)

2 tablespoons canola oil

1 cup (8 ounces) tomato sauce

1/2 cup packed brown sugar

2 tablespoons cider vinegar

1-1/2 teaspoons Worcestershire sauce

1 teaspoon celery salt

1/2 teaspoon ground nutmeg

1/2 teaspoon pepper

1. In a large skillet, brown pork chops in oil. Combine the remaining ingredients; add to skillet. Bring to a boil. Reduce heat; simmer, uncovered, for 8-10 minutes or until meat is tender. Spoon sauce over pork chops.

Yield: 4 servings.

Pork Chops with Apple Dressing

Donna Garvin • Glens Falls, New York

When we first purchased our microwave years ago, I could not wait to cook with it! This is the first recipe I tried. My husband loves it.

1-1/2 cups crushed seasoned stuffing

1 medium tart apple, peeled and chopped

3 tablespoons butter, melted

2 tablespoons chopped onion

1 tablespoon sugar

1/4 teaspoon rubbed sage

1/4 teaspoon salt

1/4 cup raisins

4 boneless pork loin chops (1/2 inch thick and 6 ounces *each*)

1 envelope pork gravy mix

1. In a small bowl, combine the first eight ingredients. Place in a greased 11-in. x 7-in. microwave-safe dish. Top with pork chops. Cover and microwave on high for 8-12 minutes or until a meat thermometer reads 160°. Prepare gravy mix according to package directions. Serve with pork chops.

Yield: 4 servings.

EDITOR'S NOTE: This recipe was tested in a 1,100-watt microwave.

Pork Tenderloin Medallions

Gerry Holcomb • Fairfax, California

Tender pork with cranberry sauce is on the top of my list of best recipes to serve family and guests. Pine nuts make a nice, crunchy garnish.

2 pork tenderloins (1 pound *each*), cut into 1-inch slices

Salt and pepper to taste

2 tablespoons olive oil

CRANBERRY SAUCE:

1/3 cup finely chopped red onion

1 garlic clove, minced

1 can (14 ounces) whole-berry cranberry sauce

2/3 cup white wine *or* chicken broth

2 tablespoons *each* orange juice concentrate and balsamic vinegar

2 tablespoons Dijon mustard

1 teaspoon reduced-sodium chicken bouillon granules

1/4 teaspoon salt

1/8 teaspoon pepper

1. Flatten pork slices to 1/2-in. thickness; sprinkle with salt and pepper. In a large skillet over medium heat, cook pork in oil in batches until meat is no longer pink. Remove and keep warm.

2. In the same skillet, saute onion in drippings until tender. Add garlic; saute 1 minute longer. Stir in the cranberry sauce, wine, orange juice concentrate, vinegar, mustard, bouillon, salt and pepper; heat through. Serve with pork.

Yield: 8 servings.

TIP

Medallion is just an elegant name for a small oval or round slice of meat. It can refer to pork, beef, veal, lamb or fish. Medallions also save time because the smaller pieces often cook faster than when left in a larger cut.

busy family favorites

Pork Chops with Onion Gravy

Amy Radyshewsky • Great Falls, Montana

I came up with this recipe as a quick dinner for a finicky husband who's not too fond of pork chops. These are so tender and good, he gives them a thumbs up!

4 boneless pork loin chops (1/2 inch thick and 4 ounces *each*)

1/4 teaspoon pepper

1/8 teaspoon salt

1 small onion, sliced and separated into rings

1 tablespoon canola oil

1/4 cup reduced-sodium chicken broth

1 envelope pork gravy mix

1/8 teaspoon garlic powder

3/4 cup water

1. Sprinkle the pork chops with pepper and salt. In a large skillet, cook chops and onion in oil over medium heat for 2-3 minutes on each side or until chops are lightly browned; drain.

2. Add the broth. Bring to a boil. Reduce heat; cover and simmer for 7-8 minutes on each side or until a meat thermometer reads 160°.

3. In a small bowl, whisk the gravy mix, garlic powder and water. Pour over pork. Bring to a boil. Reduce heat; simmer, uncovered, for 3-4 minutes or until thickened, stirring occasionally.

Yield: 4 servings.

Italian Sausage With Bow Ties

Janelle Moore • Federal Way, Washington

Here's a family favorite that's requested monthly in our house. The Italian sausage paired with creamy tomato sauce tastes out of this world. Not only is this dish simple to make, it tastes like you slaved over a hot stove for hours!

1 package (16 ounces) bow tie pasta
1 pound bulk Italian sausage
1/2 cup chopped onion
1/2 teaspoon crushed red pepper flakes
1-1/2 teaspoons minced garlic
2 cans (14-1/2 ounces *each*) Italian stewed tomatoes, drained and chopped
1-1/2 cups heavy whipping cream
1/2 teaspoon salt
1/4 teaspoon dried basil
Shredded Parmesan cheese

1. Cook the pasta according to package directions. Meanwhile, in a Dutch oven, cook the sausage, onion and pepper flakes over medium heat for 4-5 minutes or until meat is no longer pink. Add garlic; cook for 1 minute. Drain.

2. Stir in the tomatoes, cream, salt and basil. Bring to a boil over medium heat. Reduce heat; simmer, uncovered, for 6-8 minutes or until thickened, stirring occasionally. Drain pasta; toss with sausage mixture. Garnish with cheese.

Yield: 5 servings.

Ham 'n' Cheese Pizzas

Taste of Home Test Kitchen

With leftover ham, cheese and Alfredo sauce, these pizzas are sure to please. Best of all, they're very kid-friendly.

1/4 cup refrigerated Alfredo sauce
4 pita breads (6 inches)
1 cup (4 ounces) shredded Swiss cheese
1-3/4 cups cubed fully cooked ham
1/2 cup shredded part-skim mozzarella cheese
1 tablespoon minced chives

1. Spread Alfredo sauce over pita breads. Top with Swiss cheese, ham, mozzarella cheese and chives.

2. Place on an ungreased baking sheet. Bake at 350° for 10-15 minutes or until cheese is melted.

Yield: 4 servings.

busy family favorites

Busy-Day Pork Chops

Dee Maltby • Wayne, Ohio

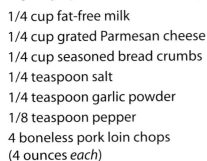

I developed this recipe one day when I had thawed pork chops and needed to find a quick fix for them. It's extremely simple, and the response was a rave review!

1/4 cup fat-free milk

1/4 cup grated Parmesan cheese

1/4 cup seasoned bread crumbs

1/4 teaspoon salt

1/4 teaspoon garlic powder

1/8 teaspoon pepper

4 boneless pork loin chops
(4 ounces *each*)

Cooking spray

1. Place milk in a shallow bowl. In another shallow bowl, combine the cheese, bread crumbs, salt, garlic powder and pepper. Dip the pork chops in milk, then coat with the crumb mixture.

2. Place chops on a baking sheet coated with cooking spray; spritz the chops with cooking spray. Bake at 375° for 9-11 minutes on each side or until a meat thermometer reads 160°.

Yield: 4 servings.

Lemon-Pecan Pork Chops

Katie Sloan • Charlotte, North Carolina

This delicious dish is quick to make and unforgettable to taste. I serve the chops with garlic mashed potatoes and sweet peas or a colorful mix of vegetables.

4 boneless pork loin chops (7 ounces *each*)

1 teaspoon lemon-pepper seasoning

1/2 teaspoon garlic salt

1 tablespoon butter

1 cup chopped pecans

1/4 cup lemon juice

1. Sprinkle the pork chops with lemon-pepper and garlic salt. In a large skillet over medium heat, cook chops in butter for 8-10 minutes on each side or until a meat thermometer reads 160°. Remove chops and keep warm.

2. Add the pecans and lemon juice to the skillet; cook and stir for 1 minute or until heated through. Spoon over pork chops.

Yield: 4 servings.

Skillet Barbecued Pork Chops

Tammy Messing • Ruth, Michigan

On days I volunteer at church or shuttle between after-school activities, I'm glad this dinner comes together in one skillet. The sauce makes the chops so moist and tender. I also simmer it up with other meats like beef or venison steaks.

4 boneless pork loin chops (1/2 inch thick)

1 teaspoon seasoned salt

1 tablespoon butter

1 medium onion, chopped

1/2 cup water

1/2 cup packed brown sugar

1 cup honey barbecue sauce

1 tablespoon Worcestershire sauce

2 teaspoons cornstarch

1 tablespoon cold water

1. Sprinkle the pork chops with seasoned salt. In a large skillet, brown chops on both sides in butter over medium-high heat. Remove chops.

2. In the drippings, saute onion until golden brown. Add the water, brown sugar, barbecue sauce and Worcestershire sauce. Return chops to the skillet. Bring to a boil. Reduce heat; cover and simmer for 15 minutes or until meat juices run clear. Remove chops; keep warm.

3. Combine cornstarch and cold water until smooth; gradually stir into skillet. Bring to a boil; cook and stir for 2 minutes or until thickened. Serve with pork.

Yield: 4 servings.

busy family favorites

Sweet-and-Sour Pork

Joanne Albers • Garden Grove, California

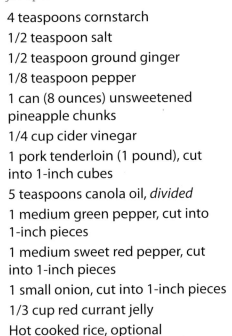

Red currant jelly gives this traditional Chinese dish a tangy kick. Your family will love it for a quick weeknight meal, and guests will be thrilled when you serve it for special occasions.

4 teaspoons cornstarch

1/2 teaspoon salt

1/2 teaspoon ground ginger

1/8 teaspoon pepper

1 can (8 ounces) unsweetened pineapple chunks

1/4 cup cider vinegar

1 pork tenderloin (1 pound), cut into 1-inch cubes

5 teaspoons canola oil, *divided*

1 medium green pepper, cut into 1-inch pieces

1 medium sweet red pepper, cut into 1-inch pieces

1 small onion, cut into 1-inch pieces

1/3 cup red currant jelly

Hot cooked rice, optional

1. In a small bowl, combine the cornstarch, salt, ginger and pepper. Drain pineapple, reserving juice; set pineapple aside. Stir juice and vinegar into cornstarch mixture until smooth; set aside.

2. In a large nonstick skillet or wok, stir-fry pork in 3 teaspoons oil until no longer pink. Remove and keep warm. In the same pan, stir-fry peppers and onion in remaining oil until crisp-tender. Stir in the pork, pineapple and jelly.

3. Stir cornstarch mixture and add to the pan. Bring to a boil; cook and stir for 2 minutes or until thickened. Serve with rice if desired.

Yield: 4 servings.

In-a-Hurry Hot Dog Dinner

Sandra Small • Niles, Ohio

I combine sliced franks with plenty of green pepper, onions and tomatoes for this well-seasoned entree. Serve it plain or over noodles or rice.

1 package (1 pound) hot dogs, halved lengthwise and sliced

2 tablespoons butter, *divided*

2 medium onions, halved and sliced

3 celery ribs, coarsely chopped

1 medium green pepper, julienned

1 garlic clove, minced

1 can (14-1/2 ounces) stewed tomatoes, undrained

1 teaspoon dried oregano

1/2 teaspoon paprika

1/4 teaspoon pepper

Hot cooked noodles *or* rice

1. In a large skillet, cook and stir hot dogs in 1 tablespoon butter over medium-high heat until lightly browned; remove and keep warm.

2. In same skillet, saute the onions, celery and green pepper in remaining butter until tender. Add garlic; cook 1 minute longer. Add the tomatoes, oregano, paprika, pepper and hot dogs. Cook and stir until heated through. Serve with noodles or rice.

Yield: 4-6 servings.

Linguine with Garlic Sauce

Taste of Home Test Kitchen

On a chilly evening, this creamy pasta toss is sure to please. It's rich and flavorful with smoky bacon, fresh spinach and toasted pine nuts.

12 ounces uncooked linguine

1/2 pound sliced bacon, diced

5 cups fresh baby spinach

1/2 cup chopped onion

1/2 teaspoon minced garlic

1-1/4 cups 2% milk

1 package (8 ounces) cream cheese, cubed

2 tablespoons butter

1/2 teaspoon salt

1/4 teaspoon ground nutmeg

1/4 teaspoon pepper

1/2 cup pine nuts, toasted

1. Cook linguine according to package directions. Meanwhile, in a large skillet, cook bacon over medium heat until crisp. Using a slotted spoon, remove to paper towels; drain, reserving 1 tablespoon drippings.

2. In the drippings, saute spinach and onion until spinach is wilted and onion is tender. Add garlic; cook 1 minute longer. Add the milk, cream cheese, butter, salt, nutmeg and pepper; stir until smooth. Stir in pine nuts and bacon; heat through. Drain pasta; toss with sauce.

Yield: 4-6 servings.

TIP

Also known as pignolia or pinon, the pine nut is the small seed from one of several pine tree varieties. They are small elongated ivory-colored nuts measuring about 3/8 inch long and have a soft texture and a buttery flavor. Store in an airtight container in the refrigerator for up to 3 months or in the freezer for up to 9 months.

busy family favorites

Pork Fajita Kabobs

Bea Westphal • Slidell, Louisiana

This has become my favorite way to cook pork loin. The grilled vegetable and meat chunks, seasoned with a homemade Southwestern-style spice blend, are appropriately served in a flour tortilla. Just top with salsa and enjoy!

2 teaspoons paprika

1-1/2 teaspoons ground cumin

1-1/2 teaspoons dried oregano

1 teaspoon garlic powder

1/8 to 1/4 teaspoon crushed red pepper flakes

1-1/2 pounds boneless pork loin chops, cut into 1-inch cubes

1 small green pepper, cut into 1-inch pieces

1 small onion, cut into eight wedges

8 large fresh mushrooms

16 grape tomatoes

8 flour tortillas (8 inches), warmed

3/4 cup chunky salsa

1. In a large resealable plastic bag, combine paprika, cumin, oregano, garlic powder and pepper flakes; add pork. Seal bag and toss to coat. On eight metal or soaked wooden skewers, alternately thread the pork, green pepper, onion, mushrooms and tomatoes.

2. Grill kabobs, covered, over medium heat for 5-8 minutes on each side or until meat is no longer pink and vegetables are tender. Place each kabob on a tortilla; remove skewers and fold tortillas in half. Serve with the salsa.

Yield: 4 servings.

Glazed Pork Chops And Apples

Kathy Barry • Lake Forest, California

This hearty dish was always a family favorite when I was growing up. Now it's a favorite meal with my own family.

4 boneless pork loin chops (4 ounces *each*)

3/4 teaspoon rubbed sage

1/2 teaspoon salt

1 tablespoon canola oil

1 tablespoon all-purpose flour

1/2 cup reduced-sodium chicken broth

1 tablespoon cider vinegar

2 medium tart apples, thinly sliced

4 teaspoons brown sugar

1. Sprinkle pork chops with sage and salt. In a large skillet, brown chops in oil on both sides. Transfer to an 11-in. x 7-in. baking dish coated with cooking spray.

2. Stir flour into the pan drippings until blended. Gradually stir in broth and vinegar. Bring to a boil; cook and stir for 1-2 minutes or until thickened. Remove from the heat.

3. Arrange apples over chops; sprinkle with brown sugar. Drizzle with broth mixture. Bake, uncovered, at 350° for 20-25 minutes or until a meat thermometer reads 160°.

Yield: 4 servings.

Creamed Ham in Toast Cups

Catherine Crandall • Amity, Oregon

My grandmother taught me many of her recipes in show-and-cook sessions. Usually, we had this dish on Mondays, following a Sunday lunch of ham, peas and corn.

8 slices bread

1/2 cup butter, softened, *divided*

1/4 cup all-purpose flour

1/8 teaspoon white pepper

1 cup 2% milk

1 cup heavy whipping cream

2 cups chopped fully cooked ham

1 cup frozen green peas, thawed

1 cup whole kernel corn

Paprika

1. Remove and discard crusts from bread; using a rolling pin, flatten to 1/8-in.

thickness. Butter both sides of each slice, using 1/4 cup of butter. Press into eight greased muffin cups . Bake at 350° for 15-18 minutes or until golden brown.

2. In a saucepan, melt the remaining butter. Stir in flour and pepper. Gradually stir in milk and cream. Bring to a boil; cook and stir for 2 minutes or until thickened. Reduce heat.

3. Stir in ham, peas and corn. Cook and stir for 5 minutes or until heated through. Pour into warm toast cups; sprinkle with paprika.

Yield: 4 servings.

busy family favorites

Pizza Pork Chops

Vance Werner Jr. • Franklin, Wisconsin

Pepperoni and mozzarella cheese punch up this easy skillet recipe with the pizza taste that kids love.

2 cups sliced fresh mushrooms

2 tablespoons butter

4 boneless pork loin chops (1/2 inch thick and 4 ounces *each*)

1/4 teaspoon salt

1/4 teaspoon pepper

2 tablespoons olive oil

2 cups marinara *or* spaghetti sauce

16 slices pepperoni

1 cup (4 ounces) shredded part-skim mozzarella cheese

1. In a large skillet, saute mushrooms in butter until tender. Remove and keep warm. Sprinkle pork chops with salt and pepper. In the same skillet, brown chops in oil on both sides; drain.

2. Add marinara sauce; bring to a boil. Reduce heat; simmer, uncovered, for 4-5 minutes on each side or until a meat thermometer reads 160°. Layer pork with pepperoni, mushrooms and cheese. Remove from the heat. Cover and let stand for 2-3 minutes or until cheese is melted.

Yield: 4 servings.

Pork Kiev

Jeanne Barney • Saratoga Springs, New York

My pork Kiev provides the same great experience of traditional chicken Kiev but in a fraction of the time! This recipe is so easy, and it's always a big hit.

4 teaspoons butter, softened

2 teaspoons minced chives

2 teaspoons dried parsley flakes

1 teaspoon minced garlic

1/2 teaspoon pepper

4 boneless pork loin chops (4 ounces each)

1 egg

1 teaspoon water

1/2 cup all-purpose flour

1/2 cup dry bread crumbs

2 tablespoons canola oil

1. In a small bowl, combine the butter and seasonings.

Cut a pocket in each pork chop. Fill with butter mixture; secure with toothpicks.

2. In a shallow bowl, beat egg and water. Place flour and bread crumbs in separate shallow bowls. Dip chops in flour, then in egg mixture; coat with crumbs.

3. In a large skillet over medium heat, cook the chops in oil for 6-8 minutes on each side or until meat juices run clear.

Yield: 4 servings.

Ginger Pork Stir-Fry

Jackie Hannahs • Fountain, Michigan

My recipe box is full of delicious pork recipes, but this fast-to-fix stir-fry really stands out from the rest. My gang loves the citrus glaze that coats the tender pork and vegetables. Ginger, garlic and orange juice provide its terrific taste.

1 tablespoon cornstarch

1 cup orange juice

2 tablespoons soy sauce

2 garlic cloves, minced

1/4 teaspoon ground ginger

1 pork tenderloin (1 pound), cut into thin strips

1 tablespoon canola oil

1 small onion, chopped

1/4 pound fresh snow peas

1/4 cup chopped sweet red pepper

Hot cooked rice

1. In a small bowl, combine the first five ingredients until smooth; set aside. In a large skillet or wok, stir-fry pork in oil for 5 minutes or until lightly browned; drain. add the onion, peas and red pepper; cook and stir for 3-5 minutes or until crisp-tender.

2. Stir orange juice mixture and stir into the pan. Bring to a boil; cook and stir for 2 minutes or until thickened. Serve with rice.

Yield: 4 servings.

busy family favorites

Pork Parmigiana

Julee Wallberg • Salt Lake City, Utah

I bring home the flavors of Italy with this tantalizing Parmigiana. Baked in mere minutes, the crispy yet moist pork tenderloin makes an easy dinner, which your family will surely savor!

1-1/3 cups uncooked spiral pasta

2 cups meatless spaghetti sauce

1 pork tenderloin (1 pound)

1/4 cup egg substitute

1/3 cup seasoned bread crumbs

3 tablespoons grated Parmesan cheese, *divided*

1/4 cup shredded part-skim mozzarella cheese

1. Cook pasta according to package directions. Place spaghetti sauce in a small saucepan; cook over low heat until heated through, stirring occasionally.

2. Meanwhile, cut tenderloin into eight slices; flatten to 1/4-in. thickness. Place egg substitute in a shallow bowl. In another shallow bowl, combine bread crumbs and 1 tablespoon Parmesan cheese. Dip pork slices in egg substitute, then roll in the crumb mixture.

3. Place on a baking sheet coated with cooking spray. Bake at 425° for 5-6 minutes on each side or until meat is tender. Drain pasta; serve with spaghetti sauce and pork. Sprinkle with mozzarella cheese and remaining Parmesan cheese.

Yield: 4 servings.

Family-Pleasing Pizza

Judy Sellgren • Grand Rapids, Michigan

This is great as is but can easily be adapted to fit your family's tastes. Add whatever fresh veggies you have on hand.

1/2 pound bulk pork sausage

1 tube (13.8 ounces) refrigerated pizza crust

2 teaspoons butter, melted

2 tablespoons grated Parmesan cheese

1 teaspoon garlic powder

2 cups (8 ounces) shredded part-skim mozzarella cheese

2 medium Roma tomatoes, thinly sliced

2 teaspoons Italian seasoning

1. In a large skillet, cook sausage over medium heat until no longer pink. Drain and set aside.

2. Meanwhile, press pizza dough into a greased 13-in. x 9-in. baking dish. Brush with butter; sprinkle with Parmesan cheese and garlic powder. Layer with 1 cup mozzarella, sausage and tomatoes. Sprinkle with remaining mozzarella and Italian seasoning.

3. Bake at 400° for 20-25 minutes or until crust is golden brown and cheese is melted.

Yield: 6 servings.

German Bratwurst

Taste of Home Test Kitchen

What a tasty use for bacon drippings! The tangy mustard and brown sugar make this quick-and-easy bratwurst recipe something special.

4 bacon strips, diced

5 uncooked bratwurst links

1 teaspoon cornstarch

1/4 cup chicken broth

2 tablespoons Dijon mustard

1 tablespoon brown sugar

1 tablespoon white wine *or* additional chicken broth

1 tablespoon cider vinegar

1/8 teaspoon celery seed

1. In a large skillet, cook bacon over medium heat until crisp. Using a slotted spoon, remove to paper towels (save for another use). Drain, reserving 4 tablespoons drippings. In the drippings, cook bratwurst for 10-15 minutes or until no longer pink. Remove and keep warm. Drain skillet.

2. In a bowl, combine cornstarch and broth until smooth; set aside. Add the mustard, brown sugar, wine, vinegar and celery seed to skillet; cook and stir over medium heat until mixture is hot and bubbly.

3. Gradually add cornstarch mixture. Bring to a boil; cook and stir for 2 minutes or until thickened. Return bratwurst to the pan; cook and stir for 1-2 minutes or until glazed.

Yield: 5 servings.

Cranberry Pork Chops with Rice

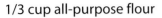

Mary Bilyeu • Ann Arbor, Michigan

This is an easy, nutritious and, most important, a delicious dinner! Even better, it goes together in minutes and looks lovely enough to serve company. Keep the ingredients on hand for last-minute dinner guests.

1/3 cup all-purpose flour

1/2 teaspoon salt

1/2 teaspoon seasoned salt

1/4 teaspoon pepper

4 boneless pork loin chops (1/2 inch thick and 4 ounces *each*)

2 tablespoons olive oil

1 can (14 ounces) whole-berry cranberry sauce

1 tablespoon balsamic vinegar

CRANBERRY RICE:

1-3/4 cups chicken broth

2 cups instant brown rice

1/2 cup dried cranberries

1. In a large resealable plastic bag, combine the flour, salt, seasoned salt and pepper. Add pork chops, one at a time, and shake to coat. In a large skillet, cook pork in oil over medium-high heat for 4-5 minutes on each side or until juices run clear. In a small bowl, combine cranberry sauce and vinegar; pour over chops. Bring to a boil. Reduce heat; cover and simmer for 10 minutes.

2. Meanwhile, in a large saucepan, bring broth to a boil. Add rice and cranberries. Return to a boil. Reduce heat; cover and simmer for 5 minutes. Remove from the heat. Let stand for 5 minutes or until broth is absorbed. Serve pork chops with sauce and rice.

Yield: 4 servings.

Microwave Potato Ham Dinner

Sharon Price • Caldwell, Idaho

I've had this recipe for 15 years. From the first time I made it, my family couldn't get enough. Now that our three daughters are grown and married, they fix it for their families, too.

2 cups cubed peeled potatoes
1 cup sliced carrots
1 cup chopped celery
1/2 cup water
2 tablespoons chopped green pepper
2 tablespoons chopped onion
2 tablespoons reduced-fat margarine
3 tablespoons all-purpose flour
1/4 teaspoon salt
1/8 teaspoon pepper
1-1/2 cups 2% milk
1/2 cup shredded reduced-fat cheddar cheese
2 cups cubed fully cooked lean ham

1. In a large microwave-safe bowl, combine the potatoes, carrots, celery and water. Cover and microwave on high for 5-1/2 minutes, stirring once. Add green pepper and onion; cover and microwave on high for 3-4 minutes or until crisp-tender, stirring once. Pour into a 2-qt. microwave-safe baking dish coated with cooking spray; set aside.

2. In a microwave-safe bowl, heat the margarine, covered, on high for 30-40 seconds or until melted. Stir in the flour, salt and pepper until smooth. Gradually add milk.

3. Cook, uncovered, on high for 1-1/2 to 2 minutes or until thickened and bubbly; stir after each minute. Stir in cheese until melted. Pour over vegetables. Stir in ham. Cover and microwave on high for 3-4 minutes or until heated through.

Yield: 4 servings.

EDITOR'S NOTE: This recipe was tested in a 1,100-watt microwave.

busy family favorites

Dijon-Honey Pork Chops

Shirley Goehring • Lodi, California

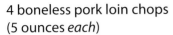

You won't need to season with salt when you serve these tasty chops. They're treated to a flavorful honey-orange-Dijon sauce in this quick entree.

4 boneless pork loin chops
(5 ounces *each*)

1 teaspoon salt-free lemon-pepper seasoning

2 teaspoons canola oil

1/2 cup orange juice

1 tablespoon Dijon mustard

1 tablespoon honey

1. Sprinkle pork chops with lemon-pepper. In a large nonstick skillet coated with cooking spray, cook chops in oil over medium heat for 2-3 minutes on each side or until lightly browned.

2. In a small bowl, combine the orange juice, mustard and honey; pour over pork. Bring to a boil. Reduce heat; cover and simmer for 5-8 minutes or until a meat thermometer reads 160°.

3. Remove chops and keep warm. Cook sauce, uncovered, for 2-3 minutes or until reduced to 1/4 cup. Spoon over chops.

Yield: 4 servings.

Sausage and Vegetable Skillet

Ruby Williams • Bogalusa, Louisiana

This hearty stovetop entree has been a family favorite for many years. The combination of vegetables makes this dish very appealing.

1 pound fresh Italian sausage links, cut into 1/2-inch slices

2 tablespoons canola oil

2 cups cubed yellow summer squash

1 cup chopped green onions

3 to 4 garlic cloves, minced

3 cups chopped tomatoes

4 teaspoons Worcestershire sauce

1/8 teaspoon cayenne pepper

1. In a large skillet over medium heat, cook the sausage in oil until no longer pink; drain.

2. Add the squash and onions; cook for 3 minutes. Add the garlic; cook 1 minute longer. Stir in the tomatoes, Worcestershire sauce and cayenne; heat through.

Yield: 4 servings.

Pizza Pasta Dinner

Claudia Malone • Louisville, Kentucky

The flavors found in this delicious supper are always welcome in my house. Packed with pasta, three kinds of meats, veggies and cheese, it makes a hearty and filling meal.

2 cups uncooked spiral pasta

1/2 pound ground beef

1/2 pound bulk Italian sausage

1 small green pepper, chopped

1 small onion, chopped

3 ounces sliced pepperoni

1 can (14-1/2 ounces) diced tomatoes, undrained

1 jar (14 ounces) spaghetti sauce

1 jar (4-1/2 ounces) sliced mushrooms

1 can (4-1/4 ounces) chopped ripe olives, drained

1 cup (4 ounces) shredded part-skim mozzarella cheese

1. Cook the pasta according to the package directions. Meanwhile, in a skillet, cook the beef, sausage, green pepper and onion until meat is no longer pink; drain. Add the pepperoni, tomatoes, spaghetti sauce, mushrooms and ripe olives; cook and stir for 5 minutes.

2. Drain pasta; stir into meat mixture. Heat through. Sprinkle with cheese. Remove from the heat; cover and let stand until cheese is melted.

Yield: 6 servings.

busy family favorites

Ham with Pineapple Salsa

Dawn Wilson • Buena Vista, Colorado

A dear friend shared this dinner when she moved from Hawaii to Colorado. Now I think it's one of the best ways to eat ham. I get lots of requests for the recipe when I make it for guests.

1 can (8 ounces) crushed pineapple, drained
2 tablespoons orange marmalade
1 tablespoon minced fresh cilantro
2 teaspoons lime juice
2 teaspoons chopped jalapeno pepper
1/4 teaspoon salt
1 bone-in fully cooked ham steak (1-1/2 pounds)

1. For salsa, in a small bowl, combine the first six ingredients; set aside.

2. Place the ham steak on an ungreased rack in a broiler pan. Broil 4-6 in. from the heat for 4-5 minutes on each side or until a meat thermometer reads 140°. Cut into serving-size pieces; serve with salsa.

Yield: 4 servings.

EDITOR'S NOTE: When cutting hot peppers, disposable gloves are recommended. Avoid touching your face.

Potato Kielbasa Skillet

Taste of Home Test Kitchen

Smoky kielbasa steals the show in this home-style all-in-one meal that can be on the table in half an hour!

1 pound red potatoes, cubed

3 tablespoons water

3/4 pound smoked kielbasa *or* Polish sausage, cut into 1/4-inch slices

1/2 cup chopped onion

1 tablespoon olive oil

2 tablespoons brown sugar

2 tablespoons cider vinegar

1 tablespoon Dijon mustard

1/2 teaspoon dried thyme

1/4 teaspoon pepper

4 cups fresh baby spinach

5 bacon strips, cooked and crumbled

1. Place potatoes and water in a microwave-safe dish. Cover and microwave on high for 4 minutes or until tender; drain.

2. In a large skillet, saute kielbasa and onion in oil until onion is tender. Add potatoes; saute 3-5 minutes longer or until kielbasa and potatoes are lightly browned.

3. Combine the brown sugar, vinegar, mustard, thyme and pepper; stir into skillet. Bring to a boil. Reduce heat; simmer, uncovered, for 2-3 minutes or until heated through. Add spinach and bacon; cook and stir until spinach is wilted.

Yield: 4 servings.

Country Skillet

Terri Adrian • Lake City, Florida

When I need a fast flavorful dinner, I turn to this filling combination of kielbasa, rice and veggies. It's a hearty dish for cool weather.

1 pound fully cooked kielbasa *or* Polish sausage, cut into 1/2-inch slices

1/2 cup chopped onion

1 tablespoon canola oil

1-1/2 cups water

1 can (10-3/4 ounces) condensed cream of celery soup, undiluted

1/2 teaspoon dried basil

1/4 teaspoon dried thyme

1/4 teaspoon pepper

1 package (10 ounces) frozen cut broccoli, thawed

1 jar (4-1/2 ounces) sliced mushrooms, drained

1 cup uncooked instant rice

1/4 cup grated Parmesan cheese

1. In a large skillet, cook sausage and onion in oil until onion is tender; drain. Combine the water, soup, basil, thyme and pepper; add to skillet.

2. Stir in broccoli and mushrooms. Bring to a boil. Stir in rice. Cover and remove from the heat. Let stand for 5-7 minutes or until rice is tender. Sprinkle with cheese.

Yield: 4-6 servings.

Harvest Ham Skillet

Jann Van Massenhoven • Hensall, Ontario

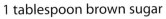

It's easy to dress up ordinary ham with speedy stovetop recipes like mine. The eye-catching sauce features diced apple, green onions and dried cranberries, so it tastes as special as it looks.

1 tablespoon brown sugar

1-1/2 teaspoons cornstarch

2/3 cup apple juice

1-1/2 teaspoons Dijon mustard

1 teaspoon lemon juice

1 fully cooked ham slice (about 1-1/2 pounds and 1 inch thick), quartered

1 tablespoon butter

1 medium tart apple, peeled and diced

1/4 cup dried cranberries

2 green onions, chopped

1. In a bowl, combine the brown sugar and cornstarch. Stir in the apple juice, mustard and lemon juice until smooth; set aside.

2. In a large skillet, brown the ham slice on both sides in butter. Remove and set aside. Add the apple, cranberries and onions to the skillet; cook for 2-3 minutes or until apple is tender. Stir in the apple juice mixture. Bring to a boil; cook and stir for 2 minutes or until thickened. Return the ham to the skillet; heat through.

Yield: 4 servings.

Prosciutto Pasta Toss

Laura Murphy-Ogden • Charlotte, North Carolina

I love quick, simple pasta dishes, and this is one of my favorites. I prepare a tossed green salad while the pasta cooks and serve up a lovely light supper in minutes!

1 package (16 ounces) linguine

1/2 cup frozen peas

2 tablespoons minced garlic

1 tablespoon Italian seasoning

1 teaspoon pepper

1/4 cup olive oil

1/2 pound thinly sliced prosciutto *or* deli ham, chopped

1/4 cup shredded Parmesan cheese

1. Cook linguine according to package directions, adding peas during the last 3 minutes. Meanwhile, in a large skillet, saute the garlic, Italian seasoning and pepper in oil for 1 minute or until garlic is tender. Stir in prosciutto.

2. Drain linguine; add to skillet and toss to coat. Sprinkle with cheese.

Yield: 6 servings.

Zippy Calzones

Mary Addy • West Point, Nebraska

My husband loves pizza and these make a fast alternative to the real thing. They're a great football game party snack, too, and always a hit.

1 tube (13.8 ounces) refrigerated pizza crust

1 cup (4 ounces) shredded part-skim mozzarella cheese

32 slices pepperoni

3/4 cup 1% cottage cheese

3/4 cup julienned green, sweet red *and/or* yellow pepper

1/4 cup finely chopped onion

1. Unroll pizza crust; roll into a 12-in. square. Cut into four 6-in. squares. Sprinkle 2 tablespoons mozzarella cheese over half of each square to within 1/2 in. of edges. Top each with eight slices pepperoni and 3 tablespoons cottage cheese.

2. Combine pepper and onion; place 1/4 cup mixture on each square; top with 2 tablespoons cottage cheese. Fold dough over filling; press edges with a fork to seal.

3. Transfer to a lightly greased baking sheet. Bake at 400° for 13-18 minutes or until golden brown.

Yield: 4 servings.

Honey-Dijon Pork Tenderloin

Trisha Kruse • Eagle, Idaho

It's hard to believe such an elegant dish is table-ready in half an hour. To cut prep time, use a food processor to slice onions and mushrooms. Mixed vegetables make a quick side dish.

1 pound pork tenderloin, cut into 1-inch slices

1/4 teaspoon salt

1/4 teaspoon pepper

1 tablespoon olive oil

1 small onion, chopped

1/2 cup sliced fresh mushrooms

1 tablespoon butter

2 garlic cloves, minced

1/2 cup evaporated milk

2 tablespoons Dijon mustard

1 tablespoon soy sauce

1 tablespoon honey

Hot cooked pasta

1. Flatten pork slices to 1/2-in. thickness; sprinkle with salt and pepper. In a large skillet over medium heat, cook pork in oil in batches until meat is no longer pink. Remove and keep warm.

2. In the same skillet, saute onion and mushrooms in butter until tender. Add garlic; saute for 1 minute. Stir in milk, mustard, soy sauce and honey. Return pork to pan; heat through. Serve with noodles.

Yield: 4 servings.

busy family favorites

Sausage Rice Skillet

Connie Putnam • Clayton, North Carolina

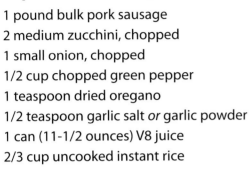

Flavorful pork sausage, fresh zucchini and instant rice make this stovetop sensation a favorite with my family and friends. Everyone I have shared this recipe with tells me how good it tastes.

1 pound bulk pork sausage

2 medium zucchini, chopped

1 small onion, chopped

1/2 cup chopped green pepper

1 teaspoon dried oregano

1/2 teaspoon garlic salt *or* garlic powder

1 can (11-1/2 ounces) V8 juice

2/3 cup uncooked instant rice

1. In a large skillet, cook the sausage until no longer pink; drain. Add the zucchini, onion, green pepper, oregano and garlic salt; cook and stir until onion is tender, about 5 minutes. Stir in V8 juice; bring to a boil. Reduce heat; cover and simmer for 10-14 minutes or until vegetables are tender.

2. Return to a boil. Stir in the rice; cover and remove from the heat. Let stand for 5-7 minutes or until the rice is tender. Fluff with a fork.

Yield: 6 servings.

Ham 'n' Cheese Pasta

Taste of Home Test Kitchen

Kids and adults alike will love this dressed-up version of creamy macaroni and cheese.

3 cups uncooked bow tie pasta

3/4 pound fresh asparagus, trimmed and cut into 1-inch pieces

2 tablespoons butter

1 teaspoon minced garlic

2 tablespoons all-purpose flour

1/4 teaspoon onion powder

1/4 teaspoon pepper

1/8 to 1/4 teaspoon dried thyme

2 cups milk

2 cups (8 ounces) shredded cheddar cheese

1/2 cup grated Parmesan cheese

1/2 pound sliced deli ham, chopped

1. Cook pasta according to package directions, adding asparagus during the last 3 minutes.

2. Meanwhile, in a large saucepan, melt butter; add garlic. Stir in the flour, onion powder, pepper and thyme until blended; gradually add milk. Bring to a boil; cook and stir for 2 minutes or until thickened.

3. Reduce the heat. Add cheeses; stir until melted. Stir in the ham; heat through. Drain the pasta and asparagus; toss with the cheese mixture.

Yield: 4 servings.

TIP Cooking vegetables along with pasta not only saves time, but it also eliminates another dirty pot. Subtract the amount of time the veggies need from the total time for the pasta. Then set the timer for the shorter time to alert you to add the veggies.

pork

109

Pork 'n' Penne Skillet

Dawn Goodison • Rochester, New York

I enjoy this one-pan skillet supper because it's quick, and the cleanup is easy. But best of all, my family enjoys these flavorful and nutritious dinners. Add a salad for a complete filling meal.

2 tablespoons all-purpose flour

1 teaspoon chili powder

3/4 teaspoon salt

3/4 teaspoon pepper

1 pound boneless pork loin chops, cut into strips

2 cups sliced fresh mushrooms

1 cup chopped onion

1 cup chopped sweet red pepper

1 teaspoon dried oregano

1 tablespoon canola oil

1 tablespoon butter

1 teaspoon minced garlic

3 cups 2% milk

1 can (15 ounces) tomato sauce

2 cups uncooked penne

1. In a large resealable plastic bag, combine the flour, chili powder, salt and pepper. Add pork, a few pieces at a time, and shake to coat.

2. In a large skillet, cook the pork, mushrooms, onion, red pepper and oregano in oil and butter over medium heat for 4-6 minutes or until pork is browned. Add garlic; cook 1 minute longer.

3. Add the milk, tomato sauce and pasta. Bring to a boil. Reduce heat; simmer, uncovered, for 15-20 minutes or until meat is tender.

Yield: 8 servings.

TIP Pork loin is a tender cut of pork. It usually has a thin strip of fat on one edge. Trim the fat off before cutting the chops into strips. Once it is cut into strips, the pork will cook very quickly. Care should be taken not to overcook and dry out the pork.

busy family favorites

Poultry

Chutney Turkey Burgers, p. 115

Chicken Stew

Taste of Home Test Kitchen

Try this satisfying stew with tender chicken and veggies in a creamy gravy. There are only a handful of ingredients, but it still delivers that old-fashioned flavor. Serve it with fresh-from-the-oven biscuits.

1 pound boneless skinless chicken breasts, cut into 1-inch cubes
1 tablespoon olive oil
1 package (16 ounces) frozen vegetables for stew
1 jar (12 ounces) chicken gravy
1/2 teaspoon dried thyme
1/4 teaspoon rubbed sage
1/4 teaspoon pepper

1. In a large saucepan, brown chicken in oil over medium heat for 4-6 minutes or until no longer pink. Drain if necessary.

2. Stir in the remaining ingredients. Bring to a boil. Reduce heat; cover and simmer for 15 minutes or until vegetables are tender.

Yield: 4 servings.

Turkey Noodle Supper

Lori Tinkler • Richland, Washington

This was one of my favorites made by my mom when I was growing up. I lightened it up by using lean ground turkey, fat-free cream cheese, reduced-fat soup and fat-free milk. And it still tastes as good as Mom's!

8 ounces yolk-free extra-wide noodles
1 pound lean ground turkey
1 medium onion, chopped
1 can (10-3/4 ounces) reduced-fat reduced-sodium condensed cream of mushroom soup, undiluted
1 package (8 ounces) fat-free cream cheese, cubed
1 cup fat-free milk
1-1/2 cups frozen whole kernel corn, thawed
1 jar (4 ounces) chopped pimientos, drained
3/4 teaspoon salt
1/8 teaspoon pepper

1. Cook noodles according to package directions; drain. Meanwhile, crumble turkey into a large nonstick skillet. Add onion, cook over medium heat until meat is no longer pink; drain.

2. Return to pan. Add the soup, cream cheese and milk. Cook and stir until blended. Stir in the noodles, corn, pimientos, salt and pepper; cook until heated through.

Yield: 6 servings.

busy family favorites

Sweet Onion 'n' Sausage Spaghetti

Mary Relyea • Canastota, New York

Sweet onion seasons turkey, adding a richness to this wholesome pasta dish. It takes only minutes to toss it together with light cream, basil and tomatoes for a quick, springy meal in minutes.

6 ounces uncooked whole wheat spaghetti

3/4 pound Italian turkey sausage links, casings removed

2 teaspoons olive oil

1 sweet onion, thinly sliced

1 pint cherry tomatoes, halved

1/2 cup loosely packed fresh basil leaves, thinly sliced

1/2 cup half-and-half cream

Shaved Parmesan cheese, optional

1. Cook spaghetti according to package directions. Meanwhile, in a large nonstick skillet over medium heat, cook sausage in oil for 5 minutes. Add onion; cook 8-10 minutes longer or until meat is no longer pink and onion is tender.

2. Stir in tomatoes and basil; heat through. Add cream; bring to a boil. Drain spaghetti; toss with sausage mixture. Garnish with cheese if desired.

Yield: 5 servings.

Southwest Smothered Chicken

Debbie Schaefer • Durand, Michigan

There's a fiesta in every bite of this tasty chicken dish. Let it spice up dinner tonight! If you're worried about the heat, simply reduce the amount of jalapenos.

4 boneless skinless chicken breast halves (6 ounces *each*)
1/2 teaspoon ground cumin
1/2 teaspoon cayenne pepper
1 tablespoon canola oil
1 cup fresh *or* frozen corn
1 cup salsa
1 cup (4 ounces) shredded pepper Jack cheese
1/4 cup pickled jalapeno slices
1/4 cup sour cream

1. Flatten chicken to 1/2-in. thickness. Sprinkle both sides with cumin and cayenne. In a large skillet, cook chicken in oil over medium heat for 4-5 minutes on each side or until no longer pink.

2. Meanwhile, combine corn and salsa; spoon over chicken. Top with cheese and jalapenos. Cover and cook for 3-5 minutes or until heated through and cheese is melted. Top each chicken breast with a dollop of sour cream.

Yield: 4 servings.

Best Chicken 'n' Biscuits

Judith Whitford • East Aurora, New York

Quick and comforting, this delicious dish is guaranteed to warm your family to their toes!

6 individually frozen biscuits
1 can (49-1/2 ounces) chicken broth, *divided*
1-1/2 pounds boneless skinless chicken breasts, cubed
5 medium carrots, coarsely chopped
2 celery ribs, chopped
1/2 cup chopped onion
1/2 cup frozen corn
3 teaspoons dried basil
1/4 teaspoon pepper
1 cup all-purpose flour
3/4 teaspoon browning sauce, optional

1. Bake biscuits according to package directions. Meanwhile, in a Dutch oven, combine 4 cups broth, chicken, carrots, celery, onion, corn, basil and pepper. Bring to a boil. Reduce heat; cover and simmer for 7-10 minutes or until vegetables are tender.

2. In a small bowl, combine flour and remaining broth until smooth. Stir into chicken mixture. Bring to a boil; cook and stir for 2 minutes or until thickened. Stir in browning sauce if desired. Split biscuits; top with chicken mixture.

Yield: 6 servings.

busy family favorites

Chutney Turkey Burgers

Jeanne Lueders • Waterloo, Iowa

The secret to these burgers is the tangy mango chutney, but the arugula adds a special wow to the plate. I get lots of compliments when I serve these at cookouts.

1/2 cup chutney, *divided*

1 tablespoon Dijon mustard

2 teaspoons lime juice

1/4 cup minced fresh parsley

2 green onions, chopped

1/2 teaspoon salt

1/4 teaspoon pepper

1 pound lean ground turkey

4 hamburger buns, split

16 fresh arugula *or* baby spinach leaves

4 slices red onion

1. Combine 1/4 cup chutney, mustard and lime juice; set aside. In a large bowl, combine the parsley, onions, salt, pepper and remaining chutney. Crumble the turkey over mixture and mix well. Shape mixture into four patties.

2. Using long-handled tongs, moisten a paper towel with cooking oil and lightly coat the grill rack. Grill burgers, covered, over medium heat or broil 4 in. from the heat for 5-7 minutes on each side or until a meat thermometer reads 165° and juices run clear.

3. Serve on buns with arugula, onion and reserved chutney mixture.

Yield: 4 servings.

Turkey with Cran-Orange Sauce

Mary Relyea • Canastota, New York

Packed with protein, this turkey dish is a weekday throwback to Thanksgiving. You'll love the flavor combination and how fast this entree comes together.

1 package (17.6 ounces) turkey breast tenderloins, cut into 1/4-inch slices

1 tablespoon canola oil

1/2 cup reduced-sodium chicken broth

1/2 cup orange juice

1 tablespoon Dijon mustard

1 tablespoon honey

1/2 teaspoon dried tarragon

1 tablespoon cornstarch

1 tablespoon cold water

1/3 cup dried cranberries

1. In a large skillet, brown turkey in oil. In a small bowl, combine the broth, orange juice, mustard, honey and tarragon; pour over turkey. Bring to a boil. Reduce heat; cover and simmer for 7 minutes or until turkey juices run clear.

2. Combine cornstarch and water until smooth; stir into turkey mixture. Stir in cranberries. Bring to a boil; cook and stir for 2 minutes or until thickened.

Yield: 4 servings.

TIP

To keep sauces velvety smooth, always make sure the cornstarch or flour is completely dissolved in the liquid before adding it to the hot mixture in the pan. Whisk or stir before you pour in the cornstarch mixture, and continue stirring while it comes to a boil. Boil and stir for 2 minutes.

Ginger Mushroom Chicken

Christina Shape • Swartz Creek, Michigan

If you love fresh ginger, you're sure to adore this dish. The stir-fry is so quick to prepare. It's perfect for a busy weeknight.

1 cup fresh snow peas
2 teaspoons cornstarch
1/2 teaspoon salt
1/8 teaspoon pepper
3/4 cup 2% milk
3/4 pound boneless skinless chicken breasts, cut into thin strips
3 teaspoons canola oil, *divided*
1/2 pound sliced baby portobello mushrooms
1 teaspoon minced fresh gingerroot
2 cups hot cooked brown rice
1/4 cup minced fresh parsley

1. Place snow peas in a small saucepan; cover with water. Bring to a boil; boil for 1 minute. Drain and set aside.

In a small bowl, combine the cornstarch, salt, pepper and milk until smooth; set aside.

2. In a large nonstick skillet or wok coated with cooking spray, stir-fry chicken in 1 teaspoon hot oil for 5 minutes or until no longer pink. Remove and keep warm.

3. In the same pan, stir-fry mushrooms and ginger in remaining oil for 2 minutes. Add the peas; stir-fry 2 minutes longer.

4. Stir cornstarch mixture and add to the pan. Return chicken to pan. Bring to a boil; cook and stir for 2 minutes or until thickened. Serve with rice. Sprinkle with parsley.

Yield: 4 servings.

TIP

Before mincing your fresh parsley, rinse it under cold running water. Shake off the excess water and pat dry. Then place the parsley in a small glass container, and snip sprigs with kitchen shears until minced.

busy family favorites

Nutty Chicken Strips

Betsy Baertlein • Mazeppa, Minnesota

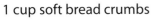

I enjoy cooking for my parents and two brothers. I usually prepare things that are a little out of the ordinary. These strips, seasoned with curry, are great.

1 cup soft bread crumbs

1/2 cup chopped almonds

2 tablespoons minced fresh cilantro

1-1/2 teaspoons curry powder

1/4 cup all-purpose flour

1 egg

1/2 cup 2% milk

1-1/2 pounds boneless skinless chicken breasts, cut into 1-inch strips

1/4 cup canola oil

YOGURT DIPPING SAUCE:

1 cup (8 ounces) plain yogurt

2 tablespoons minced fresh cilantro

1 tablespoon honey

1. In a large resealable plastic bag, combine the bread crumbs, almonds, cilantro and curry powder. Place flour in a shallow bowl.

2. In another shallow bowl, beat the egg and milk. Dip chicken strips in flour, then in egg mixture. Place in bag and shake to coat.

3. In a large skillet, cook chicken in oil for 5-6 minutes on each side or until no longer pink. Drain on paper towels.

4. In a small bowl, combine the sauce ingredients. Serve with chicken.

Yield: 6 servings.

Garlic Ranch Chicken

Taste of Home Test Kitchen

The simple ingredients in this recipe give it flavor the whole family will enjoy. A no-nonsense salad will round out the meal.

4 boneless skinless chicken breast halves (5 ounces *each*)
1/4 cup 2% milk
1/2 teaspoon minced garlic
1/4 cup all-purpose flour
1 tablespoon ranch salad dressing mix
1/8 teaspoon pepper
1 tablespoon olive oil
1 tablespoon butter

1. Flatten chicken slightly; set aside. In a shallow bowl, combine milk and garlic. In another shallow bowl, combine the flour, salad dressing mix and pepper. Dip chicken in milk mixture, then coat with flour mixture.

2. In a large skillet, cook chicken in oil and butter over medium heat for 6-8 minutes on each side or until no longer pink.

Yield: 4 servings.

Pan-Glazed Chicken

Margaret Wilson • Sun City, California

Honey and balsamic vinegar lend a sweet taste to chicken in this stovetop supper. Served over rice, the tangy chicken combination makes a delicious entree on a busy night.

1 package (6 ounces) instant long grain and wild rice mix
4 boneless skinless chicken breast halves (4 ounces *each*)
1/4 teaspoon salt
1/4 teaspoon pepper
2 teaspoons olive oil
2 tablespoons balsamic vinegar
1 tablespoon honey
2 teaspoons dried basil

1. Prepare rice according to package directions. Meanwhile, sprinkle chicken with salt and pepper. In a large skillet, cook chicken in oil over medium-high heat for 5 minutes on each side or until a meat thermometer reads 170°.

2. Combine the vinegar, honey and basil; pour over chicken. Cook for 1-2 minutes or until sauce is heated through. Serve with rice.

Yield: 4 servings.

Fiesta Ranch Burgers

Carol Brewer • Fairborn, Ohio

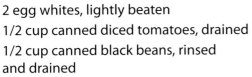

Depending on how spicy you like your burgers, add more or less chipotle pepper, which also gives it a nice smoky quality.

2 egg whites, lightly beaten

1/2 cup canned diced tomatoes, drained

1/2 cup canned black beans, rinsed and drained

1 small onion, chopped

1 tablespoon lime juice

1 to 2 tablespoons chopped chipotle peppers in adobo sauce

1 garlic clove, minced

1/4 teaspoon salt

1-1/4 pounds lean ground turkey

1/3 cup fat-free ranch salad dressing

1 tablespoon minced fresh cilantro

5 lettuce leaves

5 hamburger buns, split

1. In a large bowl, combine the first eight ingredients. Crumble turkey over mixture and mix well. Shape into five burgers.

2. Broil 4 in. from the heat for 7-9 minutes on each side or until a meat thermometer reads 165° and juices run clear.

3. In a small bowl, combine the salad dressing and cilantro. Serve burgers with dressing on lettuce-lined buns.

Yield: 5 servings.

Chicken Veggie Wraps

Kendra Katt • Albuquerque, New Mexico

I gathered bits and pieces of things I like about Southwest cooking to come up with this economical recipe. Serve with a green salad and vinaigrette dressing for a delightful meal.

1-1/2 cups uncooked instant rice

1 medium tomato, chopped

2 cans (4 ounces *each*) chopped green chilies

7 tablespoons lime juice, *divided*

1-1/2 teaspoons chili powder

1-1/2 teaspoons ground cumin

1/2 teaspoon salt

1 pound boneless skinless chicken breasts, cubed

3 teaspoons canola oil, *divided*

1 large onion, halved and sliced

1 large *each* green pepper, julienned and large sweet red pepper, julienned

3 garlic cloves, minced

1 tablespoon brown sugar

6 flour tortillas (8 inches), warmed

1. Cook rice according to package directions. Stir in the tomato, chilies and 3 tablespoons lime juice.

2. Meanwhile, combine the chili powder, cumin and salt; sprinkle over chicken. In a large nonstick skillet coated with cooking spray, saute chicken in 2 teaspoons oil until no longer pink. Remove and keep warm.

3. In the same skillet, cook onion and peppers in remaining oil until crisp-tender. Add garlic; cook 1 minute longer. Stir in the brown sugar, chicken and remaining lime juice; heat through.

4. Spoon 2/3 cup each of rice mixture and chicken mixture down the center of each tortilla; roll up.

Yield: 6 servings.

TIP To pack a little more fiber into your diet, substitute instant brown rice for the instant rice and use whole wheat flour tortillas for the flour tortillas.

Rotisserie Chicken Ragout

Paula Marchesi • Lenhartsville, Pennsylvania

Deli-roasted chicken is the secret to this super-quick family favorite. It's especially good after a long day of shopping, when you're tired or the kids have a game and time's tight. I like to serve this fail-proof meal-in-one with crusty Italian bread.

1 cup chopped yellow summer squash
1 cup chopped zucchini
1/2 cup chopped onion
2 tablespoons olive oil
1-1/2 teaspoons minced garlic
2 cups cubed cooked rotisserie chicken
1 can (15 ounces) white kidney *or* cannellini beans, rinsed and drained
1 tablespoon heavy whipping cream
1 tablespoon minced fresh thyme

1/8 teaspoon *each* salt and pepper
1/2 cup shredded Parmesan cheese

1. In a large skillet, saute the yellow squash, zucchini and onion in oil for 4-6 minutes or until tender. Add garlic; cook 1 minute longer.

2. Add the chicken, beans, cream, thyme, salt and pepper. Cook and stir 3-4 minutes longer or until heated through. Sprinkle with cheese.

Yield: 5 servings.

Easy Chicken Potpie

Amy Briggs • Gove, Kansas

Why look for potpie in the frozen food aisle when this easy, homemade version tastes much better? Under its golden-brown crust, you'll find the ultimate comfort food for kids and adults.

1 medium onion, chopped
2 tablespoons canola oil
1/2 cup all-purpose flour
1 teaspoon poultry seasoning
1 can (14-1/2 ounces) chicken broth
3/4 cup 2% milk
3 cups cubed cooked chicken
2 cups frozen mixed vegetables, thawed
1 sheet refrigerated pie pastry

1. In a large saucepan, saute onion in oil until tender. Stir in flour and poultry seasoning until blended; gradually add broth and milk. Bring to a boil; cook and stir for 2 minutes or until thickened. Add chicken and vegetables.

2. Transfer to a greased 9-in. deep-dish pie plate. Top with pastry. Trim, seal and flute edges. Cut slits in pastry. Bake at 450° for 15-20 minutes or until crust is golden brown and filling is bubbly.

Yield: 6 servings.

Apricot Chicken Drumsticks

Mary Ann Sklanka • Blakely, Pennsylvania

During the summer months, you can find my family gathered around the grill enjoying delicious bites like this. You can serve the drumsticks hot off the grill or chilled.

12 chicken drumsticks
(3 pounds)

1 teaspoon salt

1/4 teaspoon pepper

1/4 cup canola oil

1/4 cup apricot jam, warmed

1/4 cup prepared mustard

1 tablespoon brown sugar

1. Sprinkle chicken with salt and pepper. For sauce, in a small bowl, combine the remaining ingredients.

2. Using long-handled tongs, moisten a paper towel with cooking oil and lightly coat the grill rack. Grill chicken, covered, over medium heat for 15-20 minutes or until a meat thermometer reads 180°, turning and basting occasionally with sauce.

3. Serve immediately. Or, cool for 5 minutes, then cover and refrigerate until chilled.

Yield: 6 servings.

EDITOR'S NOTE: To bake drumsticks, coat a foil-lined baking sheet with cooking spray. Arrange drumsticks in a single layer. Baste with sauce. Bake at 400° for 25 minutes or until a meat thermometer reads 180°. Serve warm or chilled.

Broiled Turkey Tenderloins

Jean Komlos • Plymouth, Michigan

This recipe is ideal for weekday meals or special dinners… even though it's ready in 30 minutes! The simple sauce gets its tang from citrus, a little kick from cayenne and subtle sweetness from molasses. The sauce keeps well in the refrigerator, so it can be made ahead. I often fix extra to use later with other meats.

3/4 cup thawed orange juice concentrate

1/3 cup molasses

1/4 cup ketchup

3 tablespoons prepared mustard

2 tablespoons soy sauce

1/2 teaspoon garlic powder

1/4 teaspoon cayenne pepper

1/8 teaspoon ground cumin

3 turkey breast tenderloins
(about 1-1/2 pounds),
cut lengthwise in half

1. In a small saucepan, whisk the first eight ingredients; bring to a boil. Set aside 3/4 cup for serving. Brush tenderloins on both sides with remaining sauce.

2. Broil 6 in. from the heat for 5 minutes, basting once. Turn and broil 5-8 minutes longer or until juices run clear. Serve with the reserved sauce.

Yield: 6 servings.

busy family favorites

Turkey Portobello Pasta

Heather Fergeson • Idaho Springs, Colorado

With portobellos and a host of seasoning, this turkey pasta dish is truly special. It's perfect for guests, but since it's so quick, you can make it any time!

6 ounces uncooked spaghetti

2 cups cubed cooked turkey breast

1 can (10-3/4 ounces) reduced-fat reduced-sodium condensed cream of mushroom soup, undiluted

1 cup water

3/4 cup sliced baby portobello mushrooms

1 teaspoon dried rosemary, crushed

1 teaspoon Italian seasoning

1/2 teaspoon onion powder

1/2 teaspoon garlic powder

1/2 cup shredded Italian cheese blend

1/2 cup reduced-fat sour cream

2 tablespoons shredded Parmesan cheese

1 tablespoon dried parsley flakes

1. Cook spaghetti according to the package directions. Meanwhile, in a large saucepan, combine the turkey, soup, water, mushrooms, rosemary, Italian seasoning, onion powder and garlic powder. Bring to a boil. Reduce heat; simmer uncovered, for 5-7 minutes or until heated through and mushrooms are tender.

2. Remove from the heat. Whisk in the Italian cheese and sour cream until smooth. Drain spaghetti; place in a serving bowl. Top with the turkey mixture, Parmesan cheese and parsley.

Yield: 4 servings.

Breaded Turkey Slices

Julie Jahnke • Green Lake, Wisconsin

Serve these turkey slices with a vegetable and side salad for a complete and satisfying meal!

2 eggs
3 tablespoons 2% milk
2 cups seasoned bread crumbs
1/2 teaspoon salt
1-1/2 pounds turkey breast cutlets
1/2 cup butter, cubed

1. In a shallow bowl, beat the eggs and milk. In another shallow bowl, combine bread crumbs and salt. Dip turkey slices in egg mixture, then coat with crumb mixture.

2. In a large skillet, melt butter; brown turkey for about 2 minutes on each side or until juices run clear.

Yield: 6 servings.

Garlic-Mushroom Turkey Slices

Rick Fleishman • Beverly Hills, California

Even my daughter likes this turkey dish, and she is such a picky eater! It makes a delicious entree and takes just minutes to make.

1/2 cup all-purpose flour
1/2 teaspoon dried oregano
1/2 teaspoon paprika
3/4 teaspoon salt, *divided*
1/4 teaspoon pepper, *divided*
1 package (17.6 ounces) turkey breast cutlets
1 tablespoon olive oil
3/4 cup reduced-sodium chicken broth
1/4 cup white wine *or* additional reduced-sodium chicken broth
1/2 pound sliced fresh mushrooms
2 garlic cloves, minced

1. In a large resealable plastic bag, combine the flour, oregano, paprika, 1/2 teaspoon salt and 1/8 teaspoon pepper. Add turkey, a few pieces at a time, and shake to coat.

2. In a large nonstick skillet coated with cooking spray, cook turkey in oil in batches over medium heat for 1-2 minutes on each side or until no longer pink. Remove and keep warm.

3. Add broth and wine to the skillet; stir in mushrooms and remaining salt and pepper. Cook and stir for 4-6 minutes or until mushrooms are tender. Add garlic; cook 1 minute longer. Return turkey to the pan; heat through.

Yield: 4 servings.

busy family favorites

Chicken Orzo Skillet

Kathleen Farrell • Rochester, New York

As a busy homemaker with a home-based business, I try to make quick meals that are healthy for my husband and children. I combined two recipes to come up with this family favorite.

1 cup uncooked orzo pasta

1 pound boneless skinless chicken breasts, cubed

3 teaspoons olive oil, *divided*

3 garlic cloves, minced

2 cans (14-1/2 ounces *each*) stewed tomatoes, cut up

1 can (15 ounces) white kidney *or* cannellini beans, rinsed and drained

1-1/2 teaspoons Italian seasoning

1/2 teaspoon salt

1 package (16 ounces) frozen broccoli florets, thawed

1. Cook orzo according to package directions. Meanwhile, in a large nonstick skillet coated with cooking spray, cook chicken in 2 teaspoons oil for 6-7 minutes or until no longer pink. Remove and keep warm.

2. In the same skillet, cook garlic in remaining oil for 1 minute or until tender. Stir in the tomatoes, beans, Italian seasoning and salt. Bring to a boil. Stir in the broccoli and reserved chicken; heat through. Drain the orzo and stir into chicken mixture.

Yield: 6 servings.

Turkey Chop Suey

Ruth Peterson • Jenison, Michigan

I use leftover turkey for my fast-to-fix chop suey. Canned bean sprouts and water chestnuts add a nice crunch to the mix.

1 small onion, sliced

2 celery ribs, sliced

1 tablespoon butter

2 cups cubed cooked turkey breast

1 can (8 ounces) sliced water chestnuts, drained

1-1/4 cups reduced-sodium chicken broth

2 tablespoons cornstarch

1/4 cup cold water

3 tablespoons reduced-sodium soy sauce

1 can (14 ounces) canned bean sprouts, drained

Hot cooked rice

1. In a large skillet, saute onion and celery in butter until tender. Add the turkey, water chestnuts and broth; bring to a boil. Reduce heat.

2. In a small bowl, combine the cornstarch, water and soy sauce until smooth; add to turkey mixture. Bring to a boil; cook and stir for 2 minutes or until thickened. Add bean sprouts. Serve with rice.

Yield: 4 servings.

Turkey Sweet Potato Supper

Margaret Wilson • Sun City, California

This streamlined but elegant version of a traditional turkey dinner is a quick meal that's sure to brighten any table!

2 turkey breast tenderloins (8 ounces *each*)

1 tablespoon butter

1 can (2 pounds, 8 ounces) sweet potatoes, drained

1/3 cup dried cranberries

1/3 cup maple syrup

1/4 cup orange juice

1/4 teaspoon ground cinnamon

1/2 teaspoon cornstarch

1 tablespoon cold water

1. In a large skillet, brown turkey in butter on each side. Arrange sweet potatoes around turkey. Combine the cranberries, maple syrup, orange juice and cinnamon; pour over top. Bring to a boil. Reduce heat; cover and simmer for 15-20 minutes or until turkey juices run clear.

2. Remove the turkey and sweet potatoes to a serving platter. Combine cornstarch and cold water until smooth; stir into skillet. Bring to a boil. Cook and stir for 1 minute or until thickened. Serve with turkey and sweet potatoes.

Yield: 4 servings.

busy family favorites

Spinach and Mushroom Smothered Chicken

Katrina Wagner • Grain Valley, Missouri

Chicken breasts stay nice and moist with a mushroom and spinach topping tucked under a blanket of melted cheese. It's extra special but is not tricky to make.

3 cups fresh baby spinach

1-3/4 cups sliced fresh mushrooms

3 green onions, sliced

2 tablespoons chopped pecans

1-1/2 teaspoons olive oil

4 boneless skinless chicken breast halves (4 ounces *each*)

1/2 teaspoon rotisserie chicken seasoning

2 slices reduced-fat provolone cheese, halved

1. In a large skillet, saute the spinach, mushrooms, onions and pecans in oil until the mushrooms are tender. Set aside and keep warm.

2. Sprinkle chicken with seasoning. Using long-handled tongs, moisten a paper towel with cooking oil and lightly coat the grill rack.

3. Grill chicken, covered, over medium heat or broil 4 in. from the heat for 4-5 minutes on each side or until a meat thermometer reads 170°.

4. Top with cheese. Cover and grill or broil 2-3 minutes longer or until cheese is melted. To serve, top each chicken breast with reserved spinach mixture.

Yield: 4 servings.

Chicken Lo Mein

Taste of Home Test Kitchen

This simple but scrumptious chicken dish is perfect for family or company. You'll find it's so easy, you'll serve it often.

4 ounces uncooked angel hair pasta

2 teaspoons cornstarch

1/4 cup reduced-sodium soy sauce

2 tablespoons rice vinegar

2 tablespoons hoisin sauce

1 tablespoon minced fresh gingerroot

1 teaspoon minced garlic

1 pound boneless skinless chicken breasts, cut into strips

2 tablespoons canola oil, *divided*

2 cups fresh broccoli florets

1 cup julienned carrots

1/4 cup salted peanuts, finely chopped

1. Cook pasta according to package directions. Meanwhile, in a small bowl, combine the cornstarch, soy sauce, vinegar, hoisin sauce, ginger and garlic; set aside.

2. In a large skillet or wok, stir-fry chicken in 1 tablespoon oil for 5-8 minutes or until no longer pink. Remove with a slotted spoon. Drain pasta and set aside.

3. Stir-fry broccoli and carrots in remaining oil for 5-6 minutes or until crisp-tender. Stir cornstarch mixture and add to the pan. Bring to a boil; cook and stir for 2 minutes or until thickened. Stir in chicken and pasta; heat through. Sprinkle with peanuts.

Yield: 4 servings.

Saucy Apricot Chicken

Tanya McKay • Wells, Nevada

On days when I help my husband and his crew with the cows, I need a no-fuss supper like my apricot chicken. I often make the sauce ahead of time and use precooked chicken.

8 boneless skinless chicken breast halves (4 ounces *each*)

1 tablespoon butter

1 tablespoon canola oil

1 cup apricot jam

1 cup Catalina salad dressing

2 to 3 tablespoons onion soup mix

1. In a large skillet, brown chicken in butter and oil over medium heat for 3 minutes on each side or until lightly browned. Combine the jam, salad dressing and soup mix; pour over chicken.

2. Cover and simmer for 10 minutes or until a meat thermometer reaches 170°.

Yield: 8 servings.

Almond Turkey Stir-Fry

Lori Johnson • Four Corners, Wyoming

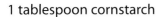

When I want to stir things up in my kitchen, I pull out this quick recipe.

1 tablespoon cornstarch

1 cup reduced-sodium chicken broth

1/4 cup water

2 tablespoons reduced-sodium soy sauce

1 teaspoon sugar

1/4 teaspoon *each* salt and pepper

1 pound turkey breast tenderloin, cubed

4 teaspoons canola oil, *divided*

1 cup chopped celery

1/2 cup shredded carrot

1/2 cup chopped onion

1/2 cup sliced fresh mushrooms

1/2 cup sliced green onions

1 garlic clove, minced

1 can (8 ounces) sliced water chestnuts, drained

1/2 cup slivered almonds, toasted

Hot cooked rice, optional

1. In a small bowl, combine the first seven ingredients until smooth; set aside. In a nonstick skillet, stir-fry turkey in 2 teaspoons hot oil until no longer pink. Remove and keep warm.

2. In the skillet, stir-fry the celery, carrot, onion, mushrooms and green onions in remaining oil until crisp-tender, about 5-6 minutes. Add garlic; cook 1 minute longer. Add water chestnuts and reserved turkey; heat through.

3. Stir broth mixture and stir into the pan. Bring to a boil; cook and stir for 1-2 minutes or until thickened. Sprinkle with almonds. Serve with hot cooked rice if desired.

Yield: 4 servings.

Country Barbecued Chicken

Taste of Home Test Kitchen

This moist chicken takes minutes to cook using the direct grilling method. The thick, zesty sauce is equally tasty over pork. If you'd like, make a double batch of sauce and reserve half of it to serve at the table.

3/4 cup ketchup

1 tablespoon molasses

2 teaspoons brown sugar

1 teaspoon chili powder

1 teaspoon canola oil

1/2 teaspoon Worcestershire sauce

1 garlic clove, minced

1-1/2 to 2 pounds boneless skinless chicken breast halves

2 tablespoons butter, melted

1. In a small bowl, combine the first seven ingredients. Cover and refrigerate until ready to use.

2. If grilling the chicken, lightly coat grill rack using long-handled tongs with a paper towel moistened with cooking oil. Brush chicken with butter. Grill, uncovered, over medium heat or broil 4 in. from heat for 3-4 minutes on each side or until browned. Baste with barbecue sauce. Grill or broil 4-6 minutes longer or until a meat thermometer reads 170°, basting and turning often.

Yield: 4-6 servings (3/4 cup barbecue sauce).

Autumn Turkey Tenderloins

Brenda Lion • Warren, Pennsylvania

This out-of-the-ordinary meal is perfect for cool nights with family, friends or company. With cinnamon and brown sugar, it's slightly sweet, and the walnuts add a wonderful toasty-nutty crunch.

1-1/4 pounds turkey breast tenderloins

1 tablespoon butter

1 cup unsweetened apple juice

1 medium apple, sliced

1 tablespoon brown sugar

2 teaspoons chicken bouillon granules

1/4 teaspoon ground cinnamon

1/4 teaspoon ground nutmeg

1 tablespoon cornstarch

2 tablespoons cold water

1/2 cup chopped walnuts, toasted

1. In a large skillet, brown turkey in butter. Add the apple juice, apple, brown sugar, bouillon, cinnamon and nutmeg. Bring to a boil. Reduce heat; cover and simmer for 10-12 minutes or until a meat thermometer reads 170°.

2. Using a slotted spoon, remove turkey and apple slices to a serving platter; keep warm. Combine cornstarch and water until smooth; stir into pan juices. Bring to a boil; cook and stir for 2 minutes or until thickened. Spoon over turkey and apple. Sprinkle with walnuts.

Yield: 5 servings.

Barbecued Chicken Bake

Taste of Home Test Kitchen

You can find ready-to-heat barbecued chicken in the refrigerated meat section of your local grocery store. Just add three ingredients and you have a tasty casserole.

1 carton (32 ounces) refrigerated shredded barbecued chicken

1 can (15-1/2 ounces) hominy, rinsed and drained

1/4 cup canned chopped green chilies

1 package (11-1/2 ounces) refrigerated corn bread twists

1. In a large bowl, combine the chicken, hominy and chilies. Pour into an 11-in. x 7-in. baking dish coated with cooking spray.

2. Separate the corn bread twists into strips. Place four strips diagonally in each direction over chicken mixture, forming a lattice crust. Press ends against sides of baking dish. Bake at 375° for 20-25 minutes or until crust is golden brown.

Yield: 6 servings.

busy family favorites

Country Chicken with Gravy

Ruth Helmuth • Abbeville, South Carolina

This lightened-up entree is so simple! It's always a hit when guests try it!

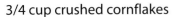

3/4 cup crushed cornflakes

1/2 teaspoon poultry seasoning

1/2 teaspoon paprika

1/4 teaspoon dried thyme

1/4 teaspoon salt

1/4 teaspoon pepper

2 tablespoons fat-free evaporated milk

4 boneless skinless chicken breast halves (4 ounces each)

2 teaspoons canola oil

GRAVY:

1 tablespoon butter

1 tablespoon all-purpose flour

1/4 teaspoon pepper

1/8 teaspoon salt

1/2 cup fat-free evaporated milk

1/4 cup condensed chicken broth, undiluted

1 teaspoon sherry, optional

2 tablespoons minced chives

1. In a shallow bowl, combine the first six ingredients. Place milk in another shallow bowl. Dip chicken in milk, then roll in cornflake mixture.

2. In a large nonstick skillet coated with cooking spray, cook chicken in oil over medium heat for 6-8 minutes on each side or until a meat thermometer reads 170°.

3. Meanwhile, in a small saucepan, melt butter. Stir in the flour, pepper and salt until smooth. Gradually stir in the milk, broth and sherry if desired. Bring to a boil; cook and stir for 1-2 minutes or until thickened. Stir in chives. Serve with chicken.

Yield: 4 servings.

Chicken Fingers with Lemon Sauce

Amanda Donnelly • Fairborn, Ohio

My husband turned up his nose when he saw me making this the first time, but he absolutely flipped when he tasted it. I like to serve the chicken with an apple rice pilaf salad.

1 jar (10 ounces) lemon curd
1/4 cup chicken broth
1/2 teaspoon soy sauce
1/4 teaspoon ground ginger
1 cup buttermilk
1 tablespoon grated lemon peel
1 cup all-purpose flour
1/2 cup cornstarch
1-1/4 pounds boneless skinless chicken breasts, cut into strips
Oil for frying

1. In a small saucepan, combine the lemon curd, broth, soy sauce and the ginger. Cook and stir until combined and heated through; keep warm.

2. In a shallow bowl, combine buttermilk and lemon peel. In another bowl, combine flour and cornstarch. Dip chicken in buttermilk mixture, then coat with flour mixture.

3. In an electric skillet, heat oil to 375°. Fry chicken, a few strips at a time, for 2-3 minutes on each side or until no longer pink. Drain on paper towels. Serve with lemon sauce.

Yield: 4 servings (1-1/4 cups sauce).

Individual Buffalo-Style Chicken Pizza

Taste of Home Cooking School

Buffalo chicken fans will love the spicy pizza version of their favorite party food. The blue cheese dressing mellows the flavor of the pepper sauce, giving every bite that can't-be-beat buffalo-style taste.

4 prebaked mini pizza crusts
2 cups cubed *or* shredded cooked chicken
2 tablespoons butter, melted
1/4 cup hot pepper sauce
1 cup blue cheese *or* ranch salad dressing
1 cup (4 ounces) shredded cheddar cheese
1 cup (4 ounces) shredded part-skim mozzarella cheese

1. Place crusts on an ungreased 15-in. x 10-in. x 1-in. baking pan. In a large bowl, combine the chicken, butter and pepper sauce. Spread salad dressing over crusts. Top with chicken mixture; sprinkle with cheeses.

2. Bake at 425° for 10-15 minutes or until the edges are lightly browned. Let stand for 5 minutes.

Yield: 4 servings.

busy family favorites

Curry Chicken

Tracy Simiele • Chardon, Ohio

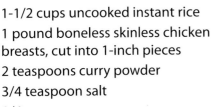

This is a top pick in our home. My young son and daughter gobble it up. With its irresistible blend of curry and sweet coconut milk, your family will, too.

1-1/2 cups uncooked instant rice

1 pound boneless skinless chicken breasts, cut into 1-inch pieces

2 teaspoons curry powder

3/4 teaspoon salt

1/4 teaspoon pepper

1/2 cup chopped onion

1 tablespoon canola oil

1 can (14 ounces) coconut milk

2 tablespoons tomato paste

3 cups fresh baby spinach

1 cup chopped tomato

1. Cook rice according to package directions. Meanwhile, sprinkle the chicken with curry, salt and pepper. In a large skillet, saute chicken and onion in oil until chicken is no longer pink.

2. Stir in the coconut milk and tomato paste. Bring to a boil. Reduce the heat; simmer, uncovered, for 5 minutes or until thickened. Add spinach and tomato; cook 2-3 minutes longer or until spinach is wilted. Serve with rice.

Yield: 4 servings.

Monterey Barbecued Chicken

Linda Coleman • Cedar Rapids, Iowa

It's easy to turn regular chicken into a savory dish with barbecue sauce, crisp bacon and melted cheese. It gets even better with a sprinkling of fresh tomatoes and green onions.

4 bacon strips

4 boneless skinless chicken breast halves (4 ounces *each*)

1 tablespoon butter

1/2 cup barbecue sauce

3 green onions, chopped

1 medium tomato, chopped

1 cup (4 ounces) shredded cheddar cheese

1. Cut bacon strips in half widthwise. In a large skillet, cook bacon over medium heat until cooked but not crisp. Remove to paper towels to drain; keep warm.

2. Drain drippings from skillet; cook chicken in butter over medium heat for 5-6 minutes on each side or until a meat thermometer reads 170°.

3. Top each chicken breast with the barbecue sauce, green onions, tomato and two reserved bacon pieces; sprinkle with cheese. Cover and cook for 5 minutes or until cheese is melted.

Yield: 4 servings.

Turkey Noodle Stew

Traci Maloney • Toms River, New Jersey

I can assemble this stew, a creamy mixture of turkey, vegetables and noodles, in minutes. My husband doesn't usually go for meal-in-one dishes, but he likes this savory skillet entree.

2 turkey breast tenderloins (about 1/2 pound *each*), cut into 1/4-inch slices

1 medium onion, chopped

1 tablespoon canola oil

1 can (14-1/2 ounces) chicken broth

1 can (10-3/4 ounces) condensed cream of celery soup, undiluted

2 cups frozen mixed vegetables

1/2 to 1 teaspoon lemon-pepper seasoning

3 cups uncooked extra-wide egg noodles

1. In a large skillet, cook turkey and onion in oil for 5-6 minutes or until turkey is no longer pink; drain.

2. In a large bowl, combine the broth, soup, vegetables and the lemon-pepper. Add to the skillet; bring to a boil. Stir in noodles. Reduce the heat; cover and simmer for 10 minutes or until the noodles and vegetables are tender.

Yield: 6 servings.

busy family favorites

Chicken Tacos with Pineapple Pico de Gallo

Jenny Flake • Newport Beach, California

This recipe is not only light and tasty but also absolutely delicious. The pineapple and mango are bursting with flavor and add great taste to these zesty chicken tacos.

1 cup chopped fresh pineapple

1/2 cup chopped peeled mango

2 tablespoons minced fresh cilantro

1 tablespoon finely chopped red onion

1 tablespoon lime juice

3/4 teaspoon salt, *divided*

2 cups cubed cooked chicken breast

1/2 teaspoon ground cumin

1/4 teaspoon salt-free garlic seasoning blend

8 corn tortillas (6 inches), warmed

1. For pico de gallo, in a small bowl, combine the pineapple, mango, cilantro, onion, lime juice and 1/4 teaspoon salt. Set aside.

2. In a large nonstick skillet coated with cooking spray, cook and stir the chicken, cumin, seasoning blend and the remaining salt until heated through. Spoon 1/4 cup onto each tortilla. Fold in sides. Serve with pico de gallo.

Yield: 4 servings.

Creamed Turkey on Mashed Potatoes

Taste of Home Test Kitchen

Use leftover fresh vegetables or your favorite frozen vegetable in this quick dish.

1/2 cup chopped onion
2 tablespoons butter
2 tablespoons all-purpose flour
1/4 teaspoon salt
1/8 teaspoon white pepper
2 cups 2% milk
2 cups cubed cooked turkey breast
1 cup frozen mixed vegetables
2 cups hot mashed potatoes

1. In a large saucepan, saute the onion in butter until tender. Sprinkle with the flour, salt and pepper. Stir in the milk until blended.

2. Bring to a boil; cook and stir for 2 minutes or until thickened and bubbly. Add the turkey and vegetables; cover and simmer until heated through. Serve with mashed potatoes.

Yield: 4 servings.

French-Style Chicken

Catherine Johnston • Stafford, New York

When I have friends over, I make this classy light recipe and serve it with a tossed salad and crisp French bread. Toasted almond slices sprinkled on top add a crunchy, finishing touch.

6 boneless skinless chicken breast halves (4 ounces *each*)
3/4 teaspoon salt-free lemon-pepper seasoning
1-1/3 cups reduced-sodium chicken broth
3 medium unpeeled apples, cut into wedges
1 medium onion, thinly sliced
4 tablespoons apple cider *or* juice, *divided*
1/4 teaspoon ground cinnamon
1/8 teaspoon ground nutmeg
1 tablespoon cornstarch
Minced fresh parsley

1. Sprinkle chicken with lemon-pepper. In a large nonstick skillet coated with cooking spray, cook chicken for 5-6 minutes on each side or until a meat thermometer reads 170°. Remove and keep warm.

2. In the same skillet, combine the broth, apples, onion, 3 tablespoons cider, cinnamon and nutmeg. Bring to a boil. Combine cornstarch and remaining cider until smooth; stir into apple mixture. Bring to a boil; cook and stir for 1-2 minutes or until thickened. Top with chicken; sprinkle with parsley.

Yield: 6 servings.

busy family favorites

Swiss Turkey Tenderloin Strips

Taste of Home Test Kitchen

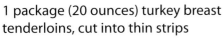

Turkey strips nestled in an easy-to-make creamy cheese sauce make a delicious weeknight dinner.

1 package (20 ounces) turkey breast tenderloins, cut into thin strips

1/2 teaspoon salt

1/4 teaspoon pepper

3 tablespoons olive oil

1 teaspoon minced garlic

2 tablespoons all-purpose flour

1 cup chicken broth

1/2 cup white wine

3 cups (12 ounces) shredded Swiss cheese

1 package (10 ounces) fresh spinach, trimmed

1/4 cup water

1. Season turkey with salt and pepper. In a large skillet, saute turkey in oil for 6-8 minutes or until no longer pink. Remove with a slotted spoon and set aside.

2. In the drippings, saute garlic until tender. Stir in the flour, broth and wine until blended. Bring to a boil over medium heat; cook and stir for 1-2 minutes or until thickened. Reduce heat to low. Slowly add cheese; cook and stir for 2 minutes or until cheese is melted and sauce is blended.

3. Add turkey; heat through. Meanwhile, in a large saucepan, cook spinach in water for 3-5 minutes or until wilted; drain. Serve turkey mixture with spinach.

Yield: 4 servings.

Italian Spinach and Chicken Skillet

Sarah Newman • Mahtomedi, Minnesota

This is a flavorful entree that is hearty enough to be a tasty one-dish meal. My husband and child both love it, even with the spinach mixed in!

2 cups uncooked yolk-free whole wheat noodles

2 cups sliced fresh mushrooms

2 teaspoons olive oil

1 garlic clove, minced

1 can (14-1/2 ounces) no-salt-added diced tomatoes, undrained

1 can (10-3/4 ounces) reduced-fat reduced-sodium condensed cream of chicken soup, undiluted

3/4 cup spaghetti sauce

2 cups cubed cooked chicken breast

1 package (10 ounces) frozen chopped spinach, thawed and squeezed dry

1/4 cup shredded Parmesan cheese

1-1/2 teaspoons Italian seasoning

1/2 cup shredded part-skim mozzarella cheese

1. Cook noodles according to package directions. Meanwhile, in a large skillet, saute mushrooms in oil until tender. Add garlic; cook 1 minute longer. Stir in the tomatoes, soup, spaghetti sauce, chicken, spinach, Parmesan cheese and Italian seasoning. Cook for 5-8 minutes or until heated through, stirring occasionally.

2. Drain noodles; toss with chicken mixture. Sprinkle with mozzarella cheese.

Yield: 4 servings.

TIP If you don't already have cooked chicken breast , take two small uncooked halves or one large uncooked half and cut the meat into cubes. Saute the poultry in a nonstick skillet for a few minutes or until the chicken is no longer pink.

Crescent Turkey Casserole

Daniela Essman • Perham, Minnesota

How did mom make a dinner of chicken and vegetables really appealing to kids? She turned it into a pie, of course! Mom knew that everyone loves pie. This classic version doesn't take anytime at all.

1/2 cup mayonnaise

2 tablespoons all-purpose flour

1 teaspoon chicken bouillon granules

1/8 teaspoon pepper

3/4 cup 2% milk

1-1/2 cups cubed cooked turkey breast

1 package (10 ounces) frozen mixed vegetables, thawed

1 tube (4 ounces) refrigerated crescent rolls

1. In a large saucepan, combine the mayonnaise, flour, bouillon and pepper. Gradually add milk; stir until smooth. Bring to a boil over medium heat; cook and stir for 2 minutes or until thickened. Add turkey and vegetables; cook 3-4 minutes longer, stirring occasionally. Spoon into a greased 8-in. square baking dish.

2. Unroll crescent dough and separate into two rectangles. Seal seams and perforations. If desired, cut a pattern in the dough using a 1-in. cookie cutter. Place over turkey mixture. Bake at 375° for 15-20 minutes or until golden brown.

Yield: 4 servings.

Turkey Sausage With Pasta

Mary Tallman • Arbor Vitae, Wisconsin

Love Italian food? You'll adore adding this good-for-you turkey dish to the menu. It balances meat, pasta and the best of the garden's bounty.

1 pound Italian turkey sausage links, casings removed

1 large onion, chopped

1 large green pepper, chopped

1-1/4 cups sliced fresh mushrooms

2 garlic cloves, minced

2 cans (14-1/2 ounces each) diced tomatoes, undrained

1 teaspoon Italian seasoning

1 teaspoon chili powder

6 cups uncooked spiral pasta

1/2 cup shredded part-skim mozzarella cheese

1. Crumble sausage into a large nonstick skillet. Add the onion, green pepper and mushrooms. Cook over medium heat until meat is no longer pink. Add garlic; cook 1 minute longer. Drain.

2. Stir in the tomatoes, Italian seasoning and chili powder. Bring to a boil. Reduce the heat; simmer, uncovered, for 10 minutes.

3. Meanwhile, cook pasta according to package directions; drain. Serve sausage mixture over pasta; sprinkle with cheese.

Yield: 6 servings.

Dijon-Crusted Chicken Breasts

Jacqueline Correa • Landing, New Jersey

If you're craving fried chicken, this dish will hit the spot! A crisp and flavorful coating makes this easy entree feel special and indulgent.

1/3 cup dry bread crumbs

1 tablespoon grated Parmesan cheese

1 teaspoon Italian seasoning

1/2 teaspoon dried thyme

1/4 teaspoon *each* salt and pepper

4 boneless skinless chicken breast halves (4 ounces *each*)

2 tablespoons Dijon mustard

1 teaspoon olive oil

1 teaspoon reduced-fat margarine

1. Place the first six ingredients in a shallow bowl. Brush chicken with mustard; roll in crumb mixture.

2. In a large skillet, cook chicken in oil and margarine over medium heat for 5-6 minutes on each side or a meat thermometer reads 170°.

Yield: 4 servings.

EDITOR'S NOTE: This recipe was tested with Parkay Light stick margarine.

busy family favorites

Tangy Turkey Saute

Amy Wenger • Severance, Colorado

Turkey breast slices really turn into something special using this recipe. With garlic, thyme and lots of fresh mushrooms, this dish is quite flavorful. But the really interesting aspect of it is the use of Marsala wine. Most of the alcohol is cooked out, leaving a delicious sauce behind. If you don't want to use the wine, feel free to substitute chicken broth.

1/4 cup all-purpose flour

8 turkey breast cutlets (2 ounces *each*)

3 tablespoons olive oil, *divided*

2 cups sliced fresh mushrooms

1/2 cup thinly sliced green onions

1/2 teaspoon minced garlic

1/2 cup chicken broth

1 cup Marsala wine *or* additional chicken broth

1/2 teaspoon salt

1/4 teaspoon dried thyme

1 tablespoon minced fresh parsley

1. Place flour in a large resealable plastic bag. Add turkey, a few pieces at a time, and shake to coat. In a large skillet, saute turkey in 2 tablespoons oil in batches for 2 minutes on each side or until no longer pink; drain. Remove and keep warm.

2. In the same skillet, saute mushrooms and onions in remaining oil for 3 minutes or until crisp-tender. Add garlic; cook 1 minute longer. Stir in the broth, wine, salt and thyme. Bring to a boil; cook and stir for 3 minutes or until slightly thickened. Stir in parsley. Serve with turkey.

Yield: 4 servings.

Lemon Mushroom Chicken

Carrie Palmquist • Canova, South Dakota

There's a lot of flavor in this dish, and the best part is that it's a healthy entree that comes together in a snap!

4 boneless skinless chicken breast halves (4 ounces *each*)

1/4 cup plus 2 teaspoons all-purpose flour, *divided*

1/2 teaspoon salt

1/4 teaspoon pepper

2 tablespoons butter

1/3 cup plus 3 tablespoons reduced-sodium chicken broth, *divided*

1/2 pound sliced fresh mushrooms

1 tablespoon lemon juice

1. Flatten chicken to 1/2-in. thickness. In a large resealable plastic bag, combine 1/4 cup flour, salt and pepper. Add chicken, one piece at a time; shake to coat.

2. In a large nonstick skillet over medium heat, cook chicken in butter for 5-6 minutes on each side or until no longer pink. Remove and keep warm.

3. Add 1/3 cup broth to the pan, stirring to loosen browned bits. Bring to a boil. Add mushrooms; cook and stir for 3-5 minutes or until tender.

4. Combine the remaining flour and broth until smooth; stir into the mushroom mixture. Bring to a boil; cook and stir for 2 minutes or until thickened. Stir in lemon juice. Serve with chicken.

Yield: 4 servings.

Sausage Zucchini Skillet

Debby Abel • Flat Rock, North Carolina

I began serving a version of this dish as a side with grilled salmon. I added sausage and rice or noodles to make a complete meal-in-one.

1 pound Italian turkey sausage links, casings removed

2 large zucchini, chopped

1 large sweet onion, chopped

2 garlic cloves, minced

1 can (14-1/2 ounces) no-salt-added diced tomatoes, undrained

1/4 teaspoon pepper

2 cups hot cooked rice

1. In a large nonstick skillet coated with cooking spray, combine the sausage, zucchini and onion; cook and stir over medium heat for 4 minutes or until meat is no longer pink. Add garlic; cook 1 minute longer. Drain.

2. Stir in tomatoes and pepper; bring to a boil. Reduce heat; simmer, uncovered, for 4-5 minutes or until liquid is evaporated. Serve with rice.

Yield: 4 servings.

busy family favorites

Curry Citrus Chicken

Marcy Hall • Visalia, California

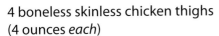

I found the recipe for this delicious chicken in a pamphlet of microwave recipes many years ago. My husband and I prefer dark meat, so we like it made with chicken thighs. But you can use boneless chicken breasts if you prefer.

4 boneless skinless chicken thighs
(4 ounces *each*)

2 tablespoons finely chopped onion

2 tablespoons lemon juice

2 tablespoons orange juice

2 tablespoons reduced-sodium soy sauce

1/2 teaspoon curry powder

1/2 teaspoon ground cumin

1/4 teaspoon poultry seasoning

1-1/2 teaspoons cornstarch

1 tablespoon water

1. Place the chicken in a microwave-safe dish coated with cooking spray. Combine the onion, juices, soy sauce, curry powder, cumin and poultry seasoning; pour over chicken.

2. Cover and microwave on high for 3 minutes; turn chicken over. Cover and microwave 2-4 minutes longer or until chicken is no longer pink and a meat thermometer reads 180°. Remove chicken and let stand for 1-2 minutes.

3. Combine cornstarch and water until smooth; stir into cooking juices. Microwave, uncovered, on high for 1 to 1-1/2 minutes or until thickened, stirring every 30 seconds. Serve with chicken.

Yield: 4 servings.

EDITOR'S NOTE: This recipe was tested in a 1,100-watt microwave.

Peanut Chicken Stir-Fry

Taste of Home Test Kitchen

It takes just 30 minutes to put this delicious peanut-buttery stir-fry on the table. Kids will love the flavor, and adults will like how quickly it comes together. For a spicier dish, add a pinch of red pepper flakes.

2 teaspoons cornstarch

3/4 cup chicken broth

1/4 cup creamy peanut butter

3 tablespoons soy sauce

1 teaspoon ground ginger

1/4 teaspoon pepper

1-1/4 pounds boneless skinless chicken breasts, cut into strips

3 teaspoons olive oil, *divided*

1 cup chopped onion

1 cup thinly sliced green pepper

1 cup thinly sliced sweet red pepper

1-1/2 cups sliced fresh mushrooms

1 teaspoon minced garlic

Hot cooked rice

1. In a small bowl, combine the cornstarch and broth until smooth. Stir in the peanut butter, soy sauce, ginger and pepper; set aside.

2. In a large skillet or wok, stir-fry chicken in 1-1/2 teaspoons oil for 3-4 minutes or until no longer pink. Remove with a slotted spoon and keep warm.

3. Stir-fry onion and peppers in remaining oil for 3 minutes. Add mushrooms; stir-fry for 3-4 minutes or until vegetables are crisp-tender. Add the garlic; cook 1 minute longer.

4. Stir cornstarch mixture and add to the pan. Bring to a boil; cook and stir for 2 minutes or until thickened. Add chicken; heat through. Serve with rice.

Yield: 4 servings.

TIP To clean mushrooms before slicing or cooking, gently remove dirt by rubbing with a mushroom brush or wipe mushrooms with a damp paper towel. Another method is to quickly rinse them under cold water, drain and pat dry with paper towels. Trim the stems.

busy family favorites

Seafood

Skillet Sea Scallops, p. 162

Crab Lo Mein

Laura Mryyan • Topeka, Kansas

I came up with this one night when I had some leftover spaghetti that I needed to use. When making the sauce, I like to use half soy sauce and half oyster sauce for a richer, more developed flavor.

4 ounces uncooked angel hair pasta *or* thin spaghetti

1 medium onion, thinly sliced

1 medium green pepper, cut into 1-inch strips

1 package (9 ounces) frozen broccoli cuts, thawed

1/4 cup sliced fresh mushrooms

2 tablespoons canola oil

1 tablespoon cornstarch

1-1/4 cups chicken broth

1/4 cup water

1/4 cup soy sauce

12 ounces imitation crabmeat, cut into 1-inch pieces

1. Cook pasta according to package directions. Meanwhile, in a large skillet or wok, stir-fry the onion, green pepper, broccoli and mushrooms in oil for 3-4 minutes or until crisp-tender.

2. In a small bowl, combine the cornstarch, broth, water and soy sauce until smooth. Gradually stir into skillet. Bring to a boil; cook and stir for 2 minutes or until thickened. Stir in crab; cook 2-3 minutes longer or until heated through. Drain pasta; toss with crab mixture.

Yield: 6 servings.

Red Clam Sauce over Pasta

Laura Valdez • Arlington, Texas

This sensational basil-seasoned clam sauce will shake up supper time. It's a nice change from typical meat-based pasta sauces.

2 teaspoons minced garlic

2 tablespoons butter

1-1/2 teaspoons olive oil

1 can (15 ounces) tomato sauce

1 can (6-1/2 ounces) chopped clams, drained

1 tablespoon dried parsley flakes

1 tablespoon dried basil

1/8 teaspoon pepper

Hot cooked linguine

1. In a large saucepan, saute garlic in butter and oil for 30 seconds. Stir in the tomato sauce, clams, parsley, basil and pepper. Bring to a boil. Reduce heat; cover and simmer for 15 minutes, stirring occasionally. Serve with linguine.

Yield: 4 servings.

Salmon with Orange Vinaigrette

Lorie Rice • Liverpool, New York

Here's my favorite way to add zip to classic salmon. The tangy vinaigrette complements the naturally sweet fish, and the golden orange color is so appealing on the plate.

1 cup orange juice

4-1/2 teaspoons finely chopped red onion

4-1/2 teaspoons lime juice

1 teaspoon chili powder

1 teaspoon honey Dijon mustard

1/2 cup fat-free Italian salad dressing

4 salmon fillets (6 ounces *each*)

Salt and pepper to taste

1 tablespoon olive oil

4 teaspoons minced fresh cilantro

1. Place orange juice in a small saucepan. Bring to a boil; cook until liquid is reduced to 1/4 cup. Cool slightly. Transfer to a blender.

Add the onion, lime juice, chili powder and mustard; cover and process until blended. While processing, gradually add salad dressing in a steady stream; process until blended.

2. Season fillets with salt and pepper. In a large skillet, cook fillets in oil over medium-high heat for 2 minutes on each side or until golden brown.

3. Transfer to a greased 15-in. x 10-in. x 1-in. baking pan. Bake at 400° for 5-10 minutes or until fish flakes easily with a fork. Serve with orange vinaigrette. Garnish with cilantro.

Yield: 4 servings.

Crumb-Topped Sole

Taste of Home Test Kitchen

Looking for a low-carb supper that's ready in a pinch? This buttery sole entree fits the bill. The moist fillets are covered with golden bread crumbs and topped with a rich sauce.

3 tablespoons reduced-fat mayonnaise

3 tablespoons grated Parmesan cheese, *divided*

2 teaspoons mustard seed

1/4 teaspoon pepper

4 sole fillets (6 ounces *each*)

1 cup soft bread crumbs

1 green onion, finely chopped

1/2 teaspoon ground mustard

2 teaspoons butter, melted

1. Combine the mayonnaise, 2 tablespoons cheese, mustard seed and pepper; spread over tops of fillets. Place on a broiler pan coated with cooking spray. Broil 4 in. from the heat for 3-5 minutes or until fish flakes easily with a fork.

2. Meanwhile, in a small bowl, combine the bread crumbs, onion, ground mustard and remaining cheese; stir in butter. Spoon over fillets; spritz topping with cooking spray. Broil 1-2 minutes longer or until golden brown.

Yield: 4 servings.

Oven-Fried Catfish

Phyllis Early • Holland, Michigan

This moist baked catfish gets its crisp golden coating from cornflake crumbs. The fillets are nicely seasoned with celery salt, onion powder and paprika.

4 catfish fillets (6 *each*)

1 cup cornflake crumbs

1 teaspoon celery salt

1/2 teaspoon onion powder

1/4 teaspoon paprika

1/8 teaspoon pepper

1 egg white

2 tablespoons fat-free milk

1. Pat fish dry with paper towels. In a shallow bowl, combine the cornflake crumbs, celery salt, onion powder, paprika and pepper. In another bowl, beat the egg white and milk. Dip fillets into egg white mixture, then coat with crumb mixture.

2. Place in a 13-in. x 9-in. baking dish coated with cooking spray. Bake, uncovered, at 350° for 25-30 minutes or until fish flakes easily with a fork.

Yield: 4 servings.

busy family favorites

Pepper-Rubbed Red Snapper

Windy Byrd • Freeport, Texas

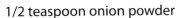

I found the recipe for this red snapper several years ago. It's often requested when guests stop over for a visit, and it sure comes in handy when the boys come home with a great catch!

1/2 teaspoon onion powder

1/2 teaspoon garlic powder

1/2 teaspoon dried thyme

1/2 teaspoon white pepper

1/2 teaspoon cayenne pepper

1/2 teaspoon pepper

1/8 teaspoon salt

4 red snapper fillets (8 ounces *each*)

3 tablespoons butter, melted

1. In a small bowl, combine the first seven ingredients. Dip fillets in butter, then rub with seasoning mixture.

2. In a large nonstick skillet, cook fillets over medium-high heat for 2-4 minutes on each side or until fish flakes easily with a fork.

Yield: 4 servings.

Tuna Crescent Ring

Julia Bivens • Martinsburg, West Virginia

This is easy to throw together, and I often make it when I've had a long, tiring day.

1 tube (8 ounces) refrigerated crescent rolls

1 can (12 ounces) white water-packed solid tuna

1 cup frozen peas and carrots

1/2 cup shredded cheddar cheese

1/4 cup mayonnaise

1 tablespoon Dijon mustard

1-1/2 teaspoons dried minced onion

1 teaspoon Italian seasoning

1. Unroll crescent dough and separate into triangles. Place on an ungreased 12-in. pizza pan, forming a ring with pointed ends facing outer edge of pan and wide ends overlapping. Lightly press wide ends together.

2. In a small bowl, combine the remaining ingredients. Spoon over wide ends of ring. Fold points over filling and tuck under wide ends (filling will be visible).

3. Bake at 375° for 15-20 minutes or until golden brown and filling is hot.

Yield: 4 servings.

Cajun Shrimp and Rice

Ruth Miller • Boyertown, Pennsylvania

I have a friend with Celiac's disease, and I serve this when she comes over. It allows her to have something besides meat and potatoes. It's become a requested recipe.

1 package (8.8 ounces) ready-to-serve long grain rice

1 pound uncooked medium shrimp, peeled and deveined

2 teaspoons Cajun seasoning

1 tablespoon olive oil

1 tablespoon butter

1-1/2 teaspoons minced garlic

1 package (6 ounces) frozen snow peas, thawed

1. Cook rice according to package directions. Meanwhile, in a large skillet, saute shrimp and Cajun seasoning in oil and butter until shrimp turn pink. Add garlic; cook 1 minute longer. Add peas and rice. Cook for 2-3 minutes or until heated through.

Yield: 4 servings.

Broiled Cod with Herb Sauce

Rachel Niemeyer • Tacoma, Washington

A flavorful white sauce dresses up cod fillets in this high-protein main dish. Pine nuts lend a little crunch for a special finishing touch.

4 cod fillets (6 ounces *each*)

1/2 teaspoon salt, *divided*

1/4 teaspoon pepper, *divided*

2 tablespoons butter

2 tablespoons all-purpose flour

1/2 teaspoon *each* dried oregano, tarragon and rosemary, crushed

1 cup fat-free milk

1/4 cup pine nuts, toasted

1. Sprinkle fillets with 1/4 teaspoon salt and 1/8 teaspoon pepper. Place on a broiler pan coated with cooking spray. Broil 3-4 in. from the heat for 8-12 minutes or until fish flakes easily with a fork.

2. Meanwhile, in a small saucepan, melt butter. Stir in the flour, herbs and remaining salt and pepper until blended. Gradually stir in milk. Bring to a boil; cook and stir for 2 minutes or until thickened. Spoon over cod; sprinkle with pine nuts.

Yield: 4 servings.

busy family favorites

Tomato Walnut Tilapia

Phyl Broich-Wessling • Garner, Iowa

Tomato, bread crumbs and crunchy walnuts top tilapia fillets in this delightful main dish. I often serve it with cooked julienned carrots and green beans.

4 tilapia fillets (4 ounces *each*)

1/4 teaspoon salt

1/4 teaspoon pepper

1 tablespoon butter

1 medium tomato, thinly sliced

TOPPING:

1/2 cup soft bread crumbs

1/4 cup chopped walnuts

2 tablespoons lemon juice

1-1/2 teaspoons butter, melted

1. Sprinkle fillets with salt and pepper. In a large ovenproof skillet coated with cooking spray, cook fillets in butter over medium-high heat for 2-3 minutes on each side or until lightly browned.

2. Place tomato slices over fish. Combine the topping ingredients; spoon over tomato. Broil 3-4 in. from the heat for 2-3 minutes or until topping is lightly browned and fish flakes easily with a fork.

Yield: 4 servings.

seafood

Southwestern Scallops

Maggie Fontenot • The Woodlands, Texas

My saucy sea scallops are popular at dinner parties—plus, they're in my repertoire of easy weekday meals. The seasoning gives the sweet shellfish a pleasant kick.

2 teaspoons chili powder
1/2 teaspoon ground cumin
1/4 teaspoon salt
1/8 teaspoon pepper
1 pound sea scallops (about 12)
2 tablespoons butter, *divided*
1/2 cup white wine *or* chicken broth

1. In a small bowl, combine the chili powder, cumin, salt and pepper. Pat scallops dry with paper towels. Rub seasoning mixture over scallops.

2. In a large heavy skillet over medium heat, melt 1 tablespoon butter. Cook scallops for 2 minutes on each side or until opaque and golden brown. Remove from the skillet; keep warm.

3. Add wine to skillet, stirring to loosen any browned bits from pan. Bring to a boil; cook until liquid is reduced by half. Stir in remaining butter until melted. Serve with scallops.

Yield: 4 servings.

Cod Delight

Nancy Daugherty • Cortland, Ohio

Though I used to whip up this delightful seasoned cod with tomatoes and onion in the oven, the microwave lets me enjoy it even faster. I like to serve the pretty main course to company. Everyone likes it and requests the recipe right away.

1 pound cod fillets
1/2 cup chopped tomatoes
1/3 cup finely chopped onion
2 tablespoons water
2 tablespoons canola oil
4-1/2 teaspoons lemon juice
1 teaspoon dried parsley flakes
1/2 teaspoon minced garlic
1/2 teaspoon minced fresh basil
1/8 teaspoon salt
1 teaspoon seafood seasoning

1. Place cod fillets in a shallow microwave-safe dish. In a small bowl, combine the tomatoes, onion, water, oil, lemon juice, parsley, garlic, basil and salt; spoon over the cod. Sprinkle with seafood seasoning.

2. Cover and microwave on high for 6 minutes or until fish flakes easily with a fork.

Yield: 4 servings.

EDITOR'S NOTE: This recipe was tested in a 1,100-watt microwave.

busy family favorites

Crab Alfredo

Susan Anstine • York, Pennsylvania

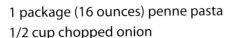

Canned soup and sour cream speed along a rich sauce that coats imitation crab. When spooned over penne pasta and garnished with grated Parmesan cheese and fresh parsley, it's an easy entree that looks and tastes elegant.

1 package (16 ounces) penne pasta

1/2 cup chopped onion

1/4 cup butter

2 cups (16 ounces) sour cream

1 can (10-3/4 ounces) condensed cream of mushroom soup, undiluted

1/2 cup 2% milk

1/2 teaspoon salt

1/2 teaspoon garlic powder

1/2 teaspoon Italian seasoning

1/4 teaspoon pepper

2 packages (8 ounces *each*) imitation crabmeat, flaked

1/4 cup grated Parmesan cheese

2 tablespoons minced fresh parsley

1. Cook pasta according to package directions. Meanwhile, in a large skillet, saute onion in butter until tender. Whisk in the sour cream, soup, milk, salt, garlic powder, Italian seasoning and pepper until blended. Cook and stir until heated through (do not boil). Stir in crab; heat through.

2. Drain pasta; top with crab sauce. Sprinkle with cheese and parsley.

Yield: 8 servings.

Shrimp 'n' Noodle Bowls

Mary Bergfeld • Eugene, Oregon

This is a great quick main dish that can be made with pick-up ingredients from the store. Cooked shrimp and bagged slaw reduce the time and work required to get it on the table.

8 ounces uncooked angel hair pasta

1 pound cooked small shrimp

2 cups broccoli coleslaw mix

6 green onions, thinly sliced

1/2 cup minced fresh cilantro

2/3 cup reduced-fat sesame ginger salad dressing

1. Cook pasta according to package directions; drain and rinse in cold water. Transfer to a large bowl. Add the shrimp, coleslaw mix, onions and cilantro. Drizzle with dressing; toss to coat. Cover and refrigerate until serving.

Yield: 6 servings.

Scallops au Gratin

Taste of Home Test Kitchen

Since scallops will continue to release their cooked juices, drain this liquid before returning scallops to the pan so your sauce does not thin out.

3 tablespoons all-purpose flour

1 cup 2% milk

1/2 cup heavy whipping cream

1/4 cup white wine

1 teaspoon Dijon mustard

1/4 teaspoon salt

1/4 teaspoon pepper

1-1/2 pounds bay scallops

1/2 cup chopped onion

2 tablespoons butter

1 jar (4-1/2 ounces) sliced mushrooms, drained

1/2 teaspoon dried tarragon

1-1/4 cups shredded Asiago cheese

TOPPING:

1/3 cup dry bread crumbs

2 tablespoons butter, melted

1 tablespoon grated Parmesan cheese

1. In a large bowl, combine the flour, milk, cream, wine, mustard, salt and pepper until smooth; set aside.

2. In a large skillet, saute scallops and onion in butter until scallops are opaque. Remove with a slotted spoon. Add milk mixture to the skillet. Bring to a boil; cook and stir for 2 minutes or until thickened.

3. Drain scallops. Add the scallops, mushrooms and tarragon to the sauce; heat through. Stir in Asiago cheese until melted.

4. Divide scallop mixture among four 10-oz. baking dishes. Combine the topping ingredients; sprinkle over scallop mixture. Broil 6 in. from the heat for 1-2 minutes or until golden brown.

Yield: 4 servings.

TIP Scallops vary in color from creamy white to tan. Fresh scallops have a sweet, fresh odor. Buy 4 ounces of scallops per serving. Scallops are best used with 24 hours of purchasing.

Tortellini with Salmon-Ricotta Sauce

Beth Dauenhauer • Pueblo, Colorado

I like to serve this entree with a colorful vegetable, such as a tomato salad or peas and carrots. It's equally good with canned salmon or tuna, too.

1 package (9 ounces) refrigerated cheese tortellini

2 green onions, sliced

1 teaspoon butter

2 garlic cloves, minced

1 teaspoon cornstarch

1 cup fat-free milk

1/2 cup shredded part-skim mozzarella cheese

1 cup fat-free ricotta cheese

1 pouch (7.1 ounces) boneless skinless pink salmon

2 tablespoons snipped fresh dill *or* 2 teaspoons dill weed

1-1/2 teaspoons grated lemon peel

1-1/2 teaspoons lemon juice

1/4 teaspoon salt

1. Cook tortellini according to package directions. Meanwhile, in a large saucepan, saute onions in butter until tender. Add garlic; cook 1 minute longer. Combine cornstarch and milk until smooth; gradually stir into the pan. Bring to a boil; cook and stir for 2 minutes or until slightly thickened.

2. Stir in mozzarella cheese until melted. Stir in the ricotta cheese, salmon, dill, lemon peel, lemon juice and salt.

3. Drain tortellini; add to ricotta sauce. Cook and stir until heated through.

Yield: 4 servings.

Easy Crab Cakes

Charlene Spelock • Apollo, Pennsylvania

Canned crabmeat makes these delicate patties simple enough for busy weeknight dinners. For a change of pace, try forming the crab mixture into four thick patties instead of eight cakes.

2 cans (6 ounces *each*) crabmeat, drained, flaked and cartilage removed
1 cup seasoned bread crumbs, *divided*
1 egg, lightly beaten
1/4 cup finely chopped green onions
1/4 cup finely chopped sweet red pepper
1/4 cup reduced-fat mayonnaise
1 tablespoon lemon juice
1/2 teaspoon garlic powder
1/8 teaspoon cayenne pepper
1 tablespoon butter

1. In a large bowl, combine the crab, 1/3 cup bread crumbs, egg, onions, red pepper, mayonnaise, lemon juice, garlic powder and cayenne.

2. Divide mixture into eight portions; shape into 2-in. balls. Roll in remaining bread crumbs. Flatten to 1/2-in. thickness. In a large nonstick skillet, cook crab cakes in butter for 3-4 minutes on each side or until golden brown.

Yield: 4 servings.

Herb Fish Fillets

Yvonne Nemec • Phillipsburg, New Jersey

Combining different types of herbs not only gives this speedy fish depth of flavor, but it also results in a beautiful presentation. This is such an easy dish and so delicious. We love it!

1/4 cup finely chopped onion
2 tablespoons butter
1/2 teaspoon minced garlic
1 tablespoon lemon juice
2 teaspoons dried parsley flakes
1/4 to 1/2 teaspoon salt
1/4 teaspoon dried tarragon
1/8 teaspoon dried thyme
1 pound whitefish *or* sole fillets
1/4 cup dry bread crumbs

1. In a small microwave-safe dish, combine the onion, butter and garlic. Microwave, uncovered, on high for 1-2 minutes or until onion is partially cooked. Stir in the lemon juice, parsley, salt, tarragon and thyme.

2. Arrange fillets in a greased 2-qt. round microwave-safe dish. Top with half of the butter mixture. Stir bread crumbs into the remaining butter mixture; sprinkle over fillets.

3. Cover and microwave on high for 4-6 minutes or until fish flakes easily with a fork.

Yield: 4 servings.

EDITOR'S NOTE: This recipe was tested in a 1,100-watt microwave.

busy family favorites

Lemon Shrimp with Parmesan Rice

Amie Overby • Reno, Nevada

I grew up in Biloxi, Mississippi, where rice, garlic and seafood are staples in Gulf Coast cuisine. This dish is an easy, long-time family favorite that's ready in minutes.

2 cups chicken broth

2 cups uncooked instant rice

1 pound uncooked medium shrimp, peeled and deveined

1/2 cup chopped green onions

2 tablespoons butter

2 tablespoons olive oil

2 teaspoons minced garlic

3 tablespoons lemon juice

1/4 teaspoon pepper

1/2 cup grated Parmesan cheese

2 tablespoons minced fresh parsley

1. In a small saucepan, bring broth to a boil. Stir in rice; cover and remove from the heat. Let stand for 5 minutes.

2. Meanwhile, in a large skillet, cook shrimp and onions in butter and oil over medium heat for 4-5 minutes. Add garlic and cook 1 minute longer or until garlic is tender and shrimp turn pink. Stir in lemon juice and pepper.

3. Stir cheese and parsley into rice; serve with shrimp.

Yield: 4 servings.

Mediterranean Seafood Stew

Virginia Anthony • Jacksonville, Florida

Mediterranean flavors make this dish special enough for company. It's loaded with orange roughy, shrimp and scallops that all bake up together easily in one dish.

1 medium onion, finely chopped

1 tablespoon olive oil

1-1/2 teaspoons minced garlic, *divided*

1/2 pound plum tomatoes, seeded and diced

1 teaspoon grated lemon peel

1/4 teaspoon crushed red pepper flakes

1 cup clam juice

1/3 cup white wine *or* additional clam juice

1 tablespoon tomato paste

1/2 teaspoon salt

1 pound orange roughy *or* red snapper fillets, cut into 1-inch cubes

1 pound uncooked large shrimp, peeled and deveined

1/2 pound sea scallops

1/3 cup minced fresh parsley

1/3 cup reduced-fat mayonnaise

1. In a Dutch oven, saute onion in oil until tender. Add 1/2 teaspoon garlic; cook 1 minute longer. Add the tomatoes, lemon peel and pepper flakes; cook and stir for 2 minutes. Add the clam juice, wine, tomato paste and salt. Bring to a boil. Reduce heat; cover and simmer for 10 minutes or until stew is heated through.

2. Add the fish, shrimp, scallops and parsley. Cover and cook for 8-10 minutes or until fish flakes easily with a fork, the shrimp turn pink and scallops are opaque. Combine mayonnaise and remaining garlic; dollop onto each serving.

Yield: 6 servings.

TIP

To peel shrimp, pull the legs off from the underside of the body. Then start loosening the shell from one side and continue to loosen going up and around to the other side. Pull off shell by tail if desired. If you buy shrimp already peeled, it will generally cost more than unpeeled shrimp, but will save you time in the kitchen.

busy family favorites

Pistachio-Crusted Salmon Cakes

Mary Lou Timpson • Colorado City, Arizona

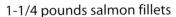

It only takes half an hour to give salmon patties glamour. These time-saving fish cakes get a rich, buttery crunch from ground pistachio nuts.

1-1/4 pounds salmon fillets

1 egg

1/2 cup soft bread crumbs

1 tablespoon Dijon mustard

1 teaspoon grated lime peel

1/4 teaspoon salt

1/4 teaspoon pepper

1 cup coarsely ground pistachios

2 tablespoons canola oil

Lime wedges

1. In a large nonstick skillet, bring 4 cups water to a boil. Reduce heat; add fillets and poach, uncovered, for 8-10 minutes or until fish flakes easily with a fork. Remove from pan and cool slightly.

2. In a large bowl, combine the egg, bread crumbs, mustard, lime peel, salt and pepper. Shred salmon with two forks; fold into bread crumb mixture. Shape into eight patties. Coat both sides with pistachios.

3. In a large skillet over medium heat, cook patties in oil in batches for 1-2 minutes on each side or until golden brown. Serve with lime wedges.

Yield: 4 servings.

Mediterranean-Style Red Snapper

Josephine Piro • Easton, Pennsylvania

This entree is both time-saving and nutritious. Seasoned with spices and served with a zesty sauce, it's a frequently-served dinner at our house.

1 teaspoon lemon-pepper seasoning

1/2 teaspoon garlic powder

1/2 teaspoon dried thyme

1/8 teaspoon cayenne pepper

4 red snapper fillets (6 ounces *each*)

2 teaspoons olive oil, *divided*

1/2 medium sweet red pepper, julienned

3 green onions, chopped

1 garlic clove, minced

1 can (14-1/2 ounces) diced tomatoes, undrained

1/2 cup chopped pimiento-stuffed olives

1/4 cup chopped ripe olives

1/4 cup minced chives

1. Combine the lemon-pepper, garlic powder, thyme and cayenne; rub over fillets. In a large nonstick skillet coated with cooking spray, cook fillets in 1 teaspoon oil over medium heat for 4-5 minutes on each side or until fish flakes easily with a fork. Remove and keep warm.

2. In the same pan, saute the red pepper and onions in remaining oil until crisp-tender. Add garlic; cook 1 minute longer. Stir in tomatoes. Bring to a boil. Reduce heat; simmer, uncovered, for 3 minutes or until liquid has evaporated. Serve with snapper. Sprinkle with olives and chives.

Yield: 4 servings.

Fish Stick Sandwiches

Cherie Durbin • Hickory, North Carolina

Make the most of convenient frozen fish sticks with these fun, family-pleasing sandwiches. My mom whipped these up whenever she wanted fish in a hurry.

1/4 cup butter, melted

2 tablespoons lemon juice

1 package (11.4 ounces) frozen breaded fish sticks

2 tablespoons mayonnaise

6 hot dog buns, split

Shredded lettuce, chopped onion and chopped tomatoes, optional

1. In a shallow bowl, combine butter and lemon juice. Dip fish sticks in butter mixture. Place in a single layer in an ungreased baking pan.

2. Bake at 400° for 15-18 minutes or until crispy. Spread mayonnaise on bottom of buns; add fish sticks. Top with lettuce, onion and tomato if desired. Replace bun tops.

Yield: 6 servings.

busy family favorites

Grilled Shrimp Fajitas

Amy Hammons • Martinez, Georgia

This dinner is assembled quickly and has very little preparation or cleanup. It's so delicious...and impressive enough to serve for guests. My family always shows up for this meal!

1/2 pound sliced bacon

1/2 pound uncooked medium shrimp, peeled and deveined

1 medium green pepper, cut into 1-inch pieces

1 medium sweet red pepper, cut into 1-inch pieces

1 medium onion, cut into 1-inch pieces

1/2 cup barbecue sauce

6 flour tortillas (8 inches), warmed

1 cup shredded lettuce

1 medium tomato, diced

1/2 cup shredded cheddar cheese

1. In a large skillet, cook bacon over medium heat until cooked but not crisp. Drain on paper towels. Wrap a strip of bacon around each shrimp; secure ends with toothpicks.

2. On six metal or soaked wooden skewers, alternately thread shrimp, peppers and onion. Grill, covered, over medium heat or broil 4 in. from the heat for 2-3 minutes on each side or until shrimp turn pink and vegetables are tender, basting frequently with barbecue sauce.

3. Remove shrimp and vegetables from skewers; discard toothpicks. Place on one side of each tortilla. Top with lettuce, tomato and cheese; fold over.

Yield: 6 servings.

Colorful Crab Stir-Fry

Lee Deneau • Lansing, Michigan

My love for seafood has carried over from childhood, when we used to fish together as a family. So I was happy to find this change-of-pace recipe that combines stir-fry with seafood. It tastes like a special treat but is a breeze to prepare.

2 teaspoons cornstarch

1 teaspoon chicken bouillon granules

3/4 cup water

1/2 teaspoon reduced-sodium soy sauce

1 cup sliced fresh carrots

1 tablespoon canola oil

1 cup fresh *or* frozen snow peas

1/2 cup julienned sweet red pepper

1 teaspoon minced fresh gingerroot

1 teaspoon minced garlic

1 package (8 ounces) imitation crabmeat

Hot cooked rice, optional

1. In a small bowl, combine the cornstarch, bouillon, water and soy sauce until smooth; set aside. In a large skillet or wok, stir-fry carrots in oil. Add the peas, red pepper, ginger and garlic; stir-fry 2 minutes longer or until vegetables are crisp-tender.

2. Stir cornstarch mixture and gradually add to the pan. Bring to a boil; cook and stir for 2 minutes or until thickened. Add crab; heat through. Serve with rice if desired.

Yield: 4 servings.

Skillet Sea Scallops

Margaret Lowenberg • Kingman, Arizona

You'll want to keep this recipe in mind for a quick-to-fix company dish. Pasta and mixed greens nicely complement the tender, citrus-flavored shellfish.

1/2 cup dry bread crumbs

1/2 teaspoon salt

1 pound sea scallops

2 tablespoons butter

1 tablespoon olive oil

1/4 cup white wine *or* reduced-sodium chicken broth

2 tablespoons lemon juice

1 teaspoon minced fresh parsley

1 garlic clove, minced

1. In a large resealable plastic bag, combine bread crumbs and salt. Add scallops, a few at a time, and shake to coat.

2. In a large skillet over medium-high heat, brown scallops in butter and oil for 1-1/2 to 2 minutes on each side or until firm and opaque. Remove and keep warm. Add the wine, lemon juice, parsley and garlic to the skillet; bring to a boil. Pour over scallops. Serve immediately.

Yield: 3-4 servings.

busy family favorites

Red Pepper & Parmesan Tilapia

Michelle Martin • Durham, North Carolina

My husband and I are always looking for light fish recipes because of their health benefits. This one's a hit with him, and we've tried it at dinner parties, too. It's a staple!

1/4 cup egg substitute

1/2 cup grated Parmesan cheese

1 teaspoon Italian seasoning

1/2 to 1 teaspoon crushed
red pepper flakes

1/2 teaspoon pepper

4 tilapia fillets (6 ounces *each*)

1. Place the egg substitute in a shallow bowl. In another shallow bowl, combine the cheese, Italian seasoning, pepper flakes and pepper. Dip fillets in egg substitute, then cheese mixture.

2. Place in a 15-in. x 10-in. x 1-in. baking pan coated with cooking spray. Bake at 425° for 10-15 minutes or until fish flakes easily with a fork.

Yield: 4 servings.

Tuna Puff Sandwiches

Stella Dobmeier • Kamloops, British Columbia

My husband and I can't get enough of this great supper sandwich. The cheese-covered tomato slices top off the mild tuna salad deliciously. Sometimes, I replace the tuna with canned salmon, ham, chicken or turkey. How could something so good be so easy?

3/4 cup mayonnaise, *divided*
2 tablespoons chopped green pepper
1-1/2 teaspoons grated onion
1-1/2 teaspoons prepared mustard
1/4 teaspoon Worcestershire sauce
1 pouch (7.1 ounces) tuna
3 hamburger buns, split
6 slices tomato
3/4 cup shredded cheddar cheese

1. In a small bowl, combine 1/4 cup mayonnaise, green pepper, onion, mustard and Worcestershire sauce; stir in tuna. Spread over each bun half; top each with a tomato slice. Arrange sandwiches on a baking sheet.

2. In another bowl, combine the cheese and remaining mayonnaise; spoon cheese mixture over tomato. Bake at 400° for 11-13 minutes or until topping is puffy and golden brown.

Yield: 6 servings.

Tilapia Wraps

Michelle Williams • Fort Worth, Texas

This savory recipe takes just minutes. If they're less expensive, I'll sometimes thaw out frozen tilapia fillets in the fridge overnight instead of using fresh fillets.

3/4 cup salsa
1 can (4 ounces) chopped green chilies
6 tilapia fillets (6 ounces *each*)
2 tablespoons olive oil
2 tablespoons steak seasoning
12 flour tortillas (6 inches), warmed
3/4 cup shredded cheddar cheese

1. In a small bowl, combine salsa and chilies; set aside. Drizzle fillets with oil; sprinkle both sides with steak seasoning. Transfer to a large skillet. Cook, uncovered, over medium heat for 5-8 minutes or until fish flakes easily with a fork. Add reserved salsa mixture, stirring gently to break up the fillets.

2. Spoon a heaping 1/3 cupful onto each tortilla; top with cheese. Roll up; serve immediately.

Yield: 6 servings.

EDITOR'S NOTE: This recipe was tested with McCormick's Montreal Steak Seasoning. Look for it in the spice aisle.

busy family favorites

BBQ Chip-Crusted Orange Roughy

Geraldine Buba • Palos Hills, Illinois

This easy and delectable entree actually converted me to a fish lover. It was given to me by a fishmonger decades ago and is frequently requested by family and friends. Even those who don't like fish, like this recipe!

4 orange roughy fillets (6 ounces *each*)

3 tablespoons lemon juice

1 tablespoon butter, melted

1/2 cup crushed barbecue potato chips

Tartar sauce, optional

1. Place orange roughy in a greased 13-in. x 9-in. baking dish. Combine lemon juice and butter; pour over fillets. Top with crushed potato chips.

2. Bake, uncovered, at 400° for 20-25 minutes or until fish flakes easily with a fork. Serve with tartar sauce if desired.

Yield: 4 servings.

Maple-Glazed Salmon

David Krisko • Becker, Minnesota

I have a few good recipes for family-favorite, heart-healthy salmon, but this one is always a hit. I serve it this way at least once a week and sometimes more!

1/4 cup ruby red grapefruit juice

2 tablespoons balsamic vinegar

2 tablespoons maple syrup

2 garlic cloves, minced

2 teaspoons olive oil

4 salmon fillets (4 ounces *each*)

1/4 teaspoon *each* salt and pepper

1. In a small saucepan, bring the grapefruit juice, vinegar, syrup and garlic to a boil. Reduce heat; simmer, uncovered, for 5 minutes. Transfer 2 tablespoons to a small bowl; add oil. Set remaining glaze aside.

2. If grilling, using long-handled tongs, moisten a paper towel with cooking oil and lightly coat the grill rack. Sprinkle salmon with salt and pepper; place skin side down on grill rack. Grill, covered, over medium heat or broil 4-6 in. from the heat for 10-12 minutes or until fish flakes easily with a fork, basting occasionally with maple-oil mixture. Drizzle with reserved glaze.

Yield: 4 servings.

Herbed Shrimp Skillet

Ruth Beller • Sun City, California

I love corn, especially in this dish. During summer, when I can use fresh corn instead of frozen, it's even better. Either way, it comes together very quickly.

1 small onion, chopped
1 small green pepper, chopped
3 tablespoons butter
3 cups frozen corn
2 teaspoons sugar
1/2 teaspoon salt
1/2 teaspoon dried basil
1/2 teaspoon dried thyme
1/4 teaspoon pepper
3/4 pound uncooked medium shrimp, peeled and deveined

1. In a large skillet, saute onion and green pepper in butter for 2 minutes. Stir in the corn, sugar, salt, basil, thyme and pepper. Cover and cook over medium-low heat for 5-8 minutes or until corn is tender.

2. Add shrimp; cook and stir for 3-4 minutes or until shrimp turn pink.

Yield: 4 servings.

Flounder with Cucumber Sauce

Carole Dishman • Toano, Virginia

We live on Chesapeake Bay and my husband goes fishing every chance he gets. This is my favorite way to fix the flounder he catches. It's also company-special.

4 flounder fillets (6 ounces *each*)
1 tablespoon butter, melted
1/8 teaspoon salt
1/8 teaspoon lemon-pepper seasoning
CUCUMBER SAUCE:
1/3 cup chopped seeded peeled cucumber
3 tablespoons reduced-fat mayonnaise
3 tablespoons reduced-fat sour cream
3/4 teaspoon minced chives
1/4 teaspoon salt
1/4 teaspoon onion powder

1. Place flounder in a 2-qt. microwave-safe dish coated with cooking spray. Drizzle with butter; sprinkle with salt and lemon-pepper. Cover and microwave on high for 5-6 minutes or until fish flakes easily with a fork.

2. Meanwhile, in a small bowl, combine the sauce ingredients. Serve with flounder.

Yield: 4 servings.

EDITOR'S NOTE: This recipe was tested in a 1,100-watt microwave.

busy family favorites

Scallops with Thai Sauce

Joe Hable • Madison, Wisconsin

Tender scallops and crunchy cashews star at dinnertime tonight! This recipe calls for sea scallops, which are about 1-1/2 inches in diameter. You could also use their sweeter, smaller relative, the bay scallop.

1 tablespoon cornstarch

1 can (14-1/2 ounces) vegetable broth

2 tablespoons creamy peanut butter

1 to 2 tablespoons Thai chili sauce

1 pound sea scallops

2 tablespoons canola oil, *divided*

1 small onion, sliced

1 large sweet red pepper, julienned

1/2 cup salted cashews

2 garlic cloves, minced

1 can (8-3/4 ounces) whole baby corn, drained

Hot cooked angel hair pasta, optional

1. In a small bowl, combine the cornstarch, broth, peanut butter and chili sauce until smooth; set aside.

2. In a large skillet, saute scallops in 1 tablespoon oil for 2-3 minutes on each side or until opaque. Remove with a slotted spoon and keep warm.

3. In the same pan, saute the onion, red pepper and cashews in remaining oil for 3-5 minutes or until vegetables are crisp-tender. Add garlic; cook 1 minute longer.

4. Stir cornstarch mixture and add to the pan. Bring to a boil; cook and stir for 1-2 minutes or until thickened. Add scallops and corn; heat through. Serve over pasta if desired.

Yield: 5 servings.

Southern Pecan Catfish

Mary Ann Griffin • Bowling Green, Kentucky

For this super fast recipe, I coat catfish in pecans, then top it with a thick, rich cream sauce. It looks like you spent all day on it, but it's actually very speedy to prepare. Garnish with lemon wedges, parsley or chopped pecans.

1 cup finely chopped pecans, *divided*

1/2 cup cornmeal

1 teaspoon salt, *divided*

1 teaspoon pepper, *divided*

4 catfish fillets (6 ounces *each*)

1/2 cup butter, *divided*

1/2 cup heavy whipping cream

2 tablespoons lemon juice

1 to 2 tablespoons minced fresh parsley

1. In a shallow bowl, combine 1/2 cup pecans, cornmeal, 1/2 teaspoon salt and 1/2 teaspoon pepper. Coat catfish with pecan mixture.

2. In a large skillet, melt 1/4 cup butter over medium-high heat; fry fillets for 6-7 minutes on each side or until fish flakes easily with a fork. Remove and keep warm.

3. In the same skillet, melt remaining butter over medium heat. Add remaining pecans; cook and stir for 1 minute. Add the cream, lemon juice and remaining salt and pepper; cook and stir for 1 minute. Stir in parsley. Serve with catfish.

Yield: 4 servings.

Crumb-Coated Red Snapper

Charlotte Elliott • Neenah, Wisconsin

I reel in compliments with these moist, crispy-coated fillets whenever I serve them. Heart-healthy omega-3 oils are an added bonus with my simple but delicious entree that's done in mere minutes! I pair this fish with instant rice and microwaved frozen beans or broccoli to keep things quick!

1/2 cup dry bread crumbs

2 tablespoons grated Parmesan cheese

1 teaspoon lemon-pepper seasoning

1/4 teaspoon salt

4 red snapper fillets (6 ounces *each*)

2 tablespoons olive oil

1. In a shallow bowl, combine the bread crumbs, cheese, lemon-pepper and salt; add fillets, one at a time, and turn to coat.

2. In a heavy skillet over medium heat, cook fillets in oil in batches for 4-5 minutes on each side or until fish flakes easily with a fork.

Yield: 4 servings.

Shrimp Scampi with Lemon Couscous

Diana Santospago • Isle au Haut, Maine

With just a few minutes of prep work, this makes an eye-catching entree. I sometimes add a handful of halved grape tomatoes to the pan during the last minute of cooking.

1 cup chicken broth

3 tablespoons lemon juice, *divided*

1 cup uncooked couscous

5 tablespoons butter, *divided*

3 tablespoons minced fresh parsley, *divided*

1 teaspoon grated lemon peel

2 tablespoons olive oil

1-1/2 teaspoons minced garlic

2 pounds cooked jumbo shrimp, peeled and deveined

1/3 cup white wine *or* additional chicken broth

1/4 teaspoon salt

1/8 teaspoon pepper

1/4 cup shredded Asiago cheese

1. In a small saucepan, bring broth and 1 tablespoon lemon juice to a boil. Stir in couscous, 1 tablespoon butter, 1 tablespoon parsley and lemon peel. Cover and remove from the heat; let stand for 5 minutes or until liquid is absorbed.

2. Meanwhile, in a large skillet, stir oil and remaining butter over medium-high heat until butter is melted. Add garlic; cook and stir until tender. Add shrimp; cook for 1 minute on each side or until shrimp turn pink.

3. Add the wine, salt, pepper and remaining lemon juice; cook 2-3 minutes longer or until heated through. Serve with couscous. Sprinkle with cheese and remaining parsley.

Yield: 6 servings.

Easy Shrimp Creole

Jean Gauthier • Rives Junction, Michigan

I found this super-quick shrimp recipe in a magazine years ago and have changed it to suit my taste. To speed things along, I cook the rice in the microwave, using chicken broth instead of water. I've only had good comments whenever I've served it.

3/4 cup *each* chopped onion, chopped celery and chopped green pepper

2 tablespoons canola oil

1 can (10-3/4 ounces) condensed tomato soup, undiluted

1 cup tomato juice

1/4 cup *each* water and salsa

2 tablespoons lemon juice

1 tablespoon minced fresh parsley

2 teaspoons chili powder

1-1/4 teaspoons garlic powder

1/4 teaspoon pepper

1 pound cooked medium shrimp, peeled and deveined

Hot cooked rice

1. In a large skillet, saute the onion, celery and green pepper in oil for 6-7 minutes or until crisp-tender. Stir in the soup, tomato juice, water, salsa, lemon juice, parsley, chili powder, garlic powder and pepper. Bring to a boil. Reduce heat to medium; cover and cook for 6-8 minutes or until heated through.

2. Add the shrimp; cook, uncovered, for 3-4 minutes or until heated through. Serve with rice.

Yield: 5 servings.

Sole Fillets in Lemon Butter

Barb Sharon • Plymouth, Wisconsin

This is such a speedy, no-fuss and delicious way to prepare fish! My son started requesting this "fish with crackers" as a little boy, and he still asks for it as an adult today.

4 sole fillets (4 ounces *each*)

1/4 teaspoon salt

1/8 teaspoon pepper

3 tablespoons butter, melted

1/2 cup minced fresh parsley

1 tablespoon lemon juice

1/4 cup crushed butter-flavored crackers

1/2 teaspoon paprika

1. Place the sole in an ungreased microwave-safe 11-in. x 7-in. dish; sprinkle with salt and pepper. Cover and microwave on high for 3-4 minutes.

2. In a small bowl, combine the butter, parsley and lemon juice; pour over fillets. Sprinkle with cracker crumbs. Microwave, uncovered, for 3-4 minutes or until fish flakes easily with a fork. Sprinkle with paprika.

Yield: 4 servings.

EDITOR'S NOTE: This recipe was tested in a 1,100-watt microwave.

busy family favorites

Fantastic Fish Tacos

Jennifer Palmer • Rancho Cucamonga, California

Searching for a lighter substitute to traditional fried fish tacos, I came up with this entree. It's been a hit with friends and family. The orange roughy fillets are so mild that even nonfish eaters are pleasantly surprised by these tasty tacos.

1/2 cup fat-free mayonnaise

1 tablespoon lime juice

2 teaspoons fat-free milk

1/3 cup dry bread crumbs

2 tablespoons salt-free lemon-pepper seasoning

1 egg, lightly beaten

1 teaspoon water

1 pound orange roughy fillets, cut into 1-inch strips

4 corn tortillas (6 inches), warmed

1 cup coleslaw mix

2 medium tomatoes, diced

1 cup (4 ounces) shredded reduced-fat Mexican cheese blend

1 tablespoon minced fresh cilantro

1. In a small bowl, combine mayonnaise, lime juice and milk; cover and refrigerate until serving.

2. In a shallow bowl, combine bread crumbs and lemon-pepper. In another shallow bowl, combine egg and water. Dip fish in egg mixture, then roll in crumbs.

3. In a large nonstick skillet coated with cooking spray, cook fish over medium-high heat for 3-4 minutes on each side or until it flakes easily with a fork. Spoon onto tortillas; top with coleslaw mix, tomatoes, cheese and cilantro. Drizzle with mayonnaise mixture.

Yield: 4 servings.

Tilapia with Corn Salsa

Brenda Coffey • Singer Island, Florida

My family loves fish, and this super-fast and wonderful dish is very popular at my house. Though it tastes like it takes a long time, it cooks in minutes under the broiler. We like it garnished with lemon wedges and couscous on the side.

4 tilapia fillets (6 ounces *each*)
1 tablespoon olive oil
1/4 teaspoon *each* salt and pepper
1 can (15 ounces) black beans, rinsed and drained
1 can (11 ounces) whole kernel corn, drained
3/4 cup Italian salad dressing
2 tablespoons chopped green onion
2 tablespoons chopped sweet red pepper

1. Drizzle both sides of fillets with oil; sprinkle with salt and pepper.

2. Broil 4-6 in. from the heat for 5-7 minutes or until fish flakes easily with a fork. Meanwhile, in a small bowl, combine the remaining ingredients. Serve with fish.

Yield: 4 servings.

Sweet 'n' Tangy Shrimp

Kathleen Davis • North Bend, Washington

With its delightfully sweet-tangy flavor, this easy entree is destined to become a hit with your gang! My husband and I adapted the recipe from one in a magazine, and we just love it.

1/2 cup ketchup
2 tablespoons sugar
2 tablespoons cider vinegar
2 tablespoons reduced-sodium soy sauce
1 teaspoon sesame oil
1/4 teaspoon crushed red pepper flakes
1-1/2 pounds uncooked medium shrimp, peeled and deveined
1 tablespoon minced fresh gingerroot
1 tablespoon canola oil
3 garlic cloves, minced
2 green onions, sliced
1 teaspoon sesame seeds, toasted
Hot cooked rice, optional

1. In a small bowl, combine the ketchup, sugar, vinegar, soy sauce, sesame oil and red pepper flakes; set aside. In a large nonstick skillet or wok, stir-fry shrimp and ginger in oil until shrimp turn pink. Add garlic; cook 1 minute longer.

2. Add the ketchup mixture; cook and stir for 2-3 minutes or until heated through. Sprinkle with onions and sesame seeds. Serve with rice if desired.

Yield: 4 servings.

busy family favorites

Meatless

Tomato Baguette Pizza, p.184

Broccoli Cheese Tortellini

Darlene Brenden • Salem, Oregon

When we lived in Seattle, my favorite restaurant served a wonderful dish I ordered every time I ate there. When we moved away, I came up with this to satisfy my craving.

2 cups heavy whipping cream

1 cup fresh broccoli florets

2 packages (9 ounces *each*) refrigerated cheese tortellini

2-1/2 cups shredded Parmesan cheese, *divided*

1/4 teaspoon coarsely ground pepper

2 teaspoons minced fresh parsley

1. In a large saucepan, cook cream and broccoli, uncovered, over medium-low heat for 5-6 minutes or until broccoli is crisp-tender.

Meanwhile, cook tortellini according to package directions.

2. Stir 2 cups cheese and pepper into broccoli mixture. Bring to a boil. Reduce heat; simmer, uncovered, for 10-12 minutes or until cheese is melted and mixture is thickened, stirring occasionally.

3. Drain tortellini; add to sauce and toss to coat. Sprinkle with parsley and remaining cheese.

Yield: 6 servings.

Lentil Burritos

Pam Masters • Wickenburg, Arizona

I'm constantly trying to incorporate healthy, but tasty meals into our menu. Both kids and adults love these mildly spiced burritos that combine filling lentils with crisp zucchini.

2 cups water

1 cup dried lentils

2 tablespoons dried minced onion

1/2 teaspoon dried minced garlic

1/2 teaspoon ground cumin

1/8 teaspoon hot pepper sauce

1 small zucchini, chopped

1 cup taco sauce

1 cup (4 ounces) shredded part-skim mozzarella cheese

8 fat-free flour tortillas (8 inches)

1. In a large saucepan, combine the first six ingredients; bring to a boil. Reduce heat; cover and simmer for 15-20 minutes or until lentils are tender. Drain if necessary.

2. Stir in the zucchini, taco sauce and cheese. Place about 1/2 cupful down the center of each tortilla. Fold sides and ends over filling and roll up.

Yield: 8 burritos.

Spicy Beans 'n' Rice

Ranae Jones • Fort Rucker, Alabama

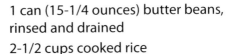

Savory Cajun flavor zips up this quick skillet dish that's loaded with beans, tomatoes, rice and seasonings. It's delicious served with corn bread muffins.

1/2 cup coarsely chopped green pepper
1/2 cup coarsely chopped onion
1 tablespoon canola oil
2 garlic cloves, minced
1 can (14-1/2 ounces) stewed tomatoes, cut up
1 can (8 ounces) tomato sauce
1/2 teaspoon Italian seasoning
1/4 teaspoon cayenne pepper
1/8 teaspoon fennel seed, crushed
1 can (16 ounces) kidney beans, rinsed and drained
1 can (15-1/4 ounces) butter beans, rinsed and drained
2-1/2 cups cooked rice

1. In a nonstick skillet, saute green pepper and onion in oil until tender. Add garlic; cook 1 minute longer. Stir in the stewed tomatoes, tomato sauce, Italian seasoning, cayenne and fennel seed. Bring to a boil. Reduce heat; cover and simmer for 10 minutes.

2. Stir in the beans. Cover and simmer 5-10 minutes longer or until beans are heated through. Serve with rice.

Yield: 5 servings.

Asian Vegetable Pasta

Mitzi Sentiff • Annapolis, Maryland

A little peanut butter and a sprinkling of peanuts give this dish plenty of flavor. While red pepper flakes offer a little kick, brown sugar balances it out with a hint of sweet.

4 quarts water

8 ounces uncooked angel hair pasta

1 pound fresh asparagus, trimmed and cut into 1-inch pieces

3/4 cup julienned carrots

1/3 cup reduced-fat creamy peanut butter

3 tablespoons rice vinegar

3 tablespoons reduced-sodium soy sauce

2 tablespoons brown sugar

1/2 teaspoon crushed red pepper flakes

1/4 cup unsalted peanuts, chopped

1. In a Dutch oven, bring the water to a boil. Add pasta and asparagus; cook for 3 minutes. Stir in carrots; cook for 1 minute or until pasta is tender. Drain and keep warm.

2. In a small saucepan, combine the peanut butter, vinegar, soy sauce, brown sugar and pepper flakes. Bring to a boil over medium heat, stirring constantly. Pour over pasta mixture; toss to coat. Sprinkle with peanuts.

Yield: 5 servings.

Veggie Fajitas

Sarah Mercer • Wichita, Kansas

For scrumptious and super-healthy party fare, these colorful, hearty fajitas packed with crisp-tender veggies are perfect. My husband prefers these to chicken or beef fajitas and I often serve them for dinner.

1 small zucchini, thinly sliced

1 medium yellow summer squash, thinly sliced

1/2 pound sliced fresh mushrooms

1 small onion, halved and sliced

1 medium carrot, julienned

1 teaspoon salt

1/2 teaspoon pepper

1 tablespoon canola oil

8 flour tortillas (8 inches), warmed

2 cups (8 ounces) shredded cheddar cheese

1 cup (8 ounces) sour cream

1 cup salsa

1. In a large skillet, saute the vegetables, salt and pepper in oil for 5-7 minutes or until crisp-tender.

2. Using a slotted spoon, place about 1/2 cup vegetable mixture down the center of each tortilla. Sprinkle each with 1/4 cup cheese; fold in sides. Top with sour cream and salsa.

Yield: 8 fajitas.

busy family favorites

Scrambled Egg Wraps

Jane Shapton • Irvine, California

This tasty morning meal, which also makes a fast dinner, will fill your family up with protein and veggies. Try using flavored wraps to jazz things up.

1 medium sweet red pepper, chopped

1 medium green pepper, chopped

2 teaspoons canola oil

5 plum tomatoes, seeded and chopped

6 eggs

1/2 cup soy milk *or* milk

1/4 teaspoon salt

6 flour tortillas (8 inches), warmed

1. In a large nonstick skillet, saute peppers in oil until tender. Add tomatoes; saute 1-2 minutes longer.

2. Meanwhile, in a large bowl, whisk the eggs, soy milk and salt. Reduce heat to medium; add egg mixture to skillet. Cook and stir until eggs are completely set. Spoon 2/3 cup mixture down the center of each tortilla; roll up.

Yield: 6 servings.

Pasta Primavera

Stephanie Marchese • Whitefish Bay, Wisconsin

This pasta is fully packed with veggies and is filled with goodness and flavor!

8 ounces uncooked linguine

1 cup thinly sliced fresh broccoli

1 medium carrot, thinly sliced

1/2 cup sliced green onions

1/4 cup butter, cubed

1-1/2 cups sliced fresh mushrooms

1 garlic clove, minced

1 teaspoon dried basil

1/2 teaspoon salt

1/4 teaspoon pepper

6 ounces fresh *or* frozen snow peas (about 2 cups), thawed

1/4 cup dry white wine *or* chicken broth

1/4 cup shredded Parmesan cheese

1. Cook linguine according to package directions. Meanwhile, in a large skillet, cook the broccoli, carrot and onions in butter for 3 minutes. Add the mushrooms, garlic, basil, salt and pepper; cook 1 minute longer. Add snow peas and wine. Cover and cook for 2 minutes or until peas are crisp-tender.

2. Drain linguine; add to skillet and toss to coat. Sprinkle with cheese.

Yield: 4 servings.

Greek Pizzas

Doris Allers • Portage, Michigan

Pita breads make crispy crusts for these individual pizzas. Topped with feta and ricotta cheese as well as spinach, tomatoes and basil, the fast pizzas are a hit with everyone who tries them.

4 pita breads (6 inches)
1 cup reduced-fat ricotta cheese
1/2 teaspoon garlic powder
1 package (10 ounces) frozen chopped spinach, thawed and squeezed dry
3 medium tomatoes, sliced
3/4 cup crumbled feta cheese
3/4 teaspoon dried basil

1. Place pita breads on a baking sheet. Combine the ricotta cheese and garlic powder; spread over pitas. Top with spinach, tomatoes, feta cheese and basil.

2. Bake at 400° for 12-15 minutes or until bread is lightly browned.

Yield: 4 servings.

Mediterranean Fettuccine

Elise Ray • Shawnee, Kansas

This wonderful recipe is quick and easy to prepare. The pasta specialty makes an impressive main course or a satisfying side dish.

1/2 cup vegetable broth
8 sun-dried tomatoes (not packed in oil), halved
6 ounces uncooked fettuccine
1 medium sweet yellow pepper, thinly sliced
1 medium sweet red pepper, thinly sliced
1 cup chopped green onions
1 tablespoon olive oil
2 garlic cloves, minced
10 Greek olives, pitted and coarsely chopped
1/4 cup minced fresh basil
1 tablespoon capers, drained
1 teaspoon dried oregano
1 package (4 ounces) crumbled feta cheese

1. In a small saucepan, bring broth to a boil. Remove from the heat; add tomatoes. Let stand for 5-7 minutes. Cut tomatoes into thin slices and return to broth; set aside.

2. Cook fettuccine according to package directions. Meanwhile, in a large nonstick skillet coated with cooking spray, saute peppers and onions in oil for 3-4 minutes or until tender. Add garlic; cook 1 minute longer. Reduce heat. Stir in the olives, basil, capers, oregano and reserved tomato mixture; heat through.

3. Drain fettuccine; place in a large serving bowl. Add the cheese and pepper mixture; toss to coat.

Yield: 4 servings.

Artichoke Ravioli

Darlene Brenden • Salem, Oregon

This dish is so quick and easy to put together, but it tastes like you spent hours preparing it. The artichokes add a gourmet flavor folks love. Serve with a salad and bread, and you're done with dinner.

2 packages (9 ounces *each*) refrigerated cheese ravioli

1 jar (26 ounces) meatless spaghetti sauce

1 can (14 ounces) water-packed artichoke hearts, rinsed, drained and chopped

1 jar (4-1/2 ounces) whole mushrooms, drained

1 can (2-1/2 ounces) sliced ripe olives, drained

1-1/2 cups (6 ounces) shredded part-skim mozzarella cheese

1. Cook ravioli according to package directions; drain and return to the pan. Add the spaghetti sauce, artichokes, mushrooms and olives; gently toss.

2. Transfer to a greased 13-in. x 9-in. baking dish. Sprinkle with cheese. Bake, uncovered, at 400° for 15-20 minutes or until heated through and cheese is melted.

Yield: 6 servings.

Blushing Penne Pasta

Margaret Wilson • Sun City, California

I reworked this recipe from an original that called for vodka and heavy whipping cream. My friends and family have a hard time believing a sauce this rich, flavorful and creamy could be light.

1 package (16 ounces) penne pasta
1 cup thinly sliced onions
2 tablespoons butter
2 tablespoons minced fresh thyme *or* 2 teaspoons dried thyme
2 tablespoons minced fresh basil *or* 2 teaspoons dried basil
1 teaspoon salt
1-1/2 cups half-and-half cream, *divided*
1/2 cup white wine *or* reduced-sodium chicken broth
1 tablespoon tomato paste
2 tablespoons all-purpose flour
1/2 cup shredded Parmigiano-Reggiano cheese, *divided*

1. Cook penne according to package directions. Meanwhile, in a large nonstick skillet over medium heat, cook onions in butter for 8-10 minutes or until lightly browned. Add the thyme, basil and salt; cook 1 minute longer. Add 1 cup cream, wine and tomato paste; cook and stir until blended.

2. Combine flour and remaining cream until smooth; gradually stir into onion mixture. Bring to a boil; cook and stir for 2 minutes or until thickened. Stir in 1/4 cup cheese. Drain penne; toss with sauce. Sprinkle with remaining cheese.

Yield: 8 servings.

busy family favorites

TIP

To prevent pasta from sticking together and avoid boil-overs, always cook pasta in a large kettle or Dutch oven. Add 1 tablespoon olive oil if desired and stir pasta. Allow 2 to 4 ounces of pasta per person for a main-dish serving.

Caribbean Quesadillas

Flori Christensen • Bloomington, Indiana

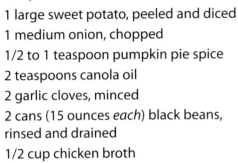

People say the sweet potato in my quesadillas makes them think of the flavor of Thanksgiving. Often, I mix and refrigerate the filling ahead, so it takes no time to layer the tortillas.

1 large sweet potato, peeled and diced

1 medium onion, chopped

1/2 to 1 teaspoon pumpkin pie spice

2 teaspoons canola oil

2 garlic cloves, minced

2 cans (15 ounces *each*) black beans, rinsed and drained

1/2 cup chicken broth

12 flour tortillas (8 inches)

1-1/2 cups (6 ounces) shredded Monterey Jack cheese

1 can (4 ounces) chopped green chilies

Sour cream and salsa

1. Place sweet potato in a microwave-safe dish. Cover and microwave on high for 5 minutes or until tender.

2. Meanwhile, in a large skillet, saute onion and pumpkin pie spice in oil until onion is tender. Add garlic; cook 1 minute longer. Stir in beans and broth. Bring to a boil. Reduce heat; simmer, uncovered, for 3 minutes or until thickened. Mash beans slightly with a fork. Stir in sweet potato. Cook until heated through.

3. Sprinkle bean mixture over one side of each of six tortillas. Top with 1/4 cup cheese and a rounded tablespoonful of chilies. Top with remaining tortillas. Cook on a griddle over low heat for 1-2 minutes on each side or until cheese is melted.

4. Cut into wedges; serve with sour cream and salsa.

Yield: 6 servings.

EDITOR'S NOTE: This recipe was tested in a 1,100-watt microwave.

Mediterranean Pizza

Deborah Prevost • Barnet, Vermont

Every year my sisters and I have a "Sister's Day," which includes a special lunch. This fast and easy pizza is one of our favorites.

1 prebaked 12-inch thin whole wheat pizza crust

3 tablespoons prepared pesto

2 medium tomatoes, thinly sliced

3/4 cup water-packed artichoke hearts, rinsed, drained and chopped

1/2 cup crumbled reduced-fat feta cheese

1/4 cup sliced ripe olives

1. Place the crust on an ungreased 12-in. pizza pan; spread with pesto. Top with tomatoes, artichokes, cheese and olives.

2. Bake at 450° for 10-12 minutes or until heated through.

Yield: 12 pieces.

meatless

Toasted PB & Banana Sandwiches

Marian Pickett • Argyle, Wisconsin

A sandwich worthy of Elvis himself, this grilled, finger-licking treat may surprise you with its flavor. I saw the recipe and thought no way...but it's delicious!

2 large ripe bananas
6 tablespoons reduced-fat peanut butter
8 slices whole wheat bread
2 tablespoons honey
Refrigerated butter-flavored spray

1. Cut each banana in half widthwise, then cut each half lengthwise into four pieces. Spread peanut butter on bread. Place banana slices on four slices of bread; drizzle with honey. Top with remaining bread.

2. Spritz outsides of sandwiches with butter-flavored spray. In a large nonstick skillet, toast sandwiches over medium heat until golden brown.

Yield: 4 servings.

Chickpea 'n' Red Onion Burgers

Lily Julow • Gainesville, Florida

This is the burger I like to make when it's chilly outdoors and the barbecue grill has been retired to the garage.

1 large red onion, thinly sliced
1/4 cup fat-free red wine vinaigrette
2 cans (15 ounces *each*) garbanzo beans *or* chickpeas, rinsed and drained
1/3 cup chopped walnuts
1/4 cup toasted wheat germ
1/4 cup packed fresh parsley sprigs
2 eggs
1 teaspoon curry powder
1/2 teaspoon pepper
1/3 cup fat-free mayonnaise
2 teaspoons Dijon mustard
6 sesame seed hamburger buns, split
6 lettuce leaves
3 tablespoons thinly sliced fresh basil leaves

1. In a small bowl, combine onion and vinaigrette; set aside. In a food processor, combine the chickpeas, walnuts, wheat germ and parsley; cover and pulse until blended. Add the eggs, curry and pepper; cover and process until smooth.

2. Shape into six patties. Place on a baking sheet coated with cooking spray. Bake at 375° for 10-15 minutes or until firm.

3. Combine mayonnaise and mustard; spread over cut sides of buns. Serve patties on buns with lettuce, basil and reserved onion mixture.

Yield: 6 servings.

busy family favorites

Black Bean Burritos

Amy Chop • Eufaula, Alabama

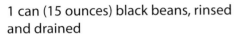

I found this recipe when searching for a quick and easy dish. After making it just once, we were hooked! The zesty flavor was a great surprise.

1 can (15 ounces) black beans, rinsed and drained

1 can (4 ounces) chopped green chilies

1/4 cup chopped onion

1/4 cup chopped green pepper

1/4 cup chopped sweet red pepper

1 tablespoon canola oil

3 teaspoons chili powder

1/2 teaspoon minced garlic

1/4 teaspoon dried oregano

1/4 teaspoon ground cumin

1/8 teaspoon salt

8 flour tortillas (8 inches), warmed

1 cup (4 ounces) shredded Monterey Jack cheese

Salsa and sour cream

1. Place beans in a large microwave-safe bowl; mash lightly. Stir in the chilies, onion, peppers, oil, chili powder, garlic, oregano, cumin and salt. Cover and microwave on high for 2-3 minutes or until heated through, stirring once.

2. Spread about 1/4 cup bean mixture down the center of each tortilla. Top with 2 tablespoons cheese; roll up. Place seam side down in an ungreased 11-in. x 7-in. microwave-safe dish.

3. Cover with a damp microwave-safe paper towel. Microwave on high for 25-40 seconds or until heated through. Serve with salsa and sour cream.

Yield: 4 servings.

EDITOR'S NOTE: This recipe was tested in a 1,100-watt microwave.

meatless

Veggie Brown Rice Wraps

Lisa Sullivan • St. Marys, Ohio

Salsa gives a bit of zip to the brown rice and bean filling in these meatless tortilla wraps.

1 medium sweet red *or* green pepper, diced

1 cup sliced fresh mushrooms

1 tablespoon olive oil

2 garlic cloves, minced

2 cups cooked brown rice

1 can (16 ounces) kidney beans, rinsed and drained

1 cup frozen corn, thawed

1/4 cup chopped green onions

1/2 teaspoon ground cumin

1/2 teaspoon pepper

1/4 teaspoon salt

6 flour tortillas (8 inches), room temperature

1/2 cup shredded reduced-fat cheddar cheese

3/4 cup salsa

1. In a nonstick skillet, saute red pepper and mushrooms in oil until tender. Add garlic; cook 1 minute longer. Add the rice, beans, corn, green onions, cumin, pepper and salt. Cook and stir for 4-6 minutes or until mixture is heated through.

2. Spoon 3/4 cup onto each tortilla. Sprinkle with cheese; drizzle with salsa. Fold sides of tortilla over filling; serve immediately.

Yield: 6 servings.

Tomato Baguette Pizza

Lorraine Caland • Thunder Bay, Ontario

When my tomatoes conspire to ripen all at once, I use them up in simple recipes like this one. Cheesy baguette pizzas, served with a salad, make an ideal lunch.

3 cups sliced fresh mushrooms

2 medium onions, sliced

2 teaspoons olive oil

2 garlic cloves, minced

1/2 teaspoon Italian seasoning

1/4 teaspoon salt

Dash pepper

1 French bread baguette (10-1/2 ounces), halved lengthwise

1-1/2 cups (6 ounces) shredded part-skim mozzarella cheese, *divided*

3/4 cup thinly sliced fresh basil leaves, *divided*

3 medium tomatoes, sliced

1. In a large skillet, saute mushrooms and onions in oil until tender. Add the garlic, Italian seasoning, salt and pepper; cook 1 minute longer.

2. Place baguette halves on a baking sheet; sprinkle with 3/4 cup cheese. Top with 1/2 cup basil, mushroom mixture, tomatoes and remaining cheese.

3. Bake at 400° for 10-15 minutes or until cheese is melted. Sprinkle with remaining basil. Cut each portion into three slices.

Yield: 6 servings.

busy family favorites

Meatless Chili

Eve Visser • South Bend, Indiana

My husband is a big meat eater, so when he's out of town, I try to cut back on meat and make this hearty chili. It's very quick and easy.

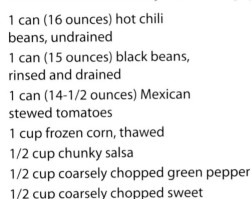

1 can (16 ounces) hot chili beans, undrained

1 can (15 ounces) black beans, rinsed and drained

1 can (14-1/2 ounces) Mexican stewed tomatoes

1 cup frozen corn, thawed

1/2 cup chunky salsa

1/2 cup coarsely chopped green pepper

1/2 cup coarsely chopped sweet red pepper

1 tablespoon ground cumin

2 teaspoons chili powder

4 tablespoons fat-free sour cream

4 tablespoons shredded reduced-fat cheddar cheese

1. In a large saucepan, combine the first nine ingredients. Bring to a boil. Reduce heat; cover and simmer for 15 minutes or until vegetables are crisp-tender. Top each serving with sour cream and cheese.

Yield: 4 servings.

Vegetable Lo Mein

Sara Tatham • Plymouth, New Hampshire

Crisp-tender veggies and soy sauce are combined with linguine noodles in this colorful main dish. I got this recipe from a radio program several years ago.

6 ounces uncooked linguine

1 teaspoon cornstarch

1/2 vegetable bouillon cube

1/2 cup water

1/4 cup reduced-sodium soy sauce

1/2 pound fresh mushrooms, quartered

2 tablespoons canola oil, *divided*

1/2 pound fresh snow peas

8 green onions, sliced

4 celery ribs with leaves, sliced

1 large sweet red pepper, thinly sliced

1 can (14 ounces) bean sprouts, rinsed and drained

1. Cook pasta according to package directions; drain and set aside. In a small bowl, combine the cornstarch and bouillon cube; stir in the water and soy sauce and set aside.

2. In a nonstick skillet, stir-fry mushrooms in 1 tablespoon oil 3 minutes or until tender; remove and keep warm. In same pan, heat remaining oil. Add remaining vegetables; stir-fry 5 minutes or until crisp-tender.

3. Stir soy sauce mixture and add to the pan. Bring to a boil; cook and stir for 2 minutes or until thickened. Add pasta and mushrooms. Heat through.

Yield: 4 servings.

TIP One-half pound of snow peas equals about 2 cups. Before using them, rinse in cold water and cut off stem end. If desired remove string.

Vegetarian Sloppy Joes

Linda Winter • Oak Harbor, Washington

The meat won't be missed in this vegetarian version of sloppy joes. I preserve the flavor of a classic dish while improving its nutritional profile.

1 small onion,
finely chopped

2 teaspoons butter

1 package (12 ounces)
frozen vegetarian
meat crumbles

1/2 teaspoon pepper

2 tablespoons all-purpose
flour

1 can (8 ounces) no-salt-
added tomato sauce

2/3 cup ketchup

6 hamburger buns,
split and toasted

1. In a large nonstick skillet coated with cooking spray, saute onion in butter until tender. Stir in meat crumbles and pepper; heat through.

2. Sprinkle flour over mixture and stir until blended. Stir in tomato sauce and ketchup. Bring to a boil; cook and stir for 1-2 minutes or until thickened. Spoon 1/2 cup onto each bun.

Yield: 6 servings.

EDITOR'S NOTE: Vegetarian meat crumbles are a nutritious protein source made from soy. Look for them in the natural foods freezer section.

Gnocchi Alfredo

Jessica Silva • East Berlin, Connecticut

This recipe's leftovers can be baked in a baking dish with a sprinkling of Parmesan cheese on top.

2 pounds frozen potato gnocchi

3 tablespoons butter, *divided*

1 tablespoon plus 1-1/2 teaspoons
all-purpose flour

1-1/2 cups milk

1/2 cup grated Parmesan cheese

Dash ground nutmeg

1/2 pound sliced baby portobello
mushrooms

Minced fresh parsley, optional

1. Cook gnocchi according to package directions. Meanwhile, in a small saucepan, melt 1 tablespoon butter. Stir in flour until smooth; gradually add milk. Bring to a boil; cook and stir for 1-2 minutes or until thickened. Remove from the heat; stir in cheese and nutmeg until blended. Keep warm.

2. Drain gnocchi. In a large heavy skillet, cook remaining butter over medium heat for 5-7 minutes or until golden brown (do not burn). Add mushrooms and gnocchi. Cook and stir 4-5 minutes or until gnocchi are lightly browned and mushrooms are tender. Serve with sauce. Sprinkle with parsley if desired.

Yield: 5 servings.

Saucy Mac & Cheese

Sara Martin • Brookfield, Wisconsin

I love the crazy noodles in this creamy recipe. If you can't find the cavatappi, it's sometimes called cellentani pasta. This dish is fun to make and it looks pretty topped with extra cheese and golden crumbs. I add ground pepper to my serving.

2 cups cavatappi *or* spiral pasta

3 tablespoons butter, *divided*

1/3 cup panko (Japanese) bread crumbs

2 tablespoons all-purpose flour

1-1/2 cups 2% milk

3/4 pound process cheese (Velveeta), cubed

1/4 cup shredded cheddar cheese

1. Cook pasta according to package directions. Meanwhile, in a large nonstick skillet, melt 1 tablespoon butter over medium-high heat. Add bread crumbs; cook and stir until golden brown. Remove to a small bowl and set aside.

2. In the same skillet, melt remaining butter. Stir in flour until smooth. Gradually add milk; bring to a boil. Cook and stir for 2 minutes or until thickened. Reduce heat. Stir in process cheese until melted.

3. Drain pasta; add to cheese mixture. Cook and stir for 3-4 minutes or until heated through. Sprinkle with cheddar cheese and bread crumbs.

Yield: 4 servings.

Pasta with Flavorful Veggies

Rachel Schmeckenbecher • Whitehall, Pennsylvania

Italian-seasoned veggies are served over pasta and topped with two types of cheese in this fast meal. It's so quick to prepare and so flavorful, but low-fat!

8 ounces uncooked whole wheat spaghetti

2 medium zucchini, halved and sliced

1/3 cup chopped onion

2 tablespoons Italian seasoning

1/2 teaspoon salt

1/2 teaspoon pepper

2 tablespoons olive oil

2 tablespoons butter

2 teaspoons minced garlic

4 medium tomatoes, quartered

1 cup (4 ounces) shredded part-skim mozzarella cheese

1/2 cup shredded Parmesan cheese

1. Cook spaghetti according to package directions. Meanwhile, in a large skillet, saute the zucchini, onion, Italian seasoning, salt and pepper in oil and butter for 4-5 minutes or until vegetables are tender. Add garlic; cook 1 minute longer.

2. Add tomatoes. Bring to a boil. Reduce heat; cook and stir for 2 minutes or until heated through. Sprinkle with cheeses; cover and simmer for 2-3 minutes or until cheese is melted.

3. Drain spaghetti; serve with vegetable mixture.

Yield: 4 servings.

TIP If you don't like the skin of the tomato in a dish you can quickly peel it by cutting a shallow "X" on the bottom of the tomato. Put it into a pot of boiling water for about 1 minute, then rinse under cold water. The skin will peel right off.

Soft Vegetable Tacos

Leona Strait • Colorado Springs, Colorado

These easy vegetarian tacos feature corn and black beans. They're easy and quick, and the heat can be adjusted depending on the type of salsa you choose.

1-2/3 cups fresh *or* frozen corn, thawed

1 small zucchini, finely chopped

1 small onion, finely chopped

1 tablespoon canola oil

1 can (15 ounces) black beans, rinsed and drained

1/4 cup salsa

8 flour tortillas (6 inches), warmed

1/2 cup sour cream

1 cup (4 ounces) shredded cheddar cheese

1. In a large skillet, saute the corn, zucchini and onion in oil until tender.

2. Stir in beans and salsa. Cook, uncovered, over medium heat for 3-4 minutes or until heated through, stirring occasionally.

3. Spoon a heaping 1/3 cupful onto half of each tortilla; top with sour cream and cheese. Fold tortilla over filling.

Yield: 4 servings.

meatless

Greek Hero

Margaret Wilson • Sun City, California

This Greek-style sandwich is made by spreading a loaf of bread with hummus, veggies, seasonings and feta cheese. With plenty of garden-fresh flavors and a hearty bean spread that packs protein, this stacked submarine makes a satisfying meal-in-one.

HUMMUS:

2 tablespoons lemon juice

1 tablespoon olive oil

1 can (15 ounces) garbanzo beans *or* chickpeas, rinsed and drained

2 garlic cloves, minced

1 teaspoon dried oregano

1/4 teaspoon salt

1/8 teaspoon pepper

SANDWICH:

1 loaf (8 ounces) unsliced French bread

2 medium sweet red peppers, cut into thin strips

1/2 medium cucumber, sliced

2 small tomatoes, sliced

1/4 cup thinly sliced red onion

1/4 cup chopped ripe olives

1/4 cup chopped pimiento-stuffed olives

1/2 cup crumbled feta cheese

4 lettuce leaves

1. For hummus, in a food processor, combine the lemon juice, oil and beans; cover and process until smooth. Stir in the garlic, oregano, salt and pepper.

2. Slice bread in half horizontally. Carefully hollow out bottom half, leaving a 1/2-in. shell. Spread hummus into shell. Layer with the red peppers, cucumber, tomatoes, onion, olives, cheese and lettuce. Replace bread top. Cut into four portions.

Yield: 4 servings.

TIP Feta is a white, salty, semi-firm cheese. Traditionally it was made from sheep or goat's milk but is now also made with cow's milk. After feta is formed in a special mold, it's sliced into large pieces, salted and soaked in brine. Although feta is mostly associated with Greek cooking, "feta" comes from the Italian word "fette," meaning slice of food.

Sides

Greek Pasta Salad, p. 197

Cheese Fries

Melissa Tatum • Greensboro, North Carolina

I came up with this recipe after my daughter had cheese fries at a restaurant and couldn't stop talking about them. She loves that I can fix them so quickly at home. Plus, the frozen fry packets can be refrigerated and reheated.

1 package (28 ounces) frozen steak fries
1 can (10-3/4 ounces) condensed cheddar cheese soup, undiluted
1/4 cup 2% milk
1/2 teaspoon garlic powder
1/4 teaspoon onion powder
Paprika

1. Arrange the steak fries in a single layer in two greased 15-in. x 10-in. x 1-in. baking pans. Bake at 450° for 15-18 minutes or until tender and golden brown.

2. Meanwhile, in a small saucepan, combine the soup, milk, garlic powder and onion powder; heat through. Drizzle over fries; sprinkle with paprika.

Yield: 8-10 servings.

Pea 'n' Mushroom Medley

Laurie LaClair • North Richland Hills, Texas

These vegetables are such a snap to throw together. Fresh mushrooms and bacon jazz up frozen peas with ease. It's pretty and impressive enough for company, so I make it often.

3 bacon strips, diced
3 cups sliced fresh mushrooms
3/4 cup finely chopped onion
3/4 cup chopped sweet red pepper
4 cups frozen peas, thawed
3/4 teaspoon pepper
1/4 to 1/2 teaspoon salt

1. In a large skillet, cook bacon over medium heat until crisp. Stir in the mushrooms, onion and red pepper. Saute for 6-8 minutes or until vegetables are crisp-tender.

2. Stir in the peas, pepper and salt. Reduce heat; cover and simmer for 3-4 minutes or until heated through.

Yield: 6 servings.

TIP Select mushrooms with fresh, firm, smooth caps and closed gills. Avoid those with cracks, brown spots or blemishes or ones that are shriveled or moist.

busy family favorites

Bacon Crescent Rolls

Jane Nearing • Indianapolis, Indiana

The mouthwatering aroma of warm bacon from these three-ingredient rolls will draw folks to the table. These are fun for children to prepare and such a cinch to assemble with precooked bacon.

1 tube (8 ounces) refrigerated
crescent rolls

6 bacon strips, cooked and crumbled

1 teaspoon onion powder

1. Separate crescent dough into eight triangles. Set aside 1 tablespoon of bacon. Sprinkle onion powder and remaining bacon over triangles; roll up and place point side down on an ungreased baking sheet. Sprinkle with reserved bacon.

2. Bake at 375° for 10-15 minutes or until golden brown. Serve warm.

Yield: 8 servings.

Quinoa Pilaf

Sonya Fox • Peyton, Colorado

I created this recipe after tasting quinoa at a local restaurant. I really enjoy rice pilaf, but I don't usually have time to make it. This quick-cooking side is a tasty alternative.

1 medium onion, chopped
1 medium carrot, finely chopped
1 teaspoon olive oil
1 garlic clove, minced
1 can (14-1/2 ounces) reduced-sodium chicken broth *or* vegetable broth
1/4 cup water
1/4 teaspoon salt
1 cup quinoa, rinsed

1. In a small nonstick saucepan coated with cooking spray, cook onion and carrot in oil for 2-3 minutes or until crisp-tender. Add garlic; cook 1 minute longer. Stir in the broth, water and salt; bring to a boil.

2. Stir in quinoa; return to a boil. Reduce heat; cover and simmer for 12-15 minutes or until liquid is absorbed. Remove from the heat; let stand for 5 minutes. Fluff with a fork.

Yield: 4 servings.

EDITOR'S NOTE: Look for quinoa in the cereal, rice or organic food aisle.

Buttered Poppy Seed Noodles

Shirley Joan Helfenbein • Lapeer, Michigan

Mom's delicious egg noodles are absolute comfort food. Mom would roll out the dough, and we kids got to cut the long noodles and hang them up to dry. Then she added a few ingredients to make a delicious side. You can enjoy this side using a package of noodles.

1 package (16 ounces) egg noodles
1 medium onion, chopped
3 tablespoons butter
2 green onions, chopped
2 tablespoons poppy seeds
Salt and pepper to taste
1 tablespoon minced fresh parsley

1. Cook noodles according to package directions. Meanwhile, in a large heavy skillet, saute onion in butter until onion begins to brown. Drain noodles; add to skillet. Cook and stir until noodles begin to brown.

2. Add the green onions, poppy seeds, salt and pepper; cook and stir 1 minute longer. Sprinkle with parsley.

Yield: 8 servings.

busy family favorites

Tomato Garden Pasta

Aileen Sheehan • Stafford, Virginia

I mix fresh tomatoes, green beans and pasta with a splash of balsamic vinaigrette, a hint of basil and chives and crumbled feta cheese for a colorful Mediterranean delight. I have served this many times using fresh tomatoes from my garden. It's a wonderful side dish.

5 cups uncooked bow tie pasta

1/2 pound fresh green beans, trimmed and cut into 1-inch pieces

2 tablespoons olive oil

2 tablespoons balsamic vinegar

1 teaspoon salt

1/4 teaspoon pepper

1-1/2 pounds tomatoes, seeded and chopped

2 garlic cloves, minced

2 tablespoons minced chives

4-1/2 teaspoons minced fresh basil

1/2 cup crumbled feta cheese

1. Cook pasta according to package directions, adding beans during the last 5-6 minutes.

2. Meanwhile, in a large bowl, whisk the oil, vinegar, salt and pepper. Stir in the tomatoes, garlic, chives and basil. Drain pasta mixture and add to tomato mixture; toss to coat. Serve warm or at room temperature. Sprinkle with cheese just before serving.

Yield: 8 servings.

Minty Sugar Snap Peas

Alice Kaldahl • Ray, North Dakota

Fresh mint is great on cooked sugar snap peas. Mint is also nice on green beans or carrots.

3 cups fresh sugar snap peas, trimmed

1/4 teaspoon sugar

2 to 3 tablespoons minced fresh mint

2 tablespoons butter

1. In a large skillet, bring 1 in. of water, peas and sugar to a boil. Reduce heat; cover and simmer for 4-5 minutes or until crisp-tender; drain. Stir in mint and butter.

Yield: 4 servings.

Colorful Pasta Salad

Mary Tallman • Arbor Vitae, Wisconsin

This colorful side dish features sweet pineapple, crunchy vegetables and refreshing cilantro in a tangy dressing with pasta. It requires just 15 minutes of prep time, so it's perfect for a quick lunch or on-the-go dinner.

1-1/2 cups uncooked tricolor spiral pasta

1 can (8 ounces) unsweetened pineapple chunks

1 cup fresh snow peas, halved

1/2 cup thinly sliced carrot

1/2 cup sliced cucumber

1 tablespoon minced fresh cilantro

1/4 cup Italian salad dressing

1. Cook pasta according to package directions. Meanwhile, drain pineapple, reserving 1/4 cup juice. In a large bowl, combine the pineapple, snow peas, carrot, cucumber and reserved pineapple juice.

2. Drain pasta and rinse with cold water. Add to pineapple mixture. Sprinkle with cilantro. Drizzle with salad dressing and toss to coat. Chill until serving.

Yield: 5 servings.

busy family favorites

Greek Pasta Salad

Laura Freeman • Ruffin, North Carolina

My mother-in-law gave me this great salad, and I have made it many times. I've taken it to church picnics and potlucks, and someone always asks for the recipe.

1-1/2 cups uncooked tricolor spiral *or* penne pasta

1/2 cup cubed cooked turkey *or* chicken

1 can (3.8 ounces) sliced ripe olives, drained

1/4 cup chopped green pepper

1/4 cup chopped sweet red pepper

1/4 cup crumbled feta cheese

1/3 cup creamy Caesar salad dressing

1. Cook pasta according to package directions; drain and rinse in cold water. In a serving bowl, combine the pasta, turkey, olives, peppers and feta cheese. Drizzle with dressing and toss to coat. Cover and refrigerate until serving.

Yield: 4 servings.

Dolloped Sweet Potatoes

Taste of Home Test Kitchen

A little microwave magic is used to turn sweet potatoes into a speedy and special side dish for hectic holiday feasts. Brown sugar and pumpkin pie spice flavor the simple but rich cream-cheese topping.

4 small sweet potatoes

1 package (3 ounces) cream cheese, softened

1 tablespoon butter, softened

2 tablespoons brown sugar

1/4 teaspoon pumpkin pie spice

1. Scrub and pierce sweet potatoes; place on a microwave-safe plate. Microwave, uncovered, on high for 10-13 minutes or until tender, turning twice. Meanwhile, in a small bowl, beat the cream cheese, butter, brown sugar and pumpkin pie spice.

2. Cut an "X" in the top of each potato; fluff pulp with a fork. Dollop with cream cheese mixture.

Yield: 4 servings.

EDITOR'S NOTE: This recipe was tested in a 1,100-watt microwave.

Tossed Salad with Pine Nuts

Alice Tremont • Rochester Hills, Michigan

This wonderful salad is easy and elegant...with lots of blue cheese flavor and crunch from the pine nuts. Topped with raspberry vinaigrette dressing, it couldn't be much easier to toss together on a busy weeknight or much nicer to serve company.

5 cups spring mix salad greens

1 small red onion, thinly sliced

1 cup (4 ounces) crumbled blue cheese

1/2 cup pine nuts, toasted

1/4 to 1/3 cup raspberry vinaigrette

1. In a large salad bowl, combine greens and onion. Sprinkle with blue cheese and pine nuts. Drizzle with vinaigrette; toss to coat.

Yield: 6-7 servings.

Mediterranean Couscous

Beth Tomlinson • Streetsboro, Ohio

With garlic, tomatoes and Parmesan cheese, this is a great side dish for just about any entree. It relies on a boxed item to keep prep simple; then all you have to do is add a few extra tasty ingredients at the end for a boost of flavor.

2 tablespoons chopped onion

2 tablespoons olive oil, *divided*

3 teaspoons minced garlic

1-1/4 cups water

1 package (5.6 ounces) couscous with toasted pine nuts

1-1/2 teaspoons chicken bouillon granules

1/2 cup cherry tomatoes, halved

2 tablespoons grated Parmesan cheese

1. In a small skillet, saute onion in 1 tablespoon oil for 3-4 minutes or until tender. Add garlic; cook 1 minute longer.

2. Meanwhile, in a large saucepan, combine the water, contents of seasoning packet from couscous mix, bouillon and remaining oil. Bring to a boil.

3. Stir in onion mixture and couscous. Cover and remove from the heat; let stand for 5 minutes. Fluff with a fork. Stir in tomatoes and cheese.

Yield: 4 servings.

Broccoli Saute

Jim MacNeal • Waterloo, New York

I invented this recipe while looking for a different way to cook broccoli that was lower in fat and sodium. Quick, colorful and tasty, it makes an easy accompaniment to a variety of meals. Don't want to throw out all those leftover broccoli stalks? Cut them up and add raw to salads or cook until tender, then puree and add to sour cream dip.

1/2 cup chopped onion
1/2 cup julienned sweet red pepper
2 tablespoons olive oil
6 cups fresh broccoli florets
2/3 cup water
1-1/2 teaspoons minced garlic
1/4 teaspoon salt
1/4 teaspoon pepper

1. In a large skillet, saute onion and red pepper in oil for 2-3 minutes or until crisp-tender. Stir in the broccoli, water, garlic, salt and pepper. Cover and cook over medium heat for 5-6 minutes or until broccoli is crisp-tender.

Yield: 5 servings.

Garlic Mashed Cauliflower

Jean Keiser • West Chester, Pennsylvania

I've always enjoyed the mashed cauliflower at a favorite restaurant we go to. So I came up with this delicious and easy recipe for the low-carb favorite that we can make at home.

5 cups fresh cauliflowerets
1 garlic clove, minced
3 tablespoons fat-free milk
3 tablespoons reduced-fat mayonnaise
1/2 teaspoon salt
1/8 teaspoon white pepper

1. Place 1 in. of water in a large saucepan; add cauliflower and garlic. Bring to a boil. Reduce heat; cover and simmer for 10-15 minutes or until tender.

2. Drain; transfer to a small bowl. Add the milk, mayonnaise, salt and pepper; beat until blended. If desired, shape into individual molds by packing 1/2 cup at a time into a 2-in. biscuit cutter.

Yield: 4 servings.

Potato Wedges

Melissa Tatum • Greensboro, North Carolina

Everyone will love the flavor of Parmesan cheese and the crunch of cornflakes on these better-than-frozen home fries. They're great for kids, but the adults will enjoy them as well!

4 medium baking potatoes
1/3 cup finely crushed cornflakes
1/3 cup grated Parmesan cheese
2 teaspoons paprika
1/2 teaspoon salt
1/4 cup ranch salad dressing
Additional ranch salad dressing, optional

1. Scrub and pierce potatoes; place on a microwave-safe plate. Microwave, uncovered, on high for 18-20 minutes or until tender, turning once. Cool slightly.

2. Meanwhile, in a small bowl, combine the cornflake crumbs, Parmesan cheese, paprika and salt. Cut each potato lengthwise into quarters; brush with salad dressing and sprinkle with cornflake mixture.

3. Place potato wedges on a broiler pan. Broil 4 in. from the heat for 2-3 minutes or until lightly browned. Serve with additional salad dressing if desired.

Yield: 4 servings.

EDITOR'S NOTE: This recipe was tested in a 1,100-watt microwave.

busy family favorites

Roasted Corn Muffins

Dorinda Bruce • Bixby, Oklahoma

I have never gone back to my old corn bread recipe after finding this one. Adding corn to the batter makes the muffins extra hearty.

1/4 cup butter, softened
1/3 cup sugar
1 egg
2 tablespoons honey
1/4 teaspoon salt
3/4 cup all-purpose flour
1/2 cup yellow cornmeal
1/4 teaspoon baking powder
1/4 cup milk
1/2 cup frozen corn

1. In a small bowl, cream the butter and sugar. Beat in the egg, honey and salt.

2. Combine the flour, cornmeal and baking powder; add to the creamed mixture alternately with the milk. Fold in the frozen corn.

3. Fill greased or paper-lined muffin cups two-thirds full. Bake at 400° for 20-25 minutes or until a toothpick comes out clean. Cool for 5 minutes before removing from pan to a wire rack. Serve warm.

Yield: 6 muffins.

Creamed Spinach

Ann Van Dyk • Wrightstown, Wisconsin

Using fresh spinach instead of frozen really enhances the taste of this classic recipe. The hint of nutmeg makes this side dish even more appealing.

3/4 pound fresh spinach, torn
2 tablespoons olive oil
6 tablespoons butter, cubed
1/4 cup chopped onion
1/4 cup all-purpose flour
1/2 teaspoon salt
1/8 teaspoon ground nutmeg
1-1/2 cups milk

1. In a Dutch oven, cook spinach in oil for 3 minutes or until wilted. Transfer to a cutting board; chop. Melt butter in the Dutch oven. Add onion; saute for 2 minutes or until crisp-tender.

2. Stir in flour, salt and nutmeg until combined. Gradually whisk in milk until blended. Bring to a boil; cook and stir for 2 minutes or until thickened. Add the chopped spinach. Reduce heat to low; cook, uncovered, for 5 minutes or until heated through.

Yield: 4 servings.

TIP Fresh spinach is a great way to add nutrition to a dish. Before using fresh spinach in a recipe, cut off any tough stems. Wash several times in cold water, drain well and pat dry.

Savory Green Beans

Carol Ann Hayden • Everson, Washington

This was my mother's favorite way to fix green beans. She always grew savory in her garden, which is the key ingredient to this recipe's fresh flavor. Not only is this dish low in fat, but it goes well with just about any main course.

3/4 cup chopped sweet red pepper

1 tablespoon canola oil

1 garlic clove, minced

1-1/2 pounds fresh green beans, trimmed and cut into 2-inch pieces

1/2 cup water

2 tablespoons minced fresh savory *or* 2 teaspoons dried savory

1 tablespoon minced chives

1/2 teaspoon salt

1. In a large skillet, saute red pepper in oil for 2-3 minutes or until tender. Add garlic; cook 1 minute longer.

2. Stir in the green beans, water, savory, chives and salt. Bring to a boil. Reduce heat; cover and simmer for 8-10 minutes or until beans are crisp-tender.

Yield: 6 servings.

Spanish Rice

Taste of Home Test Kitchen

This sensational Spanish Rice with tomatoes is seasoned with green chilies and fresh cilantro to make a colorful side. It is delicious served with tacos for an easy, streamlined supper your family is likely to request often.

1/2 cup chopped onion

1 tablespoon butter

2 cups uncooked instant rice

1 can (14-1/2 ounces) diced tomatoes with mild green chilies, undrained

1 cup water

3/4 cup beef broth

1/2 teaspoon chili powder

1/4 teaspoon salt

1/4 teaspoon sugar

1/4 teaspoon ground cumin

2 tablespoons minced fresh cilantro

1. In a large saucepan, saute onion in butter for 2-3 minutes or until tender. Add rice; cook and stir for 1-2 minutes.

2. Stir in the tomatoes, water, broth, chili powder, salt, sugar and cumin. Bring to a boil. Reduce heat; cover and simmer for 5 minutes. Remove from the heat; let stand for 5 minutes. Sprinkle with cilantro.

Yield: 4 servings.

busy family favorites

BLT Bread Salad

Tonya Vowels • Vine Grove, Kentucky

Zesty and fun, this salad always draws raves. It tastes just like a BLT, has a light vinaigrette dressing and goes well with so many main dishes.

3 cups cubed French bread

1 tablespoon water

1 tablespoon white wine vinegar

1 tablespoon reduced-fat mayonnaise

1-1/4 teaspoons sugar

1 teaspoon olive oil

1-1/2 cups torn leaf lettuce

1 large tomato, chopped

2 tablespoons crumbled cooked bacon

1 tablespoon chopped green onion

1. Place bread cubes on an ungreased baking sheet; coat lightly with cooking spray. Bake at 400° for 8-10 minutes or until golden brown.

2. For dressing, in a small bowl, whisk the water, vinegar, mayonnaise, sugar and oil until smooth. In a large salad bowl, combine the lettuce, tomato and bread cubes. Sprinkle with bacon and onion. Drizzle with dressing and toss to coat.

Yield: 4 servings.

Southwestern Sauteed Corn

Chandy Ward • Aumsville, Oregon

My mother-in-law simply came up with this dish one night. Everyone who tries it absolutely loves it!

1 package (16 ounces) frozen corn, thawed *or* 3-1/3 cups fresh corn
1 tablespoon butter
1 plum tomato, chopped
1 tablespoon lime juice
1/2 teaspoon salt
1/2 teaspoon ground cumin
1/3 cup minced fresh cilantro

1. In a large nonstick skillet, saute corn in butter until tender. Reduce heat to medium-low; add the tomato, lime juice, salt and cumin. Cook and stir for 3-4 minutes or until heated through. Remove from the heat; stir in cilantro.

Yield: 5 servings.

Three-Cheese Garlic Bread

Judy Schut • Grand Rapids, Michigan

Who doesn't like warm, gooey, cheesy bread right from the oven? Let this Three-Cheese Garlic Bread tie your dinner together. Everyone is bound to say it's a hit.

1 loaf (1 pound) unsliced Italian bread
1/4 cup butter, softened
1/2 cup shredded part-skim mozzarella cheese
1/2 cup shredded cheddar cheese
1 tablespoon grated Parmesan cheese
1/4 teaspoon garlic powder
1/8 teaspoon Worcestershire sauce
Dash paprika and pepper

1. Cut bread in half widthwise; cut one portion in half lengthwise. Save remaining bread for another use. In a small bowl, combine the remaining ingredients. Spread evenly over cut sides of bread.

2. Place on a baking sheet. Bake at 400° for 10-12 minutes or until cheese is melted. Slice and serve warm.

Yield: 4 servings.

Glazed Orange Carrots

Marilyn Hash • Enumclaw, Washington

Want your kids to eat more carrots? This tender side dish has a pleasant citrus flavor and a pretty orange glaze. It's a must at our family gatherings.

2 pounds fresh carrots, sliced

2 tablespoons butter

1/4 cup thawed orange juice concentrate

2 tablespoons brown sugar

2 tablespoons minced fresh parsley

1. Place 1 in. of water in a saucepan; add carrots. Bring to a boil. Reduce heat; cover and simmer for 7-9 minutes or until crisp-tender. Drain.

2. Melt butter in a large skillet; stir in orange juice concentrate and brown sugar. Add carrots and parsley; stir to coat. Cook and stir for 1-2 minutes or until glaze is thickened.

Yield: 6 servings.

Yogurt Fruit Salad

Sue Day • Yakima, Washington

This pretty combo is similar to an ambrosia salad. The mixture of fruits is very refreshing, and it's quick to fix, too.

2 large apples, chopped
1 cup green grapes, halved
1 cup sliced peeled peaches *or* pears
1 cup dried cherries
1/4 cup flaked coconut
1/4 cup chopped walnuts
1/2 cup vanilla yogurt
6 lettuce leaves

1. In a large bowl, combine the first six ingredients. Add yogurt; toss to coat. Serve on lettuce.

Yield: 6 servings.

Walnut Rice

Vera Whisner • Elkton, Maryland

I always get compliments whenever I serve my rice, and there are never any leftovers. The short prep and cooking time is just an added bonus.

2/3 cup chopped walnuts
1/3 cup chopped onion
1 tablespoon sesame seeds
1/4 teaspoon salt
1/4 teaspoon garlic powder
3 tablespoons butter
1-1/2 cups hot water
2 tablespoons soy sauce
1-1/2 cups frozen broccoli florets
1 cup uncooked instant rice

1. In a large skillet, saute the walnuts, onion, sesame seeds, salt and garlic powder in butter until onion is tender and sesame seeds are golden brown. Add water and soy sauce; bring to a boil. Stir in broccoli and rice. Cover and remove from the heat. Let stand for 5 minutes or until rice is tender.

Yield: 4 servings.

busy family favorites

Buttery Garlic Potatoes

Heidi Iacovetto • Phippsburg, Colorado

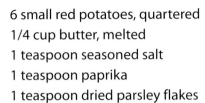

My husband and three boys love oven-roasted potatoes. But I work full-time, so once I get home and start dinner, I usually don't have time to bake potatoes in the oven. So I whipped up this quick and easy microwave recipe calling for red potatoes and seasonings. Now my family loves this version even better!

6 small red potatoes, quartered

1/4 cup butter, melted

1 teaspoon seasoned salt

1 teaspoon paprika

1 teaspoon dried parsley flakes

1 teaspoon minced garlic

1. Place the potatoes in a 2-qt. microwave-safe dish. In a small bowl, combine the butter, seasoned salt, paprika, parsley and garlic; pour over potatoes and toss to coat.

2. Microwave, uncovered, on high for 8-10 minutes or until potatoes are tender, stirring frequently.

Yield: 4 servings.

EDITOR'S NOTE: This recipe was tested in a 1,100-watt microwave.

Twice-Baked Deviled Potatoes

Karol Chandler-Ezell • Nacogdoches, Texas

This delicious side dish is flavored with bacon and cheddar, and has just a hint of Dijon mustard. And since these spuds take under 30 minutes to make, they're perfect for a quick weeknight dinner.

4 small baking potatoes
1/4 cup butter, softened
1/4 cup milk
1 cup (4 ounces) shredded cheddar cheese
1/3 cup real bacon bits
2 green onions, chopped
1 teaspoon Dijon mustard
Dash paprika

1. Scrub and pierce potatoes; place on a microwave-safe plate. Microwave, uncovered, on high for 7-10 minutes or until tender, turning once. Let stand for 5 minutes. Cut a thin slice off the top of each potato and discard. Scoop out pulp, leaving a thin shell.

2. In a large bowl, mash the pulp with butter and milk. Stir in the cheese, bacon, onions, mustard and paprika. Spoon into potato shells. Return to the microwave-safe plate. Microwave, uncovered, on high for 1-2 minutes or until cheese is melted.

Yield: 4 servings.

EDITOR'S NOTE: This recipe was tested in a 1,100-watt microwave.

Sesame Vegetable Medley

Tanya Lamb • Talking Rock, Georgia

This yummy veggie medley makes a great accompaniment to any menu.

1 cup *each* baby carrots, broccoli florets and sliced fresh mushrooms
1 cup sliced zucchini (1/2 inch thick)
1 teaspoon minced garlic
2 tablespoons water
1 tablespoon butter
2 teaspoons sesame seeds, toasted
1/8 teaspoon salt
1/8 teaspoon pepper

1. In a large microwave-safe bowl, combine the carrots, broccoli, mushrooms, zucchini, garlic and water. Cover and microwave on high for 3-5 minutes or until vegetables are tender, stirring twice; drain. Stir in the butter, sesame seeds, salt and pepper.

Yield: 4 servings.

EDITOR'S NOTE: This recipe was tested in a 1,100-watt microwave.

Cauliflower with Buttered Crumbs

Taste of Home Test Kitchen

This recipe is a home-style way to add flavor and interest to steamed cauliflower. Serve this simple side with a variety of entrees.

1 large head cauliflower, broken into florets
1/3 cup butter
1 tablespoon lemon juice
1/4 cup dry bread crumbs
1/4 cup grated Parmesan cheese
2 tablespoons minced fresh parsley
1/8 teaspoon salt
1/8 teaspoon pepper

1. Place 1 in. of water in a large saucepan; add cauliflower. Bring to a boil. Reduce heat; cover and simmer for 10-12 minutes or until crisp-tender.

2. Meanwhile, in a small heavy saucepan, cook butter over medium heat for 5 minutes or until golden brown, stirring frequently. Remove from the heat; stir in lemon juice. In a small bowl, combine the bread crumbs, cheese, parsley, salt and pepper; stir in 3 tablespoons browned butter.

3. Drain cauliflower and place in a serving dish. Drizzle with the remaining browned butter; sprinkle with bread crumb mixture.

Yield: 6 servings.

Rosemary Red Potatoes

Kelly Ward-Hartman • Cape Coral, Florida

Great with steak or any meat, this is one of our best-loved potato sidekicks. Sometimes I add sliced fresh mushrooms and sliced fresh zucchini tossed with a little olive oil after the potatoes have baked for about 15 minutes.

1-3/4 pounds small red potatoes, quartered

1 small onion, quartered

1/4 cup olive oil

1-1/2 teaspoons dried rosemary, crushed

2 garlic cloves, minced

1/4 teaspoon garlic salt

1. In a bowl, combine the potatoes, onion, oil, rosemary, garlic and garlic salt; toss to coat.

2. Transfer to a foil-lined 15-in. x 10-in. x 1-in. baking pan. Bake, uncovered, at 425° for 25-30 minutes or until potatoes are tender and browned.

Yield: 4 servings.

Sesame Breadsticks

Taste of Home Test Kitchen

Try these breadsticks...they're not too spicy and have a mild herb flavor that goes great with pasta. Your family will love them, and you'll love the quick preparation.

1 tube (11 ounces) refrigerated breadsticks

1 tablespoon butter, melted

1 tablespoon sesame seeds, toasted

1 to 2 teaspoons dried basil

1/4 to 1/2 teaspoon cayenne pepper

1. Unroll and separate breadsticks. Twist each breadstick two to three times and place on an ungreased baking sheet; brush with butter. Combine the sesame seeds, basil and cayenne; sprinkle over breadsticks.

2. Bake at 375° for 10-12 minutes or until golden brown. Serve warm.

Yield: 1 dozen.

TIP Also try a sweet version of the breadsticks. Replace the sesame seeds, basil and cayenne pepper with finely chopped nuts and a dash of cinnamon-sugar.

busy family favorites

Creamed Corn with Bacon

Tina Repak • Johnstown, Pennsylvania

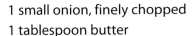

My family is addicted to this yummy, easy side. I like to make it in the summer with farm-fresh corn.

1 small onion, finely chopped

1 tablespoon butter

4 cups fresh *or* frozen corn, thawed

1 cup heavy whipping cream

1/4 cup chicken broth

4 bacon strips, cooked and crumbled

1/4 teaspoon pepper

1/4 cup grated Parmesan cheese

2 tablespoons minced fresh parsley

1. In a large skillet, saute onion in butter for 3 minutes. Add corn; saute 1-2 minutes longer or until onion and corn are tender.

2. Stir in the cream, broth, bacon and pepper. Cook and stir for 5-7 minutes or until slightly thickened. Stir in cheese and parsley.

Yield: 6 servings.

Two-Bean Salad

Ann Mulford • Lincolnville, Maine

This mixed salad is always a winner. Sometimes I make it a day or so ahead of time and let it marinate in the refrigerator until it's time to serve. Be sure to stir every 12 hours. Leftovers are great with rice or noodles.

1 can (15 ounces) garbanzo beans *or* chickpeas, rinsed and drained
1 can (15 ounces) black beans, rinsed and drained
2/3 cup shredded Swiss cheese
1/2 cup chopped onion
1 can (3.8 ounces) sliced ripe olives, drained
1/4 cup chopped celery
1/4 cup *each* chopped green, sweet red and orange peppers
1/3 cup balsamic vinaigrette

1. In a large bowl, combine the beans, cheese, onion, olives, celery and peppers. Drizzle with vinaigrette; toss evenly to coat. Refrigerate until serving.

Yield: 6 servings.

Tangy Zucchini Saute

Taste of Home Test Kitchen

You don't have to go to great lengths to zip up zucchini, as this recipe tastefully proves. You can whip up this savory saute in a jiffy!

4 medium zucchini, halved lengthwise and sliced
1 medium onion, chopped
2 tablespoons olive oil
2 garlic cloves, minced
1 teaspoon Italian seasoning
1/2 teaspoon salt
1/4 teaspoon pepper
1 to 2 tablespoons white balsamic vinegar

1. In a large skillet, saute zucchini and onion in oil until tender, about 10 minutes.

2. Stir in the garlic, Italian seasoning, salt and pepper; saute 1 minute longer. Add vinegar; saute for 1-2 minutes or until liquid is evaporated and zucchini is evenly coated.

Yield: 6 servings.

Sauteed Spinach and Peppers

Mary Lou Moon • Beaverton, Oregon

We often steam our fresh spinach and eat it plain. But this version dressed up with red pepper, onion and garlic is a nice change. It is really quick and tasty.

1 large sweet red pepper, coarsely chopped

1 tablespoon olive oil

1 small red onion, finely chopped

3 garlic cloves, minced

8 cups packed fresh spinach

1/2 teaspoon salt

1/4 teaspoon pepper

1/8 teaspoon sugar

1. In a large nonstick skillet, saute red pepper in oil for 1 minute. Add onion and garlic; saute until tender, about 1-1/2 minutes longer. Stir in the spinach, salt, pepper and sugar; saute for 1-2 minutes or until spinach is wilted and tender. Serve with a slotted spoon.

Yield: 4 servings.

Microwave Acorn Squash

Kara de la Vega • Santa Rosa, California

You'll love this sinfully good side dish that works with just about any meal. With brown sugar, butter and honey, what's not to love? Someone even said it's so good it tastes like candy. We think kids will agree.

2 medium acorn squash
1/4 cup packed brown sugar
2 tablespoons butter
4 teaspoons honey
1/4 teaspoon salt
1/4 teaspoon pepper

1. Cut squash in half; discard seeds. Place squash cut side down in a microwave-safe dish. Cover and microwave on high for 10-12 minutes or until tender.

2. Turn squash cut side up. Fill centers of squash with brown sugar, butter and honey; sprinkle with salt and pepper. Cover and microwave on high for 2-3 minutes or until heated through.

Yield: 4 servings.

EDITOR'S NOTE: This recipe was tested in a 1,100-watt microwave.

Sesame Seed Citrus Noodles

Trisha Kruse • Eagle, Idaho

I make this easy but elegant weeknight recipe often. The noodles have a wonderful citrus tang with a hint of basil and a bit of crunch from the toasted sesame seeds.

4 cups wide no-yolk noodles
2 tablespoons chopped fresh basil
or 2 teaspoons dried basil
4-1/2 teaspoons butter, melted
1 tablespoon lemon juice
1/2 teaspoon salt
1/2 teaspoon grated lemon peel
1/2 teaspoon grated orange peel
1-1/2 teaspoons sesame seeds, toasted

1. Cook noodles according to package directions. Drain, reserving 1/2 cup cooking water. Return noodles to pan.

2. Add the basil, butter, lemon juice, salt and lemon and orange peels. Toss to coat, adding reserved cooking liquid if needed to moisten the noodles. Sprinkle with the sesame seeds.

Yield: 6 servings.

busy family favorites

Swirled Dill Rolls

Taste of Home Test Kitchen

You'll need just four ingredients to bake a pan of these golden-brown rolls. With their fresh-from-the-oven aroma and mild dill flavor, they complement many types of main dishes.

1 tube (8 ounces) refrigerated crescent rolls

2 tablespoons butter, softened

1/4 teaspoon onion powder

1/4 teaspoon snipped fresh dill

1. Do not unroll crescent dough; cut into eight equal slices. Place cut side down on an ungreased baking sheet. Bake at 375° for 11-13 minutes or until golden brown. Meanwhile, in a small bowl, combine the butter, onion powder and dill. Spread over warm rolls.

Yield: 8 rolls.

Avocado Tomato Salad

Dawn McKnight • Zionsville, Indiana

We have a pitch-in lunch at work once a month and this easy, garden-fresh salad has made several popular appearances.

2-1/2 cups torn mixed salad greens

1 cup cherry tomatoes

1 medium ripe avocado, peeled and sliced

1/4 cup real bacon bits

2 tablespoons canola oil

1 tablespoon cider vinegar

1/2 teaspoon salt

1. Divide the greens, tomatoes and avocado among four salad plates; sprinkle with bacon. In a small bowl, whisk the remaining ingredients. Drizzle over salads.

Yield: 4 servings.

Bacon-Almond Green Beans

Jackie Matthews • Yucca Valley, California

I adapted this recipe from a more complicated one I saw in a magazine. My version is much quicker and easier to prepare and tastes great!

1-1/2 pounds fresh green beans, trimmed and cut into 1-1/2-inch pieces

3 tablespoons butter

3 tablespoons brown sugar

2-1/4 teaspoons soy sauce

2-1/4 teaspoons Worcestershire sauce

4 to 5 tablespoons real bacon bits

4 to 5 tablespoons sliced almonds, toasted

1. Place beans in a large saucepan and cover with water. Bring to a boil; cook, uncovered, for 8-10 minutes or until crisp-tender.

2. Meanwhile, melt butter in a large skillet over medium heat. Stir in the brown sugar, soy sauce and Worcestershire sauce. Cook for 1 minute or until sugar is dissolved.

3. Drain beans; add to the skillet. Cook and stir for 2 minutes or until heated through. Sprinkle with bacon and almonds; toss to coat. Serve with a slotted spoon.

Yield: 6 servings.

busy family favorites

Springtime Barley

Sharon Helmick • Colfax, Washington

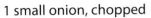

While working as a sorority house mother, I occasionally filled in for the cook. The girls really liked low-fat dishes, including this attractive medley.

1 small onion, chopped

1 medium carrot, chopped

1 tablespoon butter

1 cup quick-cooking barley

2 cups reduced-sodium chicken broth, *divided*

1/2 pound fresh asparagus, trimmed and cut into 1-inch pieces

1/4 teaspoon dried marjoram

1/8 teaspoon pepper

2 tablespoons shredded Parmesan cheese

1. In a large skillet, saute onion and carrot in butter until crisp-tender. Stir in the barley; cook and stir for 1 minute. Stir in 1 cup broth. Bring to a boil. Reduce heat; cook and stir until liquid is absorbed.

2. Add asparagus. Cook for 15-20 minutes or until barley is tender and liquid is absorbed, stirring occasionally and adding more broth as needed. Stir in marjoram and pepper; sprinkle with cheese.

Yield: 4 servings.

Parmesan Tomatoes

Marcia Orlando • Boyertown, Pennsylvania

What a great way to use up all those fresh garden tomatoes in a simple but scrumptious side for entrees of all kinds! It is sure to become a summer standard at your house, too.

3 large tomatoes

1 tablespoon chicken bouillon granules

1/4 cup grated Parmesan cheese

1 tablespoon butter

1. Remove stems from tomatoes; cut in half widthwise. Place cut side up in an 11-in. x 7-in. baking dish coated with cooking spray.

2. Sprinkle with bouillon and cheese; dot with butter. Bake, uncovered, at 400° for 20-25 minutes or until heated through.

Yield: 6 servings.

Corn Bread Dressing

Marybeth Thompson • Thurmont, Maryland

I revised a main-dish casserole recipe to make this unique stuffing side dish. I've often delivered it, along with pork or chicken, to friends who are just out of the hospital. It always is appreciated.

1 package (8 ounces) corn bread stuffing cubes

1 medium onion, finely chopped

1 celery rib, finely chopped

1 can (8-3/4 ounces) cream-style corn

1 cup water

1 tablespoon butter, melted

1 tablespoon spicy brown mustard

1. In a large bowl, combine the stuffing, onion, celery, corn and water. Spoon into a greased 8-in. square baking dish. Combine the butter and mustard; drizzle over stuffing. Bake, uncovered, at 375° for 20 minutes or until heated through.

Yield: 4-6 servings.

busy family favorites

Strawberry-Bacon Spinach Salad

Ruth Hayward • Lake Charles, Louisiana

This colorful Strawberry-Bacon Spinach Salad is sweet and crunchy with a tangy dressing. I made this recipe for our prayer group, and everyone enjoyed it.

1 package (6 ounces) fresh baby spinach
1 pint fresh strawberries, sliced
8 bacon strips, cooked and crumbled
1/4 cup chopped red onion
1/4 cup chopped walnuts
1 cup mayonnaise
1/2 cup sugar
1/4 cup raspberry vinegar

1. In a salad bowl, combine the spinach, strawberries, bacon, onion and walnuts. In a small bowl or pitcher, combine the mayonnaise, sugar and vinegar. Serve with salad.

Yield: 6-8 servings.

Winter Salad

Lynn Ganser • Oakland, California

I make this salad for special dinners. Everyone loves the flavor combination and interesting textures of the pears, walnuts, greens and Gorgonzola cheese. It's nice for winter when other fruits aren't readily available.

1 garlic clove, peeled and halved
2 tablespoons lemon juice
2 tablespoons honey
1/8 teaspoon salt
2 medium ripe pears, thinly sliced
8 cups torn mixed salad greens
1/2 cup chopped walnuts, toasted
1/3 cup crumbled Gorgonzola cheese

1. Rub garlic clove over the bottom and sides of a large salad bowl; discard garlic.

2. In the bowl, combine the lemon juice, honey and salt. Add pears; gently toss to coat. Add the greens, walnuts and cheese; toss to coat.

Yield: 6 servings.

Colorful Veggie Saute

Pamela Stewart • Belcher, Kentucky

A low-fat meal doesn't skimp on flavor with this tasty saute on its side. The medley of squash and other garden-fresh ingredients is brightened by the hearty steak seasoning.

1 small zucchini, sliced
1 yellow summer squash, sliced
1 small onion, halved and sliced
1 cup sliced fresh mushrooms
1 small green pepper, julienned
1/2 cup thinly sliced fresh carrots
1 tablespoon butter
3 cups coarsely chopped fresh spinach
1/2 teaspoon steak seasoning
1/4 teaspoon garlic salt

1. In a large skillet, saute the zucchini, yellow squash, onion, mushrooms, green pepper and carrots in butter until crisp-tender.

2. Add the spinach, steak seasoning and garlic salt; saute 3-4 minutes longer or just until spinach is wilted.

Yield: 5 servings.

EDITOR'S NOTE: This recipe was tested with McCormick's Montreal Steak Seasoning. Look for it in the spice aisle.

Cauliflower Tomato Medley

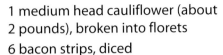

Lena Post • St. Albert, Alberta

Here's a fresh and fancy accompaniment to any buffet. It goes nicely with most meat and fish dishes and is a great way to dress up cauliflower.

1 medium head cauliflower (about 2 pounds), broken into florets

6 bacon strips, diced

1-1/2 cups soft bread crumbs

3 medium tomatoes, cut into wedges

2 tablespoons sliced green onion

1-1/2 teaspoons snipped fresh dill *or* 1/2 teaspoon dill weed

1/4 teaspoon salt

Dash pepper

3/4 cup shredded cheddar cheese

1. Place 1 in. of water and cauliflower in a large saucepan; bring to a boil. Reduce heat; cover and simmer for 5-10 minutes or until crisp-tender.

2. Meanwhile, in a large skillet, cook bacon over medium heat until crisp. Using a slotted spoon, remove to paper towels. Drain, reserving 3 tablespoons drippings. Toss bacon and bread crumbs with drippings; set aside.

3. Drain cauliflower. Arrange the tomatoes in a greased shallow 2-qt. baking dish. Sprinkle with onion, dill, salt and pepper. Top with cauliflower and bacon mixture.

4. Cover and bake at 400° for 10 minutes. Uncover; sprinkle with cheese. Bake 5 minutes longer or until cheese is melted.

Yield: 6 servings.

Orzo with Parmesan & Basil

Anna Chaney • Antigo, Wisconsin

Dried basil adds its rich herb flavor to this creamy and delicious skillet side dish that's table-ready in just minutes!

1 cup uncooked orzo pasta

2 tablespoons butter

1 can (14-1/2 ounces) chicken broth

1/2 cup grated Parmesan cheese

2 teaspoons dried basil

1/8 teaspoon pepper

1. In a large skillet, saute orzo in butter for 3-5 minutes or until lightly browned.

2. Stir in broth. Bring to a boil. Reduce heat; cover and simmer for 10-15 minutes or until liquid is absorbed and orzo is tender. Stir in the Parmesan cheese, basil and pepper.

Yield: 4 servings.

Lemon-Scented Broccoli

Dorothy Pritchett • Wills Point, Texas

If you do not like broccoli, you might change your mind after tasting this festive dish. It is simple, yet elegant, with a delightful lemon sauce.

1/4 cup coarsely chopped pecans

1-1/2 teaspoons butter

1 medium bunch broccoli, trimmed and cut into spears

1 tablespoon sugar

2 teaspoons cornstarch

1/2 cup chicken broth

3 to 4 tablespoons lemon juice

1 teaspoon grated lemon peel

1/4 teaspoon pepper

1. In a small skillet, saute pecans in butter until golden brown; set aside. Place broccoli in a large saucepan; add 1 in. of water. Bring to a boil. Reduce heat; cover and cook for 5-8 minutes or until crisp-tender.

2. Meanwhile, in a small saucepan, combine the sugar, cornstarch, broth and lemon juice until smooth. Cook and stir over medium heat for 1 minute or until thickened. Remove from the heat; stir in the lemon peel and pepper. Drain broccoli and place in a serving bowl; top with lemon sauce and pecans.

Yield: 6 servings.

busy family favorites

Desserts

Peanut Butter Chocolate Pie, p. 231

Individual Strawberry Trifles

Karen Scaglione • Nanuet, New York

These delicious little trifles are loaded with berries and pound cake cubes, then drizzled with a decadent homemade chocolate sauce. I like to sprinkle each one with a little powdered sugar.

1/2 cup semisweet chocolate chips

1/2 cup heavy whipping cream

2 tablespoons orange juice

2 cups sliced fresh strawberries

4 slices pound cake, cubed

1. In a small saucepan, melt chocolate chips with cream over low heat; stir until blended. Remove from the heat; stir in orange juice. Cool to room temperature.

2. In four dessert glasses or bowls, layer the sliced strawberries, cake cubes and chocolate mixture.

Yield: 4 servings.

Graham Cracker Cookies

Lois McKnight • Freeport, Illinois

My brother and I enjoyed these peanut butter treats when we were young. I made these cookies for my children, and now I make them for my grandchildren.

1-1/2 cups sugar

6 tablespoons butter, cubed

1/3 cup evaporated milk

1 cup marshmallow creme

3/4 cup peanut butter

1/3 cup chopped salted peanuts, optional

1/2 teaspoon vanilla extract

1 package (14.4 ounces) graham crackers

1. In a large saucepan, combine the sugar, butter and milk. Cook and stir over medium heat until mixture comes to a boil. Cook 4-5 minutes longer or until thickened and bubbly. Remove from the heat; stir in the marshmallow creme, peanut butter, peanuts if desired and vanilla.

2. Break the graham crackers in half. Spread about 2 tablespoons of the filling on the bottoms of half of the crackers; top with the remaining crackers.

Yield: 2-1/2 dozen.

Mousse Tarts

Angela Lively • Cookeville, Tennessee

Rich white chocolate and whipped cream combine in these fast-to-fix berry-topped treats. Although the tarts originally called for dark chocolate, I prepare them with white chocolate. I double the recipe when I'm asked to bring a dessert to special events. They're always a hit.

3 ounces white baking chocolate, chopped

1 cup heavy whipping cream

1/2 cup sweetened condensed milk

1/4 teaspoon vanilla extract

6 individual graham cracker tart shells

18 fresh raspberries

6 mint sprigs

1. In a microwave, melt white chocolate; stir until smooth. Cool for 1 minute, stirring several times. Meanwhile, in a small bowl, beat cream until stiff peaks form; set aside.

2. In another small bowl, combine the milk, vanilla and melted chocolate. Add half of the whipped cream; beat on low speed just until combined. Fold in remaining whipped cream. Spoon into tart shells. Garnish with raspberries and mint.

Yield: 6 servings.

Frosty Almond Dessert

Phyllis Schmalz • Kansas City, Kansas

You can treat your family to a homemade dessert without a lot of fuss when you whip up this surprise. Everyone will love its yummy flavor.

4 cups low-fat vanilla frozen yogurt

1 cup ice cubes

1/2 cup hot fudge ice cream topping

1/4 teaspoon almond extract

Whipped topping and baking cocoa, optional

1. In a blender, place half of the yogurt, ice cubes, fudge topping and extract; cover and process for 1-2 minutes or until smooth. Stir if necessary. Pour into chilled dessert glasses.

2. Repeat with remaining yogurt, ice, fudge topping and extract. Garnish with whipped topping and baking cocoa if desired.

Yield: 4 servings.

Candy Bar Parfaits

Angie Cassada • Monroe, North Carolina

My kids appreciate making their own candy and ice cream treats. These parfaits are such a favorite, we've featured them at build-your-own-parfait birthday parties. To add to the fun, try different nuts and candy bar toppings and offer a variety of ice cream flavors.

1/2 cup coarsely chopped unsalted peanuts

1/2 cup coarsely crushed pretzels

1 milk chocolate candy bar (1.55 ounces), chopped

1 pint vanilla ice cream, softened

1/3 cup chocolate syrup

2 tablespoons peanut butter

1. In a small bowl, combine the peanuts, pretzels and chopped candy bar; spoon 2 tablespoons into each of four parfait glasses. Top each with 1/4 cup ice cream, 2 tablespoons peanut mixture and another 1/4 cup ice cream.

2. Combine chocolate syrup and peanut butter; drizzle over ice cream. Sprinkle with remaining peanut mixture.

Yield: 4 servings.

busy family favorites

Layered Lemon Pie

Elizabeth Yoder • Belcourt, North Dakota

This is a great ending for almost any meal that kids and adults all enjoy. The creamy lemon filling is always a hit with my husband.

1 package (8 ounces) cream cheese, softened

1/2 cup sugar

1 can (15-3/4 ounces) lemon pie filling

1 carton (8 ounces) frozen whipped topping, thawed

1 graham cracker crust (9 inches)

1. In a small bowl, beat cream cheese and sugar until smooth. Beat in half of the pie filling. Fold in the whipped topping. Spoon into crust. Spread remaining pie filling over cream cheese layer. Refrigerate for 15 minutes or until serving. Refrigerate the leftovers.

Yield: 8 servings.

Cookie Pizza a la Mode

Dee Drew • Aliso Viejo, California

This yummy snack can't be beat—especially because it's so easy to make. It's like eating a chocolate chip cookie and ice cream sundae all in one!

1 tube (16-1/2 ounces) refrigerated chocolate chip cookie dough
Chocolate syrup
Vanilla ice cream
6 maraschino cherries, optional

1. Press the cookie dough onto an ungreased 12-in. pizza pan. Bake at 350° for 15-20 minutes or until deep golden brown. Cool on a wire rack for 5 minutes. Cut into six wedges.

2. Drizzle chocolate syrup over dessert plates. Top with warm cookie wedges, ice cream and additional chocolate syrup. Garnish with a cherry if desired.

Yield: 6 servings.

Fiesta Fruit Cups

Karen Ann Bland • Gove, Kansas

Two types of melon and other fresh fruit combine with peach preserves in this fun, best-of-the-season dish. These colorful fruit bowls are great to serve for dessert or brunch.

6 flour tortillas (6 inches)
3 tablespoons butter, melted
3 tablespoons cinnamon-sugar
2 cups halved fresh strawberries
1 cup cubed cantaloupe
1 cup cubed honeydew
1 large navel orange, peeled and sectioned
1/2 cup peach preserves
Whipped topping and additional strawberries, optional

1. Place tortillas on ungreased baking sheets. Brush with butter; sprinkle with cinnamon-sugar. Cut each tortilla into six wedges.

2. Bake at 350° for 12-15 minutes or until lightly browned. Cool on wire racks.

3. Meanwhile, in a large bowl, combine the strawberries, melons and orange. Stir in preserves. Using a slotted spoon, spoon into dessert cups.

4. Serve with tortilla chips. Garnish with whipped topping and additional strawberries if desired.

Yield: 6 servings.

busy family favorites

No-Bake Almond Bites

Taste of Home Test Kitchen

Quick and easy, these chewy no-bake treats are ideal when time is tight.

1 cup crushed reduced-fat vanilla wafers (about 30 wafers)

1 cup confectioners' sugar, *divided*

1/2 cup chopped almonds

2 tablespoons baking cocoa

2 tablespoons apple juice

2 tablespoons corn syrup

1/4 teaspoon almond extract

1. In a large bowl, combine the wafer crumbs, 1/2 cup confectioners' sugar, almonds and cocoa. Combine the apple juice, corn syrup and extract; stir into crumb mixture until blended.

2. Shape into 1-in. balls; roll in remaining confectioners' sugar. Store the cookies in an airtight container.

Yield: 1-1/2 dozen.

Cherry Mousse

Becky Lohmiller • Monticello, Indiana

This refreshing creation is a change on traditional mousse. Light and fluffy, it is the perfect ending to a heavy meal.

1 tablespoon cherry gelatin powder

1 can (14-1/2 ounces) tart cherries, drained

1 carton (8 ounces) frozen whipped topping, thawed

1. In a large bowl, combine gelatin powder and cherries; fold in the whipped topping.

Yield: 4 servings.

Strawberry Pound Cake Dessert

Linda Coleman • Cedar Rapids, Iowa

This dessert adds a pretty and refreshing finish to most any meal. The simple, classic treat comes together in moments and adds a pop of color to the dinner table.

1 loaf (10-3/4 ounces) frozen pound cake, thawed

2 containers (16 ounces *each*) frozen sweetened sliced strawberries, thawed and drained

1-1/2 cups whipped topping

1. Slice cake into eight pieces. Place a cake slice on each of four dessert plates. Top each with 1/2 cup strawberries, 3 tablespoons whipped topping and another slice of cake. Serve with remaining strawberries and whipped topping.

Yield: 4 servings.

Strawberry Cheese Bundles

Jolene Spray • Van Wert, Ohio

When I first served these turnovers, folks thought I bought them from a bakery. Everyone was surprised to hear they start with refrigerated crescent rolls and pie filling.

1 package (3 ounces) cream cheese, softened

2 tablespoons confectioners' sugar

1/4 teaspoon almond extract

1 tube (8 ounces) refrigerated crescent rolls

1/3 cup strawberry pie filling

1/3 cup crushed pineapple, drained

2 to 3 tablespoons apricot spreadable fruit

1. In a small bowl, beat the cream cheese, sugar and extract until smooth. Unroll crescent roll dough and separate into eight triangles. Place 1 heaping teaspoonful of cream cheese mixture in the center of each triangle. Top with 1 teaspoon of pie filling and 1 teaspoon of pineapple.

2. With one long side of pastry facing you, fold right and left corners over filling to top corner, forming a square. Seal edges. Place on an ungreased baking sheet. Bake at 375° for 15-17 minutes or until lightly browned. Brush with spreadable fruit. Serve warm or cold.

Yield: 8 servings.

Peanut Butter Chocolate Pie

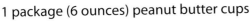

Sara Walker • Roanoke Rapids, North Carolina

This sweet and creamy pie is always popular at family reunions. Kids love it. Even better, it calls for just five ingredients and can be made in minutes!

1 package (6 ounces) peanut butter cups
1 cup cold 2% milk
1 package (3.9 ounces) instant chocolate pudding mix
1 carton (8 ounces) frozen whipped topping, thawed
1 chocolate crumb crust (8 inches)

1. Cut four peanut butter cups in half; coarsely chop remaining cups and set aside. In a large bowl, whisk milk and pudding mix for 2 minutes. Let stand for 2 minutes or until soft-set. Fold in whipped topping.

2. Fold in chopped peanut butter cups. Spoon into crust. Arrange halved peanut butter cups on top. Refrigerate for at least 15 minutes before serving.

Yield: 8 servings.

Dream Clouds

Tonya Michelle Burkhard • Englewood, Florida

Cap off any meal with this lovely dessert. With its refreshing orange flavor, the treat hits the spot and satisfies your sweet tooth. I find this to be a wonderful light dessert after a hearty meal.

1 pint vanilla ice cream, softened

1 pint orange sherbet, softened

2 cups whipped topping

1 can (11 ounces) mandarin oranges, drained

1. Place ice cream and sherbet in a large bowl. Using a knife, swirl sherbet into ice cream. Spoon 1/2 cup whipped topping into each of four serving dishes. Top with ice cream mixture and mandarin oranges.

Yield: 4 servings.

Cranberry Mallow Dessert

Cristie Hunt • Rossville, Georgia

A holiday tradition of mine is this fluffy refresher. Pretty as a picture and lighter than air, it makes a great alternative to plain old cranberry sauce. It's an easy and delicious potluck dish for seasonal get-togethers.

1 can (14 ounces) whole-berry cranberry sauce

2 cups miniature marshmallows

1 can (8 ounces) crushed pineapple, drained

1 teaspoon lemon juice

2 cups whipped topping

1. In a large bowl, combine the cranberry sauce, marshmallows, pineapple and lemon juice. Fold in the whipped topping. Transfer to a serving dish. Cover and refrigerate dessert until serving.

Yield: 6-8 servings.

busy family favorites

Black Forest Parfaits

Barbara Rudolph • Sevierville, Tennessee

These are guaranteed to sweeten up a meal, whether you're dining indoors or out. With only five ingredients, you can whip them up in no time!

2 cups cold 2% milk

1 package (3.9 ounces) instant chocolate pudding mix

1 can (21 ounces) cherry pie filling, *divided*

2 cups whipped topping, *divided*

6 maraschino cherries with stems, optional

1. In a large bowl, whisk milk and pudding mix for 2 minutes. Let stand for 2 minutes or until soft-set. Stir in 1 cup pie filling; gently fold in 1 cup whipped topping.

2. Spoon half of the pudding mixture into six tall glasses or cups. Top with remaining pie filling, pudding mixture and whipped topping. Garnish with cherries if desired.

Yield: 6 servings.

Heavenly Strawberry Tarts

Julie Jahnke • Green Lake, Wisconsin

I use convenient graham cracker tart shells that I fill with a rich cream cheese layer and cover with gorgeous glazed strawberries to create this delectable treat.

4 ounces cream cheese, softened

1/4 cup sugar

2-1/4 teaspoons 2% milk

1-1/2 teaspoons sour cream

1/2 teaspoon vanilla extract

6 individual graham cracker tart shells

1-1/2 cups sliced unsweetened strawberries

1 cup strawberry glaze

1. In a small bowl, beat the cream cheese, sugar, milk, sour cream and vanilla. Spoon into crusts. Combine the strawberries and glaze; spoon over cream cheese. Refrigerate until serving.

Yield: 6 servings.

TIP To add a touch of glamour to a parfait glass, dip the rim in melted chocolate. While the chocolate is still wet, sprinkle the rim with chocolate jimmies or even chopped nuts. Then, turn the glasses upright and let them stand until the chocolate is set.

Cake with Pineapple Pudding

Judy Sellgren • Grand Rapids, Michigan

This recipe was given to me by a dear friend, and I serve it often. It's so light and refreshing. I frequently take it to church luncheons.

2 cups cold 2% milk

1 package (3.4 ounces) instant French vanilla pudding mix

1 can (8 ounces) unsweetened crushed pineapple, drained

1 cup whipped topping

6 slices angel food cake

1. In a large bowl, whisk milk and pudding mix for 2 minutes. Let stand for 2 minutes or until soft-set. Fold in pineapple and whipped topping. Chill until serving. Serve with cake.

Yield: 6 servings.

Old-Fashioned Rice Pudding

Laura German • North Brookfield, Massachusetts

Here's a classic that's been popular through many generations. Try it and it could become a tradition in your family.

2 cups cooked long grain rice

2 cups whole milk

3 tablespoons plus 1 teaspoon sugar

1/8 teaspoon salt

1 teaspoon vanilla extract

Whipped cream, optional

1. In a large saucepan, combine the rice, milk, sugar and salt. Cook, uncovered, over medium heat for 20 minutes or until thickened, stirring often. Remove from the heat; stir in vanilla. Spoon into serving dishes. Serve warm; top with whipped cream if desired.

Yield: 4 servings.

TIP To get a head start on making rice pudding, save leftover rice from your meals. Measure the amount you have left over and place in a freezer bag. Label bag with the amount and freeze. Add to the bag until you have 2 cups, then treat your family to a comforting dessert.

busy family favorites

White Chip Cookies

Taste of Home Test Kitchen

This quick recipe is perfect when you want to bake a small batch of cookies.

1 package (9 ounces) devil's food cake mix

1 egg

2 tablespoons baking cocoa

2 tablespoons cream cheese, softened

1 tablespoon 2% milk

3/4 cup white baking chips

1. In a small bowl, combine the cake mix, egg, cocoa, cream cheese and milk until well blended (batter will be thick). Stir in the chips.

2. Drop by tablespoonfuls 2 in. apart onto a greased baking sheet. Bake at 350° for 14-16 minutes or until a toothpick comes out clean.

Yield: 1 dozen.

Butterscotch Parfaits

Judi Klee • Nebraska City, Nebraska

These yummy parfaits are impossible to turn down. You can also change the pudding flavor to suit your taste.

2 cups cold fat-free milk

1 package (1 ounce) sugar-free instant butterscotch pudding mix

18 vanilla wafers, coarsely crushed

1 carton (8 ounces) frozen reduced-fat whipped topping, thawed

1. In a large bowl, whisk milk and pudding mix for 2 minutes. Let stand for 2 minutes or until soft-set.

2. In six parfait glasses, alternate the layers of pudding, wafer crumbs and whipped topping. Refrigerate until serving.

Yield: 6 servings.

Raspberry Yogurt Pie

Margarget Schneider • Utica, Michigan

A handful of ingredients are all you need to make this no-bake pie. Try it with your favorite flavor of yogurt and the corresponding berries or fruit slices.

2 cups (16 ounces) raspberry yogurt

1 carton (8 ounces) frozen whipped topping, thawed

1 graham cracker crust (9 inches)

Fresh raspberries, optional

1. Place the yogurt in a bowl; fold in the whipped topping. Spoon into the crust. Garnish with raspberries if desired. Refrigerate until serving.

Yield: 8 servings.

Peanut Butter Cereal Bars

Denise Moore • Nepean, Ontario

I got this recipe from my mother, and it's now part of my yearly Christmas baking. For variety, I sometimes form the mixture into balls with chocolate caps. One batch is never enough!

1/4 cup packed brown sugar

1/4 cup creamy peanut butter

1/4 cup light corn syrup

2-1/2 teaspoons butter, *divided*

1 cup crisp rice cereal

1/4 cup chopped pecans

1/2 cup semisweet chocolate chips

1. In a small saucepan, combine the brown sugar, peanut butter, corn syrup and 1-1/2 teaspoons butter. Bring to a boil over medium heat, stirring constantly. Remove from the heat; stir in the cereal and pecans. Press into a 9-in. x 5-in. loaf pan coated with cooking spray.

2. In a microwave, melt chocolate chips and remaining butter; stir until smooth. Spread over cereal mixture; cool. Cut into bars. Store in the refrigerator.

Yield: 8 bars.

Mini Apricot Turnovers

Taste of Home Test Kitchen

Turnovers don't have to be time-consuming when you use prepared pie pastry and fruit preserves. These oven-fresh goodies are just right for breakfast, lunch and dinner as well as late-night snacks. Feel free to experiment with other fruit preserve flavors.

1 package (15 ounces) refrigerated pie pastry

1 jar (12 ounces) apricot *or* peach preserves

2 tablespoons 2% milk

1 tablespoon sugar

1/4 teaspoon ground cinnamon

1. Cut each pastry into four wedges. Place a rounded tablespoonful of preserves in the center of each. Moisten edges with water. Fold pastry over filling; press edges with fork to seal.

2. Place turnovers on an ungreased baking sheet. Cut a small slit in the top of each. Brush with milk. Combine sugar and cinnamon; sprinkle over turnovers.

3. Bake at 425° for 16-18 minutes or until golden brown. Serve warm.

Yield: 8 turnovers.

Puffed Apple Pastries

Taste of Home Test Kitchen

This is a perfect dessert to highlight tasty apples. It's sweet and oh-so yummy!

1 package (10 ounces) frozen pastry shells

1 can (21 ounces) apple pie filling

1/2 teaspoon ground cinnamon

1/4 teaspoon ground nutmeg

1. Prepare puff pastry according to package directions. Bake at 400° for 20-25 minutes or until golden brown. Meanwhile, in a small saucepan, combine the apple pie filling, cinnamon and nutmeg; mix well. Cook and stir over medium-low heat for about 3-4 minutes or until heated through.

2. Remove tops from shells. Fill each with about 1/3 cup of filling. Serve warm.

Yield: 6 servings.

Peach Melba Mousse Dessert

Taste of Home Cooking School

This luscious dessert combines classic Peach Melba with a heavenly white chocolate mousse. For a fun and pretty alternative, serve the dessert in small martini glasses. Garnish with a drizzle of raspberry sauce.

1/3 cup white baking chips

2 tablespoons 2% milk

1 package (3 ounces) cream cheese, softened

1/3 cup confectioners' sugar

1 teaspoon grated orange peel

1 cup heavy whipping cream, whipped

2/3 cup fresh raspberries

2 tablespoons sugar

2 cups sliced fresh *or* frozen peaches, thawed, diced

1/2 cup sliced almonds, toasted

1. In a microwave, melt 1/3 cup white chips with milk; stir until smooth. Cool to room temperature. Meanwhile, beat cream cheese and sugar in a large bowl until smooth. Beat in orange peel and melted chocolate. Fold in whipped cream. Set aside.

2. In a blender, combine the raspberries and sugar; cover and process on high until smooth. Strain and discard seeds. Set aside.

3. Place diced peaches in dessert glasses. Spoon white chocolate mousse over the peaches; smooth top surface if desired. Drizzle with raspberry sauce and sprinkle with nuts.

Yield: 8 servings.

busy family favorites

Mint Berry Blast

Diane Harrison • Mechanicsburg, Pennsylvania

What's better than a bowl of fresh-picked berries? A bowl of berries enhanced with mint, lemon juice and a dollop of whipped topping. It's quick, easy and oh, so refreshing!

1 cup *each* fresh raspberries, blackberries, blueberries *and* halved strawberries

1 tablespoon minced fresh mint

1 tablespoon lemon juice

Whipped topping, optional

1. In a large bowl, combine the berries, mint and lemon juice; gently toss to coat. Cover and refrigerate until serving. Garnish with whipped topping if desired.

Yield: 4 servings.

Pears in Orange Sauce

Audrey Friberg • Fridley, Minnesota

This is one of my favorite, easy desserts to serve guests. There is hardly any prep involved, and everyone enjoys it after a big meal.

1 can (15-1/4 ounces) pear halves

1/4 cup thawed orange juice concentrate

1 cinnamon stick (1 inch)

1/8 teaspoon salt

2 ounces cream cheese, softened

1/2 teaspoon ground cinnamon

4 Pirouette cookies *or* cookies of your choice

1. Drain pears, reserving liquid; set pears aside. Place liquid in a small saucepan; add the orange juice concentrate, cinnamon stick and salt. Bring to a boil, stirring occasionally. Add pears; cook, uncovered, for 2 minutes or until heated through.

2. Discard cinnamon stick. Spoon pears into dessert dishes; drizzle with sauce. Dollop with cream cheese and sprinkle with cinnamon. Serve with cookies.

Yield: 4 servings.

Banana Cream Pie

Perlene Hoekema • Lynden, Washington

This fluffy, no-bake pie is full of old-fashioned flavor, with only a fraction of the work. It uses instant vanilla pudding and it's whipped up in minutes.

1 cup cold 2% milk

1/2 teaspoon vanilla extract

1 package (3.4 ounces) instant vanilla pudding mix

1 carton (12 ounces) frozen whipped topping, thawed, *divided*

1 graham cracker crust (9 inches)

2 medium firm bananas, sliced

Additional banana slices, optional

Lemon juice

1. In a large bowl, whisk milk, vanilla and pudding mix for 2 minutes. Let stand for 2 minutes or until soft-set. Fold in 3 cups whipped topping.

2. Pour 1-1/3 cups of the pudding mixture into pie crust. Layer with banana slices and remaining pudding mixture. Top with remaining whipped topping. Garnish with additional banana slices dipped in lemon juice if desired. Refrigerate until serving.

Yield: 8 servings.

Lemon Angel Cake

Debbie Segate • Grande Prairie, Alberta

I rely on tangy lemon pie filling and a few other ingredients to quickly dress up a store-bought angel food cake. If there's time, I use a boxed mix to bake the cake.

1 cup heavy whipping cream
1 tablespoon confectioners' sugar
1 can (15-3/4 ounces) lemon pie filling
1 prepared angel food cake
(8 to 10 ounces)

1. In a small bowl, beat cream until it begins to thicken. Add confectioners' sugar; beat until stiff peaks form. Place pie filling in a bowl; fold in whipped cream.

2. Cut cake into two horizontal layers. Place bottom layer on a serving plate; top with 1 cup lemon mixture. Top with a second cake layer. Frost top and sides of cake with remaining lemon mixture. Chill for 15 minutes or until serving. Refrigerate the leftovers.

Yield: 10-12 servings.

Chocolate Cake with Coconut Sauce

Tabitha Freeman • Meriden, Connecticut

With the bold flavors of raspberry and coconut enhancing fudgy chocolate cake and creamy vanilla ice cream, what's not to love?

1 package (19.6 ounces) frozen chocolate fudge layer cake

1/2 cup flaked coconut

1/2 cup sweetened condensed milk

1/2 teaspoon vanilla extract

1/4 cup red raspberry preserves

4 scoops vanilla ice cream

1. Cut cake in half. Return half to the freezer. Let remaining cake stand at room temperature to thaw.

2. Meanwhile, in a small saucepan, combine the coconut, milk and vanilla. Cook and stir over medium heat for 2-3 minutes or until heated through.

3. Cut cake into four slices; place on dessert plates. Spread with preserves. Top with coconut mixture and ice cream.

Yield: 4 servings.

Berry Cheesecake Parfaits

Joyce Mart • Wichita, Kansas

I can serve up this easy dessert in no time. Impressive and delicious, it seems to be just the right touch after a full meal. We also recommend it as a great midnight snack.

1 package (8 ounces) cream cheese, softened

2 to 4 tablespoons sugar

1/2 cup vanilla yogurt

2 cups fresh raspberries *or* berries of your choice

1/2 cup graham cracker crumbs (8 squares)

1. In a large bowl, beat cream cheese and sugar until smooth. Stir in yogurt.

2. In four dessert glasses or bowls, alternate layers of berries, cream cheese mixture and cracker crumbs. Serve immediately or refrigerate for up to 8 hours.

Yield: 4 servings.

busy family favorites

Gingersnap Pears

Dodi Mahan Walker • Peachtree City, Georgia

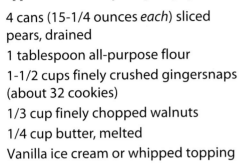

These pears combine perfectly with ice cream for one sweet treat. Guest will appreciate the tasty simplicity of the dish.

4 cans (15-1/4 ounces *each*) sliced pears, drained
1 tablespoon all-purpose flour
1-1/2 cups finely crushed gingersnaps (about 32 cookies)
1/3 cup finely chopped walnuts
1/4 cup butter, melted
Vanilla ice cream or whipped topping

1. Place the pears in a large bowl; sprinkle with flour and toss gently to combine. Divide among eight ungreased 8-oz. custard cups. Combine the gingersnaps, walnuts and butter; sprinkle over pears.

2. Place custard cups on a baking sheet. Bake at 350° for 15-20 minutes or until heated through. Serve warm with ice cream or whipped topping.

Yield: 8 servings.

Grape Nectarine Dessert Cups

Jeanette Oberholtzer • Manheim, Pennsylvania

This light, summery fruit cup is so refreshing after a heavy meal. It's drizzled with lemon-lime soda and topped with a cool scoop of pineapple sherbet. In winter, you can substitute frozen peaches for the nectarines.

7 medium nectarines, peeled and sliced
2 cups green grapes
1 cup chilled lemon-lime soda
2-1/2 cups pineapple sherbet

1. In a large bowl, combine nectarines and grapes; cover and refrigerate until chilled. Just before serving, pour soda over fruit. Spoon into dessert dishes; top with sherbet.

Yield: 10 servings.

Triple Chocolate Bundles

Taste of Home Test Kitchen

No one will be able to resist three kinds of chocolate wrapped up in a fuss-free flaky dough. Instead of sprinkling the bundles with sugar, try drizzling with melted chocolate.

3 tablespoons semisweet chocolate chips

3 tablespoons white baking chips

3 tablespoons milk chocolate chips

1 tube (8 ounces) refrigerated crescent rolls

Confectioners' sugar, optional

1. In a small bowl, combine the first three ingredients. Separate crescent dough into eight triangles. Place triangles on a work surface with the short edge toward you.

2. For each bundle, place 1 tablespoon of chips in the center of each triangle. Bring top point over chips and tuck underneath dough. Fold side points over top, pressing to seal.

3. Place on an ungreased baking sheet. Bake at 375° for 10-12 minutes or until golden brown. Cool on a wire rack until serving. Sprinkle with sugar if desired.

Yield: 8 bundles.

Easy Tiramisu

Nancy Brown • Dahinda, Illinois

Since this recipe uses frozen pound cake, it is very simple to make—but still tastes delicious!

1 package (10-3/4 ounces) frozen pound cake, thawed

3/4 cup strong brewed coffee

1 package (8 ounces) cream cheese, softened

1 cup sugar

1/2 cup chocolate syrup

1 cup heavy whipping cream, whipped

2 Heath candy bars (1.4 ounces *each*), crushed

1. Cut cake into nine slices. Arrange in an ungreased 11-in. x 7-in. dish, cutting to fit if needed. Drizzle with coffee.

2. In a small bowl, beat cream cheese and sugar until smooth. Add chocolate syrup. Fold in whipped cream. Spread over cake. Sprinkle with crushed candy bars. Refrigerate until serving.

Yield: 8 servings.

busy family favorites

Peanut Butter S'mores

Lily Julow • Gainesville, Florida

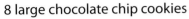

This is what I depend on when dessert is a last minute thought. It's a decadent take on campfire s'mores.

8 large chocolate chip cookies

4 teaspoons hot fudge ice cream topping

4 large marshmallows

4 peanut butter cups

1. Spread the bottoms of four cookies with fudge topping.

2. Using a long-handled fork, grill marshmallows 6 in. from medium-hot heat until golden brown, turning occasionally. Carefully place a marshmallow and a peanut butter cup on each fudge-topped cookie; top with remaining cookies. Serve immediately.

Yield: 4 servings.

Indexes

General Index

This handy index lists the recipes by food category and major ingredients, so you can easily locate recipes that suit your needs.

busy family favorites

busy family favorites

Alphabetical Index

This index lists every recipe in alphabetical order, so you can easily find your favorite recipe.

busy family favorites

busy family favorites